THE
CLANS
OF SCOTLAND
The History and Landscape of the Scottish Clans

THE
CLANS
OF SCOTLAND
The History and Landscape of the
Scottish Clans

Micheil MacDonald

**CHARTWELL
BOOKS, INC.**

Published by
Chartwell Books, Inc.
A Division of Book Sales, Inc.
Raritan Centre
114 Northfield Avenue
Edison, NJ 08818

ISBN 0–7858–0108–1

Copyright © 1991 Regency House Publishing Limited

Published 1994

Printed in Italy

Page 2: Callanish stone circle, Lewis

PICTURE ACKNOWLEDGEMENTS

Author's Collection 11, 14, 19, 20, 21, 25, 27, 28, 29, 33, 34, 35, 36, 38, 39, 41, 43, 44, 45, 66, 67, 68, 69, 85, 92, 97, 106, 116, 127, 150, 158, 161, 163, 165, 175; Environmental Concerns 37; Robert Fleming Holdings Ltd. 114-115; Glasgow University Archaeology Department 32: Images 2, 86-87, 90-91, 102-103, 119, 128, 136-137, 140, 141, 147, 159, 169, 173, 176, 178, 179, 180-181; Eslea MacDonald 24, 47, 121; National Galleries of Scotland 23; National Museum of Antiquities of Scotland 10, 18-19, 38 above, 42, 116 below; National Portrait Gallery, London 22, 28; National Trust for Scotland 18-19, 38 above, 42, 108; The Royal Collection 46; Royal Scottish Museum , Edinburgh 87; Scottish National Portrait Gallery 26; Scottish Tourist Board/Still Moving 73, 74, 76, 77, 78, 79, 80, 81, 84, 88, 89, 95, 98, 100, 105, 106-107, 110-111, 112-113, 120, 131, 132, 146, 151, 153, 155, 156, 170-171; Sotheby's 138-139, 166-167; Paul Tomkins 77, 100, 105, 106-107, 122-123, 156; Harvey Wood 98.

CONTENTS

Foreword

One of the old Highland seers – the White Lady of Lawers – prophesied in the 1560s that 'The feather of a goose will destroy the mind of the people'; an observation that owed more to common sense than second sight. But in so-called primitive societies to which I was exposed in the 1960s, I was struck by the powerful influence of oral tradition as a force for maintaining a system of values, beliefs and perceptions which were the 'glue' that kept a society stable and able to survive. When those cultural elements are handed down – and out – through the medium of the written word and disseminated without discrimination, that 'glue' begins to lose its power of adhesion. Even the ultimate audio-visual mechanism – television – lacks the power of the two-way interchange between mother and child, or the charisma of an old man entrancing the younger generations with tales of long-ago around a camp fire.

At the same time, oral tradition – handed down over thousands of years – can be amazingly accurate, once you strip away the coating of gloss and glitter acquired over the centuries. One small but significant example is the folklore surrounding the 'Little People' who lived under fairy knolls and who were terrified of anything iron. Tradition 'says' that an old scythe blade or a horseshoe over the door of your house will still keep the fairy folk at bay, but we are really 'hearing' the mangled version of a racial memory, from the times when the old pre-Celtic Bronze Age folk, who lived in underground 'wheelhouses' or turf dwellings, feared the sharper and stronger iron weapons of the tall, blond incomers.

The Masai cattle drovers in East Africa, the place-name constructions of the North American Indians, the complex totem systems of the Australian aborigines, and a host of other cultural imprints triggered in me a new understanding of the essentially tribal nature of Scottish society, which has survived intact more than any other major community in Europe. A decade and a half of establishing interactive museums and exhibitions has helped me sharpen my view of Scotland's unique cultural matrix, chiefly because of the direct and immediate involvement with a critical public – the instant correction of fallacies and the resolution of errors of thinking and judgement by discussion – which is difficult to achieve with a book. I hope that readers will respond to that challenge, especially with regard to the section on the clans, where a wealth of unrecorded oral history exists for most families, which exceeds everything previously written.

A few – and by no means complete – acknow-ledgements are due to people who gave freely of their time, knowledge and ideas. Among these are my wife Penny, who corrects any sloppy thinking; my son Peter for the quality of his Gaelic discussion and his weaver's knowledge of tartan; Kenneth Urquhart of Urquhart; Col. Arthur Lawrie; Lt. Col. John Napier of Kilmahew; Anthony Murray of Dollerie and Anthony Murray of Stirling. Among those now deceased are H.R.H. Princess Alice, Countess of Athlone; Mrs C.G. Seligman, Sir Iain Moncreiffe of that Ilk, Bt., and Donald J. Macdonald of Castleton. A chilling reminder of tribal mentality came via the doctor from Tennessee who solemnly laid a curse on me and my heirs, and declared a rift forever between his clan and the MacDonalds, merely for failing to solve the problem of a new tartan for his name before his 78-year-old father 'upped and died'. By contrast, the gentle lady from Illinois, who wanted to know more about the Scotland her great-grandfather had come from 'so that we can make him more a part of our everyday lives' reminded me of the Gaelic proverb 'Remember the Men [and Women] from whence you came'. The most memorable of those to whom I am indebted is the old Aboriginal chief in Arnhem Land in the Northern Territory of Australia, who allowed me the honour of seeing the sacred 'things' of his tribe. In return, I showed him the little piece of tartan cloth which U.S. astronaut Alan Bean had taken to the lunar surface on the 1969 Apollo XII Mission. The old chief examined this sacred object from the 'MacBean' tribe in infinite detail, and then sat talking with me far into the night about the concept of walking on the moon, which was obviously so much closer to him and his world than it was to me and mine.

The proper study of Mankind *is* Man. I hope that this book adds some new dimension to the human history of Scotland, but also encourages readers to delve deeper and always question!

Micheil MacDonald

Crieff, Scotland   August, 1991

Land and People

The Continental Shelf of Europe on which the British Isles lie is part of the European plain, flooded by rising sea levels when the last great Ice Age ended. At its furthest south the ice over Britain reached almost to the region of London, but began to recede slowly northward some 20,000 years ago. The land-bridge across the Irish Sea was breached around 9,000 BC; the Atlantic flooded the North Sea plain around 6,800 BC; the final land-bridge to France was breached, forming the English Channel, about 300 years later.

Before that time there were almost certainly no permanent settlements in Scotland where, as in Scandinavia and northern Germany, the severe cold would have made human survival impossible. Only occasional hunting forays were possible during the infrequent milder spells easing conditions on the delta shore of that great river, crossing the future bed of the future North Sea, of which the Spey, Tay, Forth and Tweed were mere tributaries, as were the Thames, the Rhine, and the Elbe.

As recently as 10,000 BC there was probably still a vast sheet of ice covering the central Highlands of Scotland, scraping and grinding the mountains to form the generally flat-topped *beinns* we see today. The glaciers flowing from the ice-caps gouged the valleys and lochs, eventually producing the 'U' shaped straths and 'V' shaped glens which are now part of the familiar scene throughout Scotland. The deeper lochs today still hold some of the original meltwater from the glaciers of the last Ice Age, generally at the levels below 30 m (100 ft). Loch Lomond, Scotland's largest body of fresh water, has a depth greater than that of the Atlantic Ocean one thousand miles out towards America.

Prehistoric families in Scotland needed to be finely tuned to the landscape around them: to the plant and animal life, to the seasons and the vagaries of everyday weather in northern climes.

This style of 'harmony with life' has survived into modern times in only a few so-called primitive peoples (whose existence is, in fact, far more sophisticated than is usually believed). From Scotland's primitive cultures, only a few subtle traces survive, and these are mainly to be found in the gene-bank inherited from our forbears: hair type and colour, facial features, physical stance, and peculiarities such as the West Highland gene for perfect pitch.

More readily perceivable, for those with eyes to see and ears to hear, are the 'sound fossils' of the tongues which invested the salient rocks, hill shapes, waterfalls, rivers, and glens with oral labels. These often seem to make little sense when merely written, but the place-names which have been handed down are every bit as expressive as those we know from, say, the American Apache and Australian Aborigines. And it is a living process, still at work. For example, *Creag Bhais Na Daoine Athar A Eireann*, 'Death Rock of the Air Men From Ireland', most poignantly records a modern-day tragedy in the Perthshire hills.

Hills and mountains used to be described in a variety of references to their physical shape – *Tom, Stob, Sron, Meall, Beinn, Carn,* and *Sliabh*. The last is an excellent example of how topographical names provide markers to the past and its people. *Sliabh*, that early Irish Gaelic word, is almost entirely associated with areas which were the heartland of the Dalriadic Scots who settled on the West Coast 1,500 years ago. Similarly, the distribution of place-names with the prefix *Pit* (a plot, or share of land) provides vital information on the limits of settlement from the south by the Celtic-speaking Picts.

Some of the oldest topographical names are so 'aboriginal' throughout Europe that they can be spotted fairly easily. *Abhainn,* the Gaelic for 'river', is pronounced 'avon' – a common river name in the English language. The basic Gaelic word for 'water', *uisge*, comes from an old Celtic stem yielding rivers named Esk, Usk, and Ouse the length of Britain. And Carnac, 'the place of the stones' in Brittany, is from the same root as the Gaelic *cairn* – and probably the English 'cone', which describes the shape of a 'cairn'. Even a limited knowledge of older Gaelic shows that modern historians missed the point when they decided that the Roman victory over the Caledonians in AD 84, recorded by Tacitus, was on the lower slopes of *Mons GRAUPIUS* – dismissing as dyslexic the 16th-century chronicler Boecce, who wrote it as *Mons GRAMPIUS*. This just happens to be the Roman translation into Latin from Old Celtic *Gruaim Pennein*, which aptly describes the Grampian Mountains as the 'Gloomy' or 'Grim Hills'.

One final example of word-lore may help encourage a continuing interest in the quest for 'fossil language'. The Gaelic word *srath* is pronounced 'strath'. This is quite probably a survival of a word meaning not 'river valley' but 'way' or 'track' from 2,000 years ago, when Scotland was clothed with thick forest, and the safest and often most direct routes for travellers were along the river valleys. (The Old Germanic word was *strata* and the Old English *straet*, giving us today's 'street' with its narrow interpretation.)

Place-name evidence reinforces the belief that there were no great influxes of Celtic peoples into Scotland before the mass migration of the Scots or *Scoti* from northern Ireland around AD 500. Before then, there seems to have been a gradual topping-up of the Celtic gene-bank – mostly by peoples fleeing from the deadly competition of other Celts who had developed superior weaponry, such as sharp iron swords instead of the earlier, less efficient, soft bronze weapons.

Shaping the Scottish Character

As the ice receded, these people and others seeking new hunting-grounds found that the nature of Highland geography encouraged the development of small family groupings, quite different from the social development encouraged by the broad central plain around the valleys of the Forth and Clyde. At the same time, a composite national temperament began to emerge. This was moulded by the territorial restraints provided by the peninsular nature of the Scottish mainland, as distinct from that of England. Even in the lowest of the Lowlands, one is never far from mountain terrain in Scotland.

Two factors, one climatic and one geophysical, have contributed to the development of the peculiarly Scottish character. In terms of latitude, most of Scotland lies well over a hundred kilometres north of Moscow. The Gulf Stream softens the climate somewhat, but few would argue seriously that the Scots share the relaxed attitude of the sun-drenched Mediterranean folk. Secondly, Scotland really *is* the 'land of the mountain and the flood'. Of the 566 peaks and tops of 914 m (3,000 ft) or more in the whole of Great Britain, no less than 545 are in Scotland, including all those over 1,219 m (4,000 ft). As for water, it is hard to find anywhere in Scotland where a body of water or a burn is not within reach – even on the east coast, where in places the annual rainfall drops to a mere 50.8 cm (20 inches) or so, compared with the 254 cm (100 inches) or more on the west coast.

This, then, is the natural setting which produced a race of tribal clansfolk who were generally thought of, by the outside world, as 'Redshanks', 'wyld Hielandmen', and generally barbaric. It took many hundreds of years for that outside world to modify its opinion.

Kings and Clans

Probably no earlier than 100 BC, a wave of Celtic invaders swept across the east coast of North Britain above the line of the Forth estuary. They found themselves confronting a long-established population of probably non-Celtic stock, whose settlements extended up the fertile eastern plains to the islands off the north coast. These islands became the Orkneys and the Shetlands in the later Viking period. By virtue of their remoteness, aided by freak climatic conditions, they have preserved some remarkable examples of the homes of these late Neolithic peoples, who date from around 2,000 BC.

Our racial memories of the encounters between the Celtic warrior aristocracy and a more brutish, primitive people, described in legends as dwelling underground and in caves, have produced tales of 'knights' with swords of power fighting club-wielding 'giants' to rescue beautiful maidens. The brutal reality would have been that the technologically superior invaders would have had an army of young warriors as their cutting edge, whose first priority after capturing new territory on which to settle would have been the abduction of wives from among the native population. These Celtic invaders – still termed *Picts* or 'painted people', from their colourful warpaint and tattoos – would themselves have been impeded from fighting their way up the British mainland by well-entrenched Celts from earlier waves of invasion. The latter had organized themselves into a nation of tribes, which the Romans called *Pritani*. With 'p' and 'b' casually interchangeable from the early Celtic language, it is easy to see how names like Brittany and the Bretons, Britain and the Britons, have evolved from the Roman *Pritani*.

From the earliest times, when population densities began to increase the danger from newcomers coveting your good land, your secure homestead with its water supply, your daughters, your lives-tock, and your hunting preserves, there was a natural urge for extended families to band together for protection. These groupings would all have claimed a common ancestor, honoured by oral tradition; to all intents and purposes, what we would call a *clan* today. The actual word 'clan' seems to have entered common usage from the Latin word *planta*, meaning a 'shoot' (in the botanical sense), and therefore dates from probably no earlier than 1,000 years ago. Before then, instead of a *Clann Dhomnuill*, for example, the more usual

reference was to the *Siol Dhomnuill* or 'the seed of Donald'.

An even earlier Celtic word as forerunner to 'clan' was *Cinel*, used more in the sense of 'kindred'. Early Irish chronicles refer to the *Cinel* into which an Antrim tribe, the *Scoti*, divided after they had invaded the west coast of Scotland. The leader of the invading Scoti was Fergus mac Erc, whose forces were supported by those of his two brothers, Loarn and Aengus. From them and from the two grandsons of Fergus sprang the four

Above: Mounted Pictish warrior from cross slab at Aberlemno

Left: Roman legionaries from a 2nd-century sculpture at the Antonine Wall

kindred groups to which many people of Scottish descent can trace their origins. The *Cinel Lorn* came to occupy a district of Argyllshire centred on Dunollia and still called Lorn. The *Cinel Aengus* controlled the key islands of Islay and Jura; the *Cinel Gabhran* occupied the rest of Argyll and Kintyre, while the *Cinel Comhgall* possessed what is known today as Cowal.

Evidence from the Irish chronicles suggests that the Scoti of the Kingdom of Dalriada in Antrim had originally been invited across the sea by their Celtic 'cousins', the Picts of Caledonia, to help repel the Roman legions of Gnaeus Julius Agricola, which were sweeping through the fertile plains of Caledonia after shattering the main Pictish army in the Battle of Mons Grampius in AD 84. (Some 800 years later, Old English tradition as recorded in the *Anglo-Saxon Chronicle* would, in identical fashion, claim that the first Jutish warbands of Hengist and Horsa had been invited across the North Sea to help defend the embattled Romano-Britons.)

In the late 1st century AD, the Picts had yet not reached their military prime, and could easily have been so desperate for the help of allies that they suspended their natural sense of caution and judgement. In the centuries after the Roman threat abated following Agricola's peremptory recall to Rome, the Picts would find that numerous colonies of Scoti would prove difficult – even impossible – to dislodge from the shores of Argyll. In any event, by the 2nd century AD much of these shores was controlled by a non-Pictish tribe referred to, by the geographer Ptolemy, as the *Epidii*. The name 'Scot' itself means 'raider' or 'predator' in Old Irish, and in the years until AD 502, when Fergus mac Erc was proclaimed King of 'New Dalriada', the Scoti truly earned their nickname across the strait between Antrim and Kintyre, which at its narrowest is a mere 21 km (13 miles).

The Clan Crucible - 13th Century

The divide between Celto-Norse and mainland Scots culture.

LEWIS

King of Man then MacLeod

THE NORTH ISLES

UIST

MacLeod

Ross

Matheson

SKYE

Ross

(K. of Man then MacLeod)

RUM

THE HEBRIDES

MacLean

MacKinnon

IONA

MULL MacDougall

THE SOUTH ISLES

Cam

MacNaughton
MacArthur
pbell

JURA

MacLachlan

La mont

Ste w

Mac Donald

ISLAY

MacDonald

Loch Fyne

Stewart

IRISH CHANNEL

Bruce

MacKay

Gunn

Sutherland

R. Oykell

Murray

Ross

(MacWilliam then Ross)

? MacKenzie

Bisset

URQUHART

Grant

Loch Ness

? Clan Chattan

Cumming

Hay

Murray

INNES

BRODIE

Murray

Crawford

Murray

Clan MacDuff

Clan MacDuff

Cumming

FORBES

LESLIE

R. Don

ABERDEEN

R. Dee

Clan MacDuff

R. Spey

Cumming

Clan MacDuff

ARBUTHNOTT

(? Murray then Stirling)

Menzies

R. Tay

RATTRAY

Clan MacDuff

OGILVIE

Loch Tay

Ruthven
Moncreiffe
Oliphant

R. Earn

Hay

CAMERON

Clan MacDuff

Graham

R. Forth

WEMYSS

DUNFERMLINE

BUCHANAN

STIRLING

Graham

Clan MacDuff

DUNBAR

DRUMMOND

DUNBARTON

COLQUHOUN

Stewart

ERSKINE

GLASGOW

Murray

Murray

Clan MacDuff

Dunbar

Sinclair

KEITH

Clan MacDuff

BERWICK

Hay

Murray

GORDON

SWINTON

R. Clyde

Cumming

Fraser

HOME

Stewart

DOUGLAS

R. Tweed

CHISHOLM

R. Nith

Cumming

Bruce

Cumming

The Kingdom or 'Lordship' of the Isle before 1493

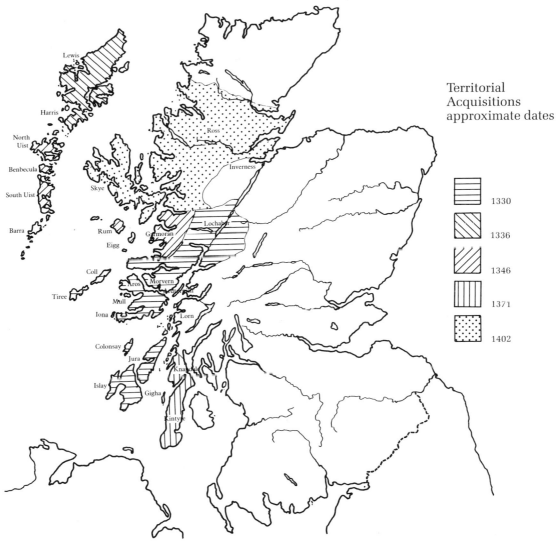

Territorial
Acquisitions
approximate dates

▤	1330
▨	1336
▨	1346
▥	1371
▦	1402

In 1493, the mainland King of Scots crushed this independent sub-kingdom, which once covered an area larger than Belgium and incorporated all the western isles and a great swathe of the western Highlands. By right of their seniority among the descendants of the great Somerled, 'King of the Isles', the Clan Donald traditionally provided their High Chief as Lord of the Isles. The title today is held by Prince Charles as heir to the Throne. Current excavations on the two islands on Finlaggan Loch in Islay confirm that this was the centre of the kingdom, at a site which seems to have been a major centre of power in the Western Isles for over 1,000 years. At a time (14th century) when many of Europe's rulers were barbaric, the Lordship was a model of the civilized exercise of power, with a system of professional district judges, a commissioner for weights and measures, hereditary physicians (the Beatons), a keeper of the records as administrator, and a Council of the Isles comprising up to 16 'privy councillors' who met in the parliament building on the smaller 'Council Isle' under the presiding Lord of the Isles. By the original Celtic (*brehon*) constitutional system, the Lord was all-powerful, but could be lawfully deposed should he become despotic. Even today, the principle that 'the clan is higher than the chief' still applies. In early times also, there was no private ownership of property (only of moveable assets), with the Lord of the Isles holding all land *in trust* for his people as their *steward*.

No wonder that Highlanders looked back on that golden age with the proverb, 'There is no Joy without Clan Donald...' The vacuum was filled by the less benign Campbells and the Mackenzies, exercising Crown authority delegated from a distant Edinburgh.

13

From the dawn of history to the present era, experience in times of danger has shown that decisions taken by councils of wise elders cannot match those made by a strong individual who possesses the trust, loyalty, and overwhelming support of his people. Ideally, that individual (almost inevitably male) needed low cunning as well as high courage, physical strength and experience in leadership as well as the business of warfare.

From primeval times, too, a series of rituals, which accompany the accession of a new leader, has developed. These are subconsciously designed to reinforce the faith in that leader of the members of the clan or tribe. As rituals evolve over a period of time, symbols are developed to strengthen faith and, at the same time, help the group to close ranks. In fact the word 'symbol' derives from a Greek word which means 'bringing together'. The simplest form of this survives today with the inauguration of a new monarch, president, company chairman, or team captain: the acclamation. This generally occurs after all the other rituals have taken place and the members of the nation, state, clan, or team can observe the trappings of ceremonial.

In AD 574, Aidan mac Gabhran was inaugurated as King of New Dalriada by the High Priest Columba, who was himself a prince of the royal house of Old Dalriada. The setting was the fortress at the summit of the great rock of Dunadd, which dominated access to present-day Knapdale and Kintyre across the Crinan isthmus. Aidan placed his foot in the footprint of his grandfather, which had been carved into the bare granite after the coronation of Fergus in 502. Aidan's ensuing consecration, with the full Christian rites, is the first so recorded. For his actual ordaining by Columba, King Gabhran crossed over to the Isle of Hy – known today as Iona. In the established Celtic tradition, Aidan would have used some of the symbols of royalty of that time. Dressed in the white robes of truth and purity, he would have been presented with the great sword of justice and the even more significant long white wand or sceptre, topped with a carved stone of quartz or crystal. The sceptre, examples of which have been found in the tombs of Bronze Age chieftains, is the ultimate symbol of chiefly power and authority. The monarch is, of course, the 'chief of chiefs', and the sceptre developed from the great stone-headed war mace, carried as a weapon by tribal leaders since the dawn of time, essentially to beat down anyone seeking to question or usurp their authority.

Possibly the oldest ritual symbol in Aidan's consecration would have been the forerunner to the 'anointing with holy oil' which became formalized for Scottish monarchs in the 14th century. In the

9th-century Celtic manuscript taken to Kells in Ireland when Vikings began raiding the east coast of Scotland.

6th century of New Dalriada, the King would have had bear grease rubbed ceremonially into his flesh, to imbue him with the strength and courage of the beast which excited universal respect and admiration above all others. Rather than the crown of later years, he would probably have had a wreath of some significant plant placed on his head, much like the laurel wreath of the Roman Caesars.

Aidan would have stood during the symbolic ritual of his inauguration, with the acclamation of his warriors expressed by wild cries and the clashing of spears on their round, studded shields. Nearly 300 years later, by which time the Scots had absorbed their reluctant Pictish hosts after centuries of warfare, their great King, Kenneth MacAlpin, established a new royal centre at the Pictish capital of Scone. Here, for the next 500 years, the ancient weapon-clashing rite of acclamation justified the description of the Hill of Kings as 'Scone of the Melodious Shields'.

With the emergence of kingdoms as larger power complexes we begin to see an erosion of the tradition of tribal authority (leaders with the necessary amalgam of physical and mental prowess evolved from a hereditary warrior aristocracy, who could rule effectively only by the support and consent of their people). When monarchies emerged with the consequent increase of wealth and power at the centre, national leaders became able to enforce their authority with a strong 'palace guard' or standing army. At the same time, factions among their subjects could be played off, one against the other, until minds could be concentrated on the real threat – genuine, or the fruit of propaganda – from an external enemy.

One of the less endearing characteristics of the Celts, right until today, has been the tendency to be constantly squabbling and feuding among themselves until a common foe appears to unite them in a common cause. Immediately that cause is removed, they revert to in-fighting. The most successful of Scotland's monarchs harnessed this tendency to their own ends, often with dramatic results.

Apart from achieving a union of Picts and Scots in the kingdom which he forged, Kenneth MacAlpin also took steps to consolidate the power and authority of the Celtic Church, which had developed separately from the Church of Rome. In the early Celtic Church, celibacy was probably practiced, in the sense of 'remaining unmarried'. In fact, many monastic abbots and abbesses passed on their holy office to their offspring by an accepted system of hereditary succession. Nor was the Church of Rome impeccable at that time; Pope Sergius III, in the reign of Kenneth MacAlpin's grandson, had two of his rivals strangled to ensure that his child by his mistress would eventually succeed him as Pope John XI.

The threat of the ecclesiastical and political domination of northern Britain by the Angles of English Northumbria was, in the year 685, dispelled by the total destruction of King Ecgfrith's army by the Picts at Nechtansmere, near Forfar in Angus. But in little more than 100 years, the menace of the English was replaced by a far more terrible foe. During the century after Nechtansmere, both the Angles and the Picts, like the Romans before them, succumbed to internal strife. This left them ill-prepared for the next, most ruthless wave of invaders from across the North Sea. In 793 the first recorded Viking raid was made on the great monastery of Lindisfarne, just to the south of Pictish territory.

The Vikings

For some 300 years, the heartlands of Scandinavia had been the crucible which produced a hardy and resourceful people, forced by competition for land and subsistence to become fierce fighters and skilled seafarers. During that period, a 'Little Ice Age' had kept the Scandinavian fjords icebound for half the year and the North Sea almost impenetrably fog-bound in summer. By the end of the 8th century, however, a dryer and warmer climate had begun to touch northern Europe, and Viking crews began to venture across the North Sea in search of plunder. Apart from the eastern Swedes, who crossed the Baltic to prey on the countries along its eastern shore, the Vikings referred to their marauding raids on Britain as sailing 'west over seas'.

The southern Vikings, from southern Sweden, Jutland, and Denmark, attacked eastern Britain from the Thames to the Moray Firth. Their rivals from Norway fell upon and annexed the Shetland and Orkney Islands, establishing their influence down the west coast of Scotland, into Ireland and the Isle of Man. The long-suffering victims of these predators referred to them by different terms; the Danes as 'Black strangers' and the Norsemen as 'White settlers'. The proliferation of Scandinavian place-names in those areas of Scotland matches that of the east and south-east of England. The very name for an estuary in Scotland, 'firth', comes from the Old Norse for fjord – fjorthr.

In 867 the 'Great Army' of the Danes, which had fallen upon East Anglia in the previous year, completed the ruin of English Northumbria. The Danes now controlled York and the north of England, but were not able to threaten the new kingdom of the Scots from the south. Wessex, last of the English kingdoms to resist (and the only one to survive) the Danish invasion was still holding out in the south, while the Dublin-based Vikings posed another threat to Danish Northumbria from the west.

16th-Century Clans of the Braelands and Highlands

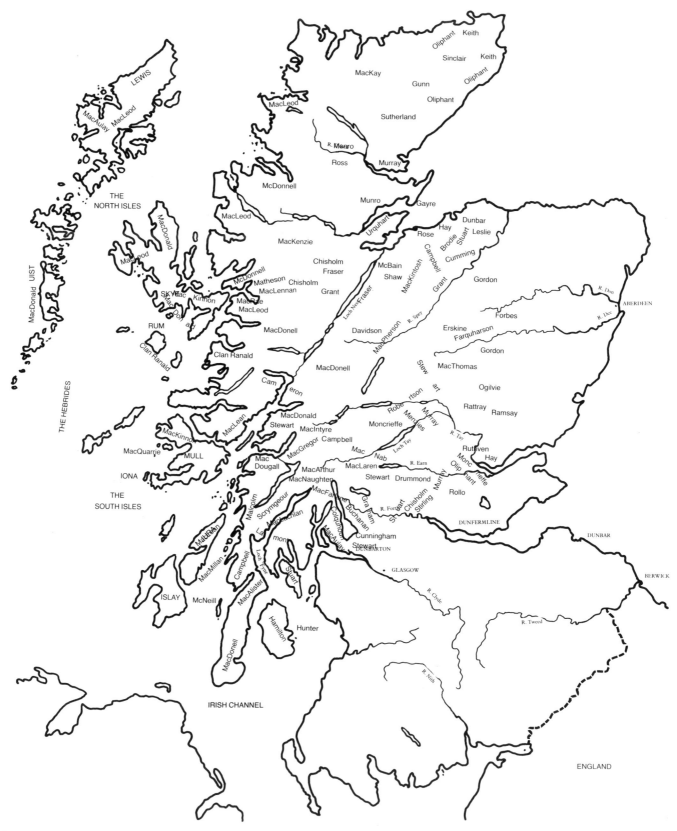

Scotland Divided – 1746

The geo-political 'Highland Line', north and west of which were most affected by post-Culloden Government measures.

Once the Vikings had fragmented the great Northumbrian kingdom, the border between England and Scotland gradually became established. In the half-century after the Danes finally lost York to the Norsemen (919), the Scots regained Dunedin (Edinburgh) and the Lothians to the east, and were ceded Cumberland in the west. By the middle of the 11th century, the ancient British kingdom of Strathclyde had effected a union with the Scots under Duncan I, who was killed in battle (1040) by the real-life Macbeth – who, despite Shakespeare's slanders, was merely establishing his claim to the throne in the only way he knew. Macbeth was killed in his turn by Duncan's son Malcolm, the third Scottish king of that name (1057–93).

The Middle Ages

Malcolm III was dubbed in Gaelic *ceann mor*, which has been Anglicized as 'Canmore' and carelessly (not to mention unflatteringly) translated as 'Big Head'. The implication is clearly 'The Head-most', or 'High King' – the head man, chief of chiefs and *capo di capos*. With Malcolm Canmore there appeared at last the monarch of a unified realm called *Scotland*, five and a half centuries after the Scots had first established their kingdom of New Dalriada in the west. Also with Malcolm Canmore, there began the process of Anglicization destined to alter Scotland's course and destiny profoundly.

In the centuries after Malcolm Canmore married a Saxon princess, the most extraordinary element in the relationship between Scotland and England is the failure of England to absorb its smaller, weaker northern neighbour. Malcolm's 36-year reign saw a programme of Anglicization at the Scottish court, implemented almost entirely by the strong will of the new Queen, Malcolm's second wife. Queen Margaret was the sister of Edgar Atheling, heir to the Old English royal line, ousted from England first by King Harold in 1066, then by the victor of Hastings: William of Normandy. A saintly woman who seems to have been totally devoid of humour, Queen Margaret phased out Gaelic as the language of the Scots court and introduced Saxon, then Norman customs and administration. Her husband was dominated by her, and was finally killed at Alnwick in one of several attempts to establish her brother's claim to the English throne.

Before his untimely demise, Malcolm had been forced to own the supremacy of William I of England, and accept a bloodless invasion of Scotland by numbers of William's barons. William had solved the problem of persistent English resistance by slaughtering every English male over the age of

12 from the River Humber to the Scottish Border and turning the country into a desert. Norman husbands were imposed on English women, and Norman lords on English manors. It was not so easy in Scotland. The old Celtic nobility was too deeply entrenched in well-defended territories, and it was by treaties and arranged marriages that the Norman heirarchy was stealthily imposed upon the Scots.

By one of the ironies of history, the incomers eventually became as Scottish as the Scots. They have left us with a range of clan names which the world regards as quintessentially Scottish, but which are principally Norman French: for example, the Bruces from Bruis, near Cherbourg, the Frasers from Frésèlière in Anjou, the Grants (from their French nickname *Le Grand*), and the Hays from the Cotentin. The most famous of these Scoto-Norman names is Stewart, which derives from the hereditary office of Steward of Scotland, borne today by

Left: Norse chessmen in walrus ivory. Isles of Lewis – 12th century.

Below: James I born 1394 and murdered in Perth in 1437.

the heir to the throne of Great Britain. The first Steward of Scotland, Walter FitzAlan, was himself descended from a long line of Breton nobles who were hereditary Stewards of Dol in Brittany.

In the years between the death of Malcolm Canmore in 1093 and the accession of Robert II, the first Stewart king, in 1371, 14 kings ruled Scotland for an average of 12 years, and for two periods totalling 12 years Edward I of England ruled Scotland himself. Edward I's nickname 'Hammer of the Scots' was not awarded lightly, but then his last and greatest opponent was also a force to be reckoned with. Robert the Bruce is still the Scottish hero of heroes, but it tends to be forgotten that he had fought both for and against Scotland on a number of occasions before having himself inaugurated as King at Scone in 1306. Bruce's brilliant generalship at Bannockburn in 1314 inflicted a crushing defeat on the English army of Edward II,

vindicating Scotland's claim to be an independent, sovereign nation and no vassal of England.

Six years later, the celebrated Declaration of Arbroath was presented to Pope John XXII at the papal court in Avignon, part of a dramatic plea for the Pope to intervene in the bloody war England was continuing to wage against Scotland. The Declaration's preamble was a masterpiece of propaganda urging the righteousness of the Scots cause. It told how the ancient Scots had made a wonderful Odyssey from Greater Scythia in Asia, through the Mediterranean and past the Pillars of Hercules to their present land. There they had defeated and absorbed the Picts before seeing off Angles, Danes, and Norsemen, since when they had 'lived under a one hundred and thirteen kings of their own stock, a line unbroken by a single foreigner'. Sealed by eight Scottish earls and 45 barons of the realm, the Declaration, with timeless eloquence, committed

19

Robert the Bruce to continue the struggle – but in language which suggests that the signatories had not forgotten Bruce's earlier tendency to change sides when it suited him:

Yet if he should give up what he has begun, and agree to make us or our kingdom subject to the King of England or the English, we should exert ourselves at once to drive him out as our enemy and a subverter of his own rights and ours, and make some other man who was well able to defend us as our King; for, as long as but a hundred of us remain alive, never will we on any conditions be brought under the English rule. It is in truth not for glory, nor riches, nor honours that we are fighting for but for freedom and for that alone, which no honest man gives up but with life itself.

When Bruce died in 1329, he was succeeded by his son David II (1329–70), who shrewdly married the daughter of Edward II of England, but failed to produce an heir. It, therefore, fell to the Bruce's daughter Marjorie to pass on those worthy genes through her son by Walter, the High Steward: Robert II (1371–90), first monarch of the Stewart dynasty.

The first Stewart kings hardly looked likely to bequeath Scotland a ruling line destined to last for the next 300 years. Robert III (1390–1406) was an ineffectual ruler, made permanently lame by the kick of a horse; his brother held the reins of power, bringing about the death of the heir to the throne to extend his own power. Robert III sent his younger son James to France for safety in 1406 and died the same year – by which time the boy had been captured by the English, who kept him under house arrest in London for 18 years. From the death of Robert III in 1406 until the accession of Charles I in 1625, every single Scottish monarch would come to the throne as a child – with all the insecurity and strife which royal minorities have tended to encourage.

When James I (1406–37) finally returned to Scotland in 1424, he arrived with firm ideas about putting the Scottish nobles in their place, and adopting other administrative improvements which he had noted were working to good effect in England. James I introduced a practice much favoured by later Stewart kings: inviting certain of the great Highland chiefs to a Parliament, then imprisoning or executing them as he saw fit. The King's own murder in Perth by Sir Robert Stewart and his accomplices left his six-year-old son to ascend the throne.

James II (1437–60) grew to be a tough and resourceful ruler who survived many plots against him (usually by the kin of nobles of whom he had disposed). The King personally stabbed to death the Earl of Douglas after dinner in Stirling Castle (1452), removing a long-standing potential rival to

the Stewart dynasty; but he seems to have died in a convenient accident in 1460, when a cannon he insisted on firing during the siege of Roxburgh blew up in his face. Yet another Stewart boy-king acceded as James III (1460–88), making one of his first adult moves a wise one by marrying the Danish heiress to Shetland and Orkney and so bringing those islands into the kingdom. But when James III chose to antagonize his nobles once too often, he was murdered after his own son led an army against him at Sauchieburn in 1488 – leaving the oldest Stewart to come to the throne for nearly 100 years to succeed at the ripe old age of 15.

From Stewart to Stuart

For a while, it seemed that James IV (1488–1513) had broken the Stewarts' run of bad luck. To settle the interminable Border feuding with England, he approached Henry VII with a view to contracting marriage with one of the English princesses and was duly betrothed to the 7-year-old Margaret Tudor, eldest sister of the future Henry VIII. Before his fiancée had reached puberty, however, James

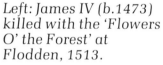

Left: James IV (b.1473) killed with the 'Flowers O' the Forest' at Flodden, 1513.

Above: Margaret Tudor (1489–1542), sister of Henry VIII; she married James IV at the age of only 12.

Above: James V (1512– 42) father of Mary Queen of Scots.

fell in love with, and secretly married, Margaret Drummond, daughter of the 1st Earl Drummond. Two other Drummond girls had been Queens of Scotland, and when this secret leaked out, it did nothing to please other ambitious Scottish noble families. In 1501, preparations for sending Princess Margaret (now 11) north to Scotland were being finalized when Margaret Drummond, with her sisters Sybilla and Euphemia, were found dead at breakfast one morning. The way was now clear for the great State marriage to go ahead. Though inconsolable for the best part of a year, James IV recovered sufficiently to take a new royal mistress in the months before Margaret Tudor finally arrived in Scotland, to become a dutiful wife of 12 years old.

(Unbeknown at the time, Margaret Tudor also brought with her the succession to the throne of England. This came about when the grandson of

her only son by James (James V) became James VI of Scotland and then James I of England, when his cousin Elizabeth died childless in 1603. Henry VIII had all but excluded his elder sisters' heirs from the Tudor succession after his death in 1547, but none of his other siblings produced surviving heirs and his only son, Edward VI, died in 1553.)

In true Stewart management style, James IV was defeated in 1513 in the Battle of Flodden Field by a considerably inferior English army, being slaughtered in company with key members of all the great families of Scotland. The famous lament *The Flowers of the Forest* preserves the memory of the national disaster, from which Scotland took a long time to recover. James V (1513–42) succeeded as a babe in arms, and died after another disastrous battle, Solway Moss, at the age of 30. He left only a six-day-old daughter to succeed him, which caused him to utter the cryptic comment on the dynasty 'It

21

James VI (1566–1625), who succeeded 'Good Queen Bess' as James I of England (1603).

began wi' a lass [Bruce's daughter Marjorie] and it will end wi' a lass.' From early in her life, his hapless daughter Mary, Queen of Scots (1542–67) did what she could to nullify the prophecy. Married to the heir to the French throne when she was 16 and Queen of France for barely a year, she came back to Scotland a childless widow of 18. But with her she brought to the history of Britain the French rendering of 'Stewart' – Stuart – made necessary by the French language's lack of 'W'.

James VI (1567–1625) was Mary's son by her second husband: her cousin Henry Stewart, Lord Darnley, who before his timely assassination (1567) enjoyed the now outmoded style and title of King-Consort. Before his coronation as King of England, James VI's apprenticeship years as King of Scotland, manipulating a ruthless and acquisitive nobility, had taught him that money and power are inseparable. Needing money to reduce his dependence on those tiresome politicians in Parliament and to buy loyal men to fill key posts in his Government, James hit on a ridiculously simple answer: milking the 'honours system' which he controlled. Between his accession to the English throne in March 1603 and the end of the year, James created 1,000 new knights. On his journey from Scotland to London, he once knighted 43 before breakfast, and on 23 July knighted 432 at one kneeling. By the end of this first year as King of

England, finding that the English squirearchy seemed to find the asking price of £40 for a knighthood quite acceptable, the King applied market forces and raised the price to £100. James also instituted a form of 'pyramid selling', whereby the Crown took 40 per cent and left 60 per cent of the price of the honour to be split among the intermediaries; and a bulk discount system whereby, for a payment of £369 1s 6d, a knighthood was secured for the dealer who could then nominate five further knights, each of whom paid him £100 direct.

This particular form of business acumen on the part of 'James Sixt and First' has largely gone unnoticed, but it had immense and indeed fatal consequences for his successor. By the time of his death in 1625 James had created 2,600 new knights and 108 new peers (making his close friend and favourite, George Villiers, Duke of Buckingham). In so doing he had transformed the English middle class and aristocracy – and the nature of both the House of Commons and House of Lords, which by the accession of Charles I in 1625 were very different bodies from what they had been in Elizabeth's time. James I could create knights and peers. What he could not do was to create an English Parliament permanently grateful and unquestionably loyal to the Crown, as Charles I later found to his cost.

John Knox (1512–72), cult figure of the Scots Protestant movement.

Reformation, Revolution and Restoration

The accession of Charles I in 1625 is a natural turning point from which to look back at how Scotland had fared under the Stewarts since the death of Robert the Bruce. By any standard, the balance sheet of the Stewart performance is an impressive one. That crisis-racked, minority-ridden dynasty had preserved the independence of Scotland and strengthened the power of the Scottish Crown. Between the reigns of Robert the Bruce and James IV, the Scots were spared the dynastic upheavals of England, which over the same period experienced the deposition and murder of four kings (Edward II, Richard II, Henry VI, and Richard III) and the 30-year power struggle between the rival dynasties of Lancaster and York.

Scotland's Stewart kings, by comparison, had not only survived but prospered. By the reign of James IV, Scotland's overseas trade was doing so well that it needed a navy. James IV built the mighty warship *Michael*, for which it was said that all the woods of Fife had been felled. The new threat of Scottish sea power helped persuade Henry VIII of England to build super-warships of his own: *Mary Rose* (which sank) and *Great Harry* (destroyed by accidental fire). The canny Scots sold *Michael* to the French after James IV's death at Flodden.

The strengthening of Crown authority and the wealth created by trade led to an early sponsoring of learning and the arts north of the Border. By 1500 Scotland had three universities (St Andrews, Glasgow, and Aberdeen) to England's two (Oxford and Cambridge). Before the 16th century was out, James VI had added another two (Edinburgh and Marischal College, Aberdeen). As for primary education, it was in Scotland, not England, that the first British statute was passed ordering the maintenance of a school in every parish (James VI again, in 1616).

By 1500, the Stewarts had earned Scotland international dignity as a recognized and respected sovereign state. This dignity was symbolized by the presentation to James IV of a royal sceptre by Pope Alexander VI, and a sword of state by Pope Julius II. It was James V who completed the Crown Regalia of Scotland (the 'Honours of Scotland', as they are correctly styled) by remodelling the reputed Crown of the Bruce in the elegant form admired by visitors to Edinburgh Castle today. In the 1650s, the politically motivated vandalism of Oliver Cromwell led to the scrapping of the English Crown Regalia, with the result that most of the Crown Jewels in the Tower of London today are of 19th century or even more recent provenance. But the Honours of Scotland were devotedly preserved from repeated English orders for their capture and destruction. Today the Crown of Scotland is, after

23

Left: The Scottish regalia, known as the 'Honours of Scotland'.

Right: The execution of King Charles I in London, 30 January, 1649.

the Crown of Hungary, the oldest royal crown in the western world.

By the time of the Union of the Crowns in 1603, the Stewarts had achieved much for their realm. But there was one thing they could not bring to or impose on Scotland: unity. The Highland Line, slicing north-east across Scotland from Dunbarton into Angus, then swinging north to the Moray Firth, was a far more obvious frontier dividing Scot from Scot than the open moorland Border between Scotland and England. The Highland/Lowland divide was not merely geographical. It was psychological, and it ran far deeper than the mutual snobbery, distrust, and condescension of Britain's modern-day 'North-South Divide'. In early 17th-century Scotland, every fruit of what we could today call 'progress' – communications, law and order, education, prosperity through trade and industry, a widening awareness of what the outside world had to offer – grew and was gathered in the Lowland towns and cities. An educated Scottish gentleman of 1625 knew more about France, Germany, or Italy than he did about the Highlands of his own country. Lowland Scots did not see the Highland clans as an integral part of Scotland's national heritage. With good reason, Lowlanders preserved a deep race-memory of centuries of ferocious raiding by the Highlanders. They regarded the Highland clans as Dark Age hangovers, long overdue for civilizing by the sword. Government crackdowns, such as James VI's outlawry and proscription of the MacGregors in 1604, aroused relief in the Lowlands, not outrage.

If the Highland/Lowland divide was one source of Scottish disunity that was (literally) as old as the hills, the other was mankind's greatest self-inflicted wound: religion, in the form of the Protestant Reformation. South of the Border, the breach with Rome and establishment of a separate Church of England was achieved by the Crown with the monarch as supreme head of the new Church. Scotland's experience was completely different. The Calvinist revolution preached by the 'Moses of Scotland', John Knox, was fiercely political right from the start. Its original aim (1559–60) was to use Old Testament fanaticism in a national uprising, to rid Scotland of the French garrison forces imposed on the country during the young Queen Mary's brief marriage to Francis II of France. (Knox's anti-French bias is always easier to understand when we remember that he had spent 19 months as a French galley-slave.)

In 1559–61 the Scottish 'Congregation of the Lord' found an unexpected ally in England, whose

new Queen Elizabeth hoped to cash in on a French defeat in Scotland and recover Calais (humiliatingly lost to France by Mary Tudor in January 1558). The English fleet sent to the Firth of Forth by Elizabeth bombarded the French out of Fife, then blockaded them into surrender at Leith. The Treaty of Edinburgh (July 1560) secured the evacuation of the French from Scotland and paved the way for the establishment of the reformed Scottish Church – the Kirk – on the dictatorial lines laid down by Knox. North of the Border, the Reformation set out to replace the centuries-old authority of Pope, bishop, and priest with the harsh new authority of the Presbyterian minister. In their zeal the ministers of the Kirk claimed tenure of the keys of Heaven and Hell, as no Pope or bishop had ever dared to do, and with them the right to preach revolution against the civil authority claiming dominion over 'God's people'.

James VI grew to manhood under a constant bombardment of lectures from the leaders of the new Kirk, whose formidable leader Andrew Melville on one memorable occasion pulled the King by his sleeve and called him 'God's silly vassal'. (It is not pleasant to contemplate the fate of any churchman foolish enough to have tried this with Henry VIII of England, or Elizabeth for that matter.) In a typical harangue, Melville told his King that:

Thair is twa Kings and twa Kingdoms in Scotland. Thair is Chryst Jesus the King and his Kingdom the Kirk, whose subject King James the Saxt is, and of whase Kingdom mocht a King nor a Lord nor a heid but a member. And they whom Chryst has callit and commandit to watch over the Kirk and govern his spirituall Kingdom has sufficient power of him and authoritie so to do.

Faced with what would nowadays be called the Old Testament fundamentalism of the Kirk (whose leaders forgot the pleas of Jesus for toleration and to 'render unto Caesar the things that are Caesar's'), James fell back on the age-old political tactic of divide and rule. His biggest danger was that Presbyterianism did indeed win devout and spiritually-intimidated adherents across the full spectrum of Scottish society, from earls to city apprentices and country ploughmen, so any frontal assault on the Kirk was out of the question. But James also knew that the more extreme political claims of the Kirk were not shared by most educated Scots, who feared any attempt to undermine civil power. And, though the Kirk was dominant in the Lowlands, its tolerance and puritanism was naturally resented by the Highland clans. It was in the Highlands and Islands that the 'Auld Religion' – Catholicism – found its natural haven north of the Border.

James VI had also learned from the lesson provided by his mother. Mary, Queen of Scots, had clung to her Catholic religion, made an undying enemy of the new Kirk and its disciples, and had lost her Kingdom (and ultimately her head) for her

Charles I, born at Dunfermline (1600), was crowned in Edinburgh in 1633.

pains. James survived, largely by convincing all parties that they could go thus far and no farther. Catholicism was finished in Scotland as the official religion. The Presbyterian Kirk was accepted (though not its politically extreme claims). But, as the new King of England from 1603, there was no way that James could root out bishops from Scotland, while accepting the duties of Supreme Head of the Church of England with its episcopalian structure. Bishops would therefore remain in the Church of Scotland, but would no longer be the mainspring of its administration.

Apart from this eminently workable political compromise, James VI and I channelled off Presbyterian energies by encouraging the forced Protestant colonization of northern Ireland, in the 'Plantation of Ulster' from 1610. If this must be judged the most fateful act of the reign, laying a powder-train of bigotry, racism, hatred and murder still burning nearly four centuries later, these were the explosives which James was seeking to dilute in his own day – and, by and large, successfully. At the same time he presided over the compilation of one of the greatest literary achievements in the history of the English language: the Authorized Version of the Bible (1611). In this 'King James Bible', God's silly vassal gave his name to a version of the acknowledged Word of God acceptable alike to the most 'Popish' High Church prelate of the Church of England, and to the most fanatical minister of the Scottish Kirk. It was an achievement of a kind wholly beyond the comprehension of his son and heir.

Charles I was not only the first adult to succeed to the throne of Scotland since 1390. He was the *only* new King of Scotland who, having been reared in England, had become King of Scotland knowing and understanding nothing of the place or its people. Lacking his father's tortuous apprenticeship in Scottish *realpolitik*, Charles I regarded Scotland very much as an unruly mongrel to be groomed and brought to heel. Compromise meant nothing to Charles I. He was the Lord's Anointed, and he was going to rule all three of his Kingdoms – England, Scotland, and Ireland – by force if that was the only way.

In the first 12 years of his reign (1625–37) Charles I showed that he had a matchless gift for making

Charles and James Stuart, sons of Charles I, who became Charles II and James VII and II.

enemies and inducing near despair in even the most faithful of his subjects and servants. The court's apparent infestation with the Catholic friends of his French Catholic Queen, Henrietta Maria, stoked religious distrust. Unable to rule with Parliament, he determined to do without – on a hand-to-mouth national economy which ruled out the expense of going to war. By then deciding to impose an Anglican prayer-book on the Scottish Church, Charles provoked the Scottish Estates into signing a National Covenant (28 February, 1638) pledged to defend the Presbyterian Kirk to the death if need be. With the signing of the Covenant the Great Civil War began in Scotland, and it began over religion.

The Covenanters of 1638–40 represented an intensity of national unity which Scotland had not known since the days of Robert the Bruce. In the so-called 'Bishops' Wars' the Army of the Covenant invaded northern England and humiliated the King, forcing him to recall Parliament to raise the money which the Covenanters demanded for their Army's pay, scrap his plans to remodel the Church of Scotland, and generally agree to all their demands. During these months of failure and humiliation, Charles I looked in vain for a single friend of influence north of the Border; all the great lords and clan chiefs were either Covenanters or supporters of the Covenant, and the clansmen on both

sides of the Highland Line followed their lairds.

Then came the outbreak of civil war in England in 1642, King versus Parliament, and a run of Royalist victories which reawakened the Covenanters' fears. If the King won his war in England, his next move would be to come north with a victorious army at his back to settle accounts with Scotland. Now came the appeal of the hard-pressed English Parliamentarians for Scottish aid, and the signing (13 October, 1643) of the 'Solemn League and Covenant'. In return for sending a Scottish army to help defeat the King in England, the Kirk demanded the scrapping of the Church of England and its replacement with a Presbyterian Church in its own image. To many formerly loyal Covenanters, who had seen the National Covenant as God's instrument for making the King see the error of his ways, the Solemn League was an outrageous breach of faith and an act of treason. It led directly to the formation of a Royalist faction in Scotland, with lords who were willing to muster their clansmen to fight the Covenant in the King's name, given the right leader.

In 1644 the main Army of the Covenant marched south to help the English Parliamentarians win the Battle of Marston Moor (2 July, 1644) which won the North of England for Parliament. The Scottish Army was still in England when, in August 1644, the Royalists in Scotland got their leader: James

Charles I was determined to establish the 'Divine Right of Kings'.

Graham, Marquess of Montrose.

Montrose perfectly summed up the feelings of his countrymen who, by the late summer of 1644, resented the fact that the Covenant had carried Scotland into outright rebellion against the King. Montrose had been a famous Covenanter himself, one of the first to sign the National Covenant in 1638. But, as he told his accusers before they hanged him in 1650, 'The Covenant which I took I own it and adhere to it. Bishops, I care not for them. I never intended to advance their interests. But when the King had granted you all your desires, and you were every one sitting under his vine and his fig tree – that then you should have taken a party in England by the hand, and entered into a League and Covenant with them against the King, was the thing I judged my duty to oppose to the yondmost.'

As the King's Lieutenant in Scotland, Montrose brought nothing to Scotland but his own military genius. The Covenant forces in Scotland, though not the equal of the main Scottish Army in England, were always better equipped and armed than Montrose's threadbare forces, and greatly superior in strength. The core of Montrose's 'army', which never numbered more than 5,000, was an expeditionary force of Irish Catholics brought across by Alastair MacDonald. The clansmen who joined the Royal Standard in 1644–45 were moti-

vated first and foremost by the desire for revenge on the Covenant's most hated weapon in the Highlands: Clan Campbell, led by Archibald Campbell, Marquess of Argyll, who fancied himself in the role of Dictator of the Covenant. This they got.

The first clans to join Montrose were Robertsons and Stewarts, followed over the ensuing year by bands of Ogilvies, Grahams, Gordons, MacDonalds, MacLeans, Macnabs, and Camerons. The main defect of the clansmen as a pool or recruits – their tendency to head for home with their loot after each victory – was more than outweighed by their amazing ability to make forced marches across mountain terrain in all weathers and all seasons, and by their ferocity in battle with the medieval armoury of broadswords, Lochaber axes, often bows and arrows and, as at Tippermuir (Montrose's first victory), with volleys of stones. Under Montrose's inspired leadership they defeated the Covenant armies in seven battles: Tippermuir, Fyvie, Inverary, Inverlochy, Auldearn, Alford, and Kilsyth, ending up in August 1645 with no more enemies to fight and Scotland effectively reconquered for the King.

It proved a fleeting victory. The King, decisively beaten at Naseby in June 1645, had no reinforcements to send to Scotland, the Highlanders refused to invade England under Montrose's banner, and the Lowlands and Border country yielded few

Oliver Cromwell fought 'God's cause' as Lord Protector of the English Commonwealth.

recruits to the Royalist army. Led by Sir David Leslie, the main Army of the Covenant returned to Scotland and overwhelmed Montrose's shrunken band at Philiphaugh on 13 September, 1645. Undaunted by the defeat, Montrose fought on until ordered by the King to disband his army in July 1646.

Although they ended in defeat, the exploits of Montrose had brought glory to the long-despised 'wyld Hielandman'. Montrose had proved that, given leadership and a cause for which to fight and endure, Highlanders could stand forth as their country's champions and as soldiers beyond compare. Never again could the clansmen of the hills be sneeringly dismissed as thieving, feuding barbarians and no more. Montrose had given the Highland warrior what Nelson was to give the Royal Navy: a legend for posterity to live up to, in defeat as well as victory. It was a legend destined to survive the defeats of the Jacobite Risings and the repression that followed them, adding to its stature from the Heights of Abraham at Quebec to Waterloo, from the Crimea to the Falklands. For the clans of the Highlands, the legacy of Montrose was a legacy beyond price.

In the 15 years after the defeat of Montrose in 1645, the Covenant plumbed the depths of ignominy. When the defeated King turned to the Scots for support, the Covenanters demanded his accept-ance of Presbyterianism as their price. When he refused, they handed him over to the English; and when the English refused to embrace Presbyterianism and pay the Scots for their services, the Scots invaded England and were thrashed by Cromwell at Preston (1648). By the 10th anniversary of the signing of the National Covenant, which had been pledged to loyalty to the Crown, freedom of Reformed worship, and defence of Scottish liberties, the Covenanters had thrown away all the national loyalty which they had enjoyed in 1638. Now they were seen as a power-mad, bloodthirsty gang who fought under revolting battle-cries like 'Jesus and No Quarter!', killed defenceless prisoners, and betrayed their King. To many Scots at the time, the two shattering defeats of the Covenant Army by Cromwell at Dunbar in 1650 and Worcester in 1651 seemed like divine punishment for the crimes of the Covenant and the execution of the King (30 January, 1649), and for the humiliations imposed on the young King Charles II, whom the Covenanting leader Argyll had crowned King of Scotland at Scone. The one gleam of honour on the Scottish side was the order of the Scots Parliament (June 1651) that the Crown Regalia, the Honours of Scotland, should be safely hidden from the advancing English Republican army under Cromwell.

With his defeat of the Covenant in 1650–51, Cromwell had succeeded where Edward I had

Left: James Francis Edward Stuart 'The Old Pretender', b.1688 (London), d.1766 (Rome).

Right: James VII of Scotland and II of England (1633–1701) 'The King o'er the Water'.

Far right: William III (of Orange), who co-reigned with James VII and II's daughter Mary.

failed. Scotland was at England's mercy, and Cromwell showed the Scots more mercy than their Covenanting leaders had. They were given all the liberties granted to the English, and freedom of worship. Cromwell's garrisons in the key Scottish towns ensured the keeping of law and order. And when he died, it was the English commander in Scotland, General Monk, who led his troops south to ensure the calling of a free Parliament to summon home King Charles II in 1660.

The return of the bishops in the Restoration Church of Scotland was another indication of the Covenanters' failure. In the 20 years after the Restoration, the Covenanters, so far from regaining the hearts and minds of the Scottish people, degenerated even further. Pretending to be martyrs for their faith (when no one was preventing them from worshipping God any way they chose), they became a clique of murdering assassins who lived by the bullet, gunning down Archbishop Sharp of St Andrews (1679) in broad daylight.

The Jacobite Wars

Covenant failure was also marked by the loyalty of the Scottish clans to the Royal House of Stewart, a loyalty remarkable for surviving 25 years of neglect from London after the Restoration. When the last of the reigning Stewarts, the Catholic James VII and II, was forced overseas in 1688, it was from his former realm of Scotland that the 'King Over the Water' and his heirs drew most support. Indeed, it could be said that the most lasting (and only real) success of James VII and II was in giving his name to all Stewart loyalists – the Jacobites.

Echoes of the Great Civil War and the prowess of the clans under the great Montrose were stirred in the first Jacobite war of 1688–89, when Montrose's descendant John Graham, 'Bonnie Dundee', led the Jacobite clansmen to victory over the army of Dutch William at Killiecrankie (1689). He added immeasurably to the Jacobite legend by getting himself killed in the moment of victory, it was said by a specially-cast silver bullet. Nor did the Highlanders forget – ever – the appalling iniquity of the Glencoe Massacre in 1692: the treacherous, government-ordered slaughterous attack by Campbell forces on their MacDonald hosts, another enduring black mark against Clan Campbell. This first Jacobite defeat did no more to weaken pro-Stewart loyalties

31

Left: Ruins of once-flourishing settlements in Glen Lochay, cleared in the 18th century.

Right: Captain Porteous was lynched by a mob after he ordered Edinburgh City Guard to fire on a protesting crowd at the Tolbooth (1736).

than had the defeat of Montrose at Philiphaugh back in 1645. Indeed, the growing Lowland pressure for full Union with England, the only move which could end Scotland's chronic economic poverty at the end of the 18th century, was fertile soil for Jacobitism in Scotland as the 17th century opened.

The real importance of Jacobitism was that it was far more than sustained nostalgia on the part of a few Highland chiefs for the return of their 'real' king. Jacobitism was the only British 'opposition party' in an age when the idea of any such thing sounded frighteningly like treason. (An equally alien new idea, also spawned in these years, was the concept of a National Debt.) Nor was Jacobitism limited to Scotland. English Catholics in particular, shut out from public office and yearning for religious toleration which they looked to the exiled Stewarts to restore, were seen as natural Jacobites (although, as in Elizabeth's time, most preferred to argue their case as loyal subjects 'from within the system' rather than resort to outright rebellion). In 1715 and 1745, Prince James Edward and Prince Charles Edward were not merely seeking to establish themselves in Scotland; their eyes, after Edinburgh, were set on London.

The clans who rallied to the Royal Standard of the Stewarts in the 'Fifteen' and the 'Forty-Five' underwent uncannily similar runs of fortune to their forebears who had fought for Montrose and Dundee. As with the initial successes from Tippermuir to Kilsyth in 1644–45, and Killiecrankie in 1689, so there were initial Jacobite victories at Sheriffmuir in 1715 and Prestonpans in 1745 before the inevitable turning of the tide. Yet though the 'Bonnie Prince' ended his life in 1788 in exile as a drunken embarrassment to all, he had, in the great days, succeeded where even the mighty Montrose had failed, and led a Highland army south into England; it got as far as Derby before the Prince realized that no English uprising in his favour was ever going to happen.

The fright which the 'Forty-Five' had given the Hanoverian regime may be measured by the subsequent Government attempt to root out the Highland clan tradition forever. Banning Highland dress, executing and exiling clan leaders, and finally driving roads into the heart of the Highlands – none of these ploys succeeded. The real damage to the Highland clans was achieved in the half-century between the death of Bonnie Prince Charlie and the accession of Queen Victoria, and this was not the result of vengeful Acts of Parliament in London. It was the mass eviction of tenants to make way for sheep: the 'Highland Clearances' which sent tens of thousands of former Highland crofters overseas to the ends of the earth – Canada, the United States, Australia, New Zealand. The emptiness of the Highlands today is mute witness to the heartbreak of the Clearances, pushed through not by English

politicians and generals but by absentee Scottish landlords looking for easy profits and low overheads.

Resolution

There is something typically British about the fact that the misery of the Highland Clearances was in full swing while the much-needed restoration of Scottish national pride was being achieved. This began with the prowess on the battlefield of the first Highland Regiments; it was sustained by the prevailing Romantic Movement with a growing worship of all things 'Scotch' (with Sir Walter Scott and his novels acting as high priest and holy writ). It was helped out of measure by the fact that the death of Bonnie Prince Charlie (1788) made it possible to be proud of Scotland without being considered a traitor – final severance, after more than four centuries, of the living link between the clans of Scotland and the Royal House of Stewart.

Full atonement for the punishment of the Scottish clans after Culloden was made by the House of Hanover in 1822, when King George IV made the first State Visit to Scotland by a reigning monarch since the humiliating coronation of Charles II in 1651. The visit was preceded by Sir Walter Scott's search for the Honours of Scotland, hidden since the Act of Union in 1707 for fear that they should

follow the Stone of Scone to London. On 4 February, 1818 the Honours were finally unearthed by Sir Walter in a giant oak chest in what is now Edinburgh Castle's Crown Room, hidden beneath a litter of ageing blankets.

When King George IV came to Edinburgh in 1822, the people had been exhorted by Scott to turn out suitably 'plaided and plumed'. It was Sir Walter, again, who chose an 'Escort to the Honours' of the MacGregor clan to convey the Regalia from the Castle to Holyrood. They were led by their chief – no longer the hunted exile he would have been barely 60 years before, but Major-General Sir Evan MacGregor of MacGregor, Bart., a respected soldier and servant of the Crown. To help him rise to the occasion, King George had been so tightly corseted to fit into the giant 'Royal Stewart' kilt he wore during the visit that he is said to have fainted three times.

There was a special irony in the restoration of Clan Gregor to 'decent society' after nearly 200 years of living as outlaws. Along with many of the more ancient clans, the MacGregors sport a cat's head crest, though theirs is crowned, to emphasize their motto 'Royal is my Blood.' After many racking and painful years, the historic marriage of Crown and clans had taken on a new lease of life from which, under seven successive monarchs, there has been no turning back.

Scottish Dress

Although whisky, golf, and bagpipes are among the more powerful symbols of Scotland's unique culture, it is undoubtedly tartan and the kilt which distinguish Scotland and its people in the eyes of the world. A Caucasian male in a tartan kilt, walking through the streets of Tokyo, is likely to bring shop assistants and their customers running into the street with admiring cries of 'Scotolando!' and 'Tartanocheck!' In New York such interest would be slightly more restrained, with maybe the added enquiry, 'Where's the parade?' But in either culture, the certain assumption would be that he who sports a tartan kilt is either Scottish, part Scottish, or contriving to appear Scottish.

Scots eccentrics have imposed their cultural imprint on every continent, often influencing local textile traditions by exposing them to the exuberance of Scottish tartan patterns, or *setts*. One such eccentric was the 18th-century explorer James Bruce of Kinnaird, discoverer of the source of the Blue Nile. He is said to have worn an extravagant tartan jacket *AND* waistcoat during some of his jaunts through Africa. The predominantly Scots management of the East India Company bequeathed a range of tartan patterns to native cotton weavers across the sub-continent of India. And tartan setts from well before 1750 have survived in areas of Sweden and Norway that still preserve tales of the Scots mercenaries whose plaids survived the battles in which they died.

Although 'tartan' and 'kilt' are cultural icons as quintessentially Scottish as Scotland itself, remember that the sovereign country known today as 'Scotland' was not known by that name until the 11th century; that 'kilt' is in fact a Scandinavian word for an item of costume wrapped or folded around the loins; and that 'tartan' is not an indigenous Scots word either. Perhaps it would be better to examine what 'tartan' means today, and

then discover the origins of both the word 'tartan' and whatever it has been used to describe in the past.

The generally accepted (and necessarily technical) description of tartan today is 'cloth woven with coloured yarns, in a sequence of bands, stripes, and lines which form a pattern that "repeats" regularly throughout the length and breadth of the cloth'. The points in the pattern where the sequence of colours begins to reverse are called the *pivots*:

blue: green: red: **black**: red: green: blue

Before 1750 there were many more patterns which were 'asymmetrical' or 'non-repeating'. In these, the sequence of colours came to an end and then merely started again with the first colour of the original sequence, with no pivots:

blue: green: red: black/ blue: green: red: black/ blue: green, etc.

Below left: Roman legionary dress, showing the 'skirted' tunic which some suggest was the origin of the Scottish kilt.

Below: The 'government tartan' (Black Watch), which was the basis for most regimental patterns. A typical 18th-century repeating sett of black, blue and green broad bands with overcheck lines.

Tartan patterns are as clever as they are simple. They give the effect of many more colours than have actually been used because, wherever two pure colours cross (for example, blue and red) a 'half-tone' is produced (for example, red/blue). Using two pure yarns gives the effect of three tones, but nine pure yarns give the effect of 45 tones. No wonder that the Gaelic word for tartan is *breacan*, which means 'speckled' or 'multicoloured'. (The Gaels also called the trout *breac*, because of its speckled colouration.) A more familiar word to describe an effect with more than one colour is *brock* from the old Celto–British word for the badger, with its black-and-white striped face.

So, in common parlance, tartan is a cloth with a (generally) regular pattern of coloured stripes, although some may perceive the patterns in terms of square islands of colours. But where does a check end and a tartan begin? Technically, they are one and the same. In practical terms, however, a check might be described as a simple pattern with squares formed by no more than three colours, and with no lines or stripes crossing the squares to produce 'overchecks'.

As for the construction of the cloth used for tartan, the simplest weave is referred to as *tabby*, using a system of 'one thread over, one thread under'. However, it is more usual today for quality cloth to be woven with the 'two threads over, two threads under' system, producing a strong weave with a distinctive diagonal effect. Its technical name is *twill*, which was spelled and pronounced in Scots as *tweel*. Ironically, the misreading of a 19th-century letter from a Highland weaver to a London draper, in which the 'l' of *tweel* was decorated with a flourish, led to the word *tweed* being given to this kind of cloth.

Even where the same pattern is being produced, tweed can be distinguished from tartan because the yarns used are not of a single colour, but a mixture. This mixture gives Scottish tweeds their distinctive visual appeal and their texture, suggesting the heathery hills, is caused by the yarn being more 'fluffy', without the smoothness of *worsted* yarns.

Until the 18th century, a fine, dense yarn was sometimes produced on the old-style 'muckle wheel', which allowed cloth to be woven at densities as high as 72 threads to the inch. (Weavers refer to e.p.i. – 'ends' per inch – or e.p.m. when obliged to think metric.) The machine-spun yarns of the late 18th and early 19th centuries also permitted cloth of similar densities to be produced. Today, however, fine woollen cloth tends to be woven at a density of between 30–40 threads per inch.

So much for what we understand by 'tartan' today. What of its origins? Here opinions vary wildly. On the one hand there are those who

Left: Unknown artist's impression of woollen checked mantle from the Pictish period.

contend that after Noah had beached the Ark on the slopes of Ben Nevis the animals emerged two by two — followed by a man and a woman from every clan, dressed in the same tartans as are found in the average tartan emporium in modern-day Edinburgh. Here one is reminded of the story that when Noah's invitation to make haste to board the Ark reached the lordly MacNeil of Barra, he promptly replied, 'Thank you kindly, but The MacNeil has a boat of his own!'

At the other end of the spectrum are those who argue that tartans were a wholly Victorian invention by the great Queen-Empress and her husband Prince Albert. Somewhere between is a body of fact incorporating elements from both extremes, which even pays a measure of tribute to one of the most devastating of all statements on the subject. This was made in a 1985 essay by the famous historian Hugh Trevor-Roper, Lord Dacre, who stated baldly that, 'The distinctive national apparatus of Scotchmen (*sic*) . . . kilt, bagpipes and clan tartans . . is, in fact, largely modern. The Highlanders of Scotland . . . were simply the overflow of Ireland.'

Before examining the history of clan tartans and the kilt as age-old badges of Scottishness, a few general comments may be made on a subject often said to generate more heat than light. Seeking more scientific assurance for the 'old as Noah' school, we know from the evidence of bodies preserved in bogs, and both written and illustrated comments from the Roman period, that the early Celts wore or were tattooed with patterns that can only be described as checks or tartans. Below the belt,

Below left: Typical border pattern on 18th-century plaid from Skye.

Below: Balmoral Castle, remodelled by Prince Albert in 1853–55, from an old mansion house first rented by Queen Victoria in 1847.

Left: The Piper to the Laird of Grant, painted by Richard Waitt in 1714. Notice the 'kilt' apron folding to left.

Below: The 'Act of Proscription' or 'Dress Act', forbidding the wearing of 'tartan, kilt or plaid' after Culloden.

Right: Colonel Alastair MacDonell of Glengarry by Raeburn. This is the first portrait of Highland dress to show the sgian dubh worn in the hose-top.

> 1004   Anno Regni vicesimo Georgii II. Regis.
>
> it is enacted, That from and after the First Day of August, One thousand seven hundred and forty seven, no Man or Boy, within that Part of Great Britain called Scotland, other than such as shall be employed as Officers and Soldiers in His Majesty's Forces, shall, on any Pretence whatsoever, wear or put on the Clothes commonly called Highland Clothes; that is to say, the Plaid, Philebeg, or little Kilt, Trowse, Shoulder Belts, or any Part whatsoever of what peculiarly belongs to the Highland Garb; and that no Tartan, or party-coloured Plaid or Stuff, shall be used for Great Coats, or for Upper Coats:

however, there is no evidence of any kilt-like garment of the kind certainly worn in the Egypt of the Pharaohs and classical Greece and Rome. The early Celts wore what we would call today *trews* (from the Gaelic *triubhas*). These were, in effect, like heavy woollen pantihose, which would seem to be sensible wear for cold mountainous regions. Such tight girding of cloth around the loins and legs has left the English language with the fossil word 'truss'.

It is therefore certain that the Celts used tartan patterns before the time of Christ, but not the elaborate patterns seen in 17th- and 18th-century Scotland. From the tribal structure of Celtic society and the importance of visual symbolism in all Celtic art forms, it is probable that the clothing patterns produced by the early Celts – restricted to geometric patterns by the limits of their weaving technology – would be more than just random, and might reflect the identity of territory or tribe. But of the kilt, there was no sign!

The 'origins in Victorian times' school of thought has definitely overstated its case. A century before Victoria and Albert acquired their Highland castle and launched the 'cult of Balmorality' on an all-too-receptive world, the British Government of 1746 felt sufficiently convinced of the emotive link between 'tartan, plaid and kilt' and the troublesome clans of Scotland, to rush through an Act of Parliament to which King George II gave his Royal Assent on (ironically) the Glorious Twelfth of August. Its wording was nothing if not explicit:

'. . . no Man or Boy, other than *f*uch as *f*hall be employed as Officers and Soldiers in his Maje*f*ty's Forces, *f*hall on any pretence what*f*oever, wear or put on the Clothes commonly called Highland Clothes (that is to *f*ay) the Plaid, Phillibeg or Little Kilt, Trow*f*e, Shoulder Belts, or any part of what*f*oever belongs to the Highland Garb, and that no Tartan or party-coloured Plaid or Stuff *f*hall be u*f*ed . . .'

Many earlier references use words close to today's 'tartan', such as *tiretaine*, *tiretana*, and *tartane*, but there is no certainty that they refer to cloth with what we now call a tartan pattern. A similar medieval word, of French or Spanish origin, referred to a type of cloth which used a strong, sometimes linen warp and a softer woollen weft. In English, this fabric was often called *linsey-woolsey*.

Surviving examples of 17th-century *plaids* show that they were sometimes produced with no pattern on them other than a decorated border, sometimes merely in herring-bone weave. References in 1355 to a tartan plaid for the Lord of the Isles, and the more commonly-quoted Lord Treasurer's accounts

for the King's clothing in 1536 – 'Heland tartane to be hoiss for the Kingis grace . . .' – offers no guarantee that they describe tartan patterns, although the term '*Heland* tartane' suggests something of that style.

There is a firm body of evidence to suggest that some loose system of identifiable patterns existed even before 1746. There is a strong implication that patterns peculiar to certain areas did develop, and may have become associated with clans who settled there. The evidence comes from Gaelic poetry in the late medieval period; the journals of numerous travellers in the Highlands; eyewitness accounts such as that of the Battle of Killiecrankie in 1689 ('. . . McDonnell's men in their triple stripe . . .'); and the intriguing letter, reputedly from Sir Robert Gordon to one of his lairds in 1618, instructing him with regard to his men to 'remove the red and white lines from the plaides so as to bring their dress into harmony with the other septs'. All in all, it seems that there is ample proof that tartans – some, if certainly not all, associated with specific clans – existed long before Queen Victoria was born.

Lord Dacre's dismissal of Highlanders as 'simply the overflow of Ireland' will surely incense those with any drop of Scots blood in their veins. But he does have a way of cutting through layers of romance masquerading as fact, and exposing the realities of the past. The popular misconception that the Battle of Culloden was fought between the troops of the English Government and an all-Scottish army is far from the truth. Lord Dacre is not far from the truth when he says that the apparatus of clan tartans, kilts, and bagpipes 'before the Union [with England in 1707] did exist but in a vestigial form; but that form was regarded by the large majority of Scotchmen as a sign of barbarism: the badge of roguish, idle, predatory, blackmailing Highlanders who were more of a nuisance than a threat to civilised, historic Scotland'. Strong words, but reinforced by the fact that most Scots in 1745–46 – namely, those in the 'civilized' areas outside the Highlands proper – were bitterly opposed to Prince Charles Edward and his savage horde. But before we are swayed completely by this argument, we must remember that no historian is infallible. Even the pronouncements of experts must be backed by facts – which, as Burns reminds us, are 'chiels that winna ding' – and this brings us to the evidence.

The evidence of history

Dictionary definitions of evidence seem to favour 'data on which a judgement may be made or by which proof or probability may be established'. Unfortunately, textiles are unlikely to survive for hundreds of years in a climate like Scotland's, other than in exceptional circumstances. Even in the wealthiest families, garments were rarely preserved for posterity, often being handed on to servants or the poor of the parish, who tended to wear them until they literally fell to pieces.

To find evidence of the aboriginal dress and textile patterns of the early inhabitants of what is now called Scotland we need to consult the pre-Roman period, before non-Celtic influences muddied the water. Unfortunately, the only sketchy surviving references are almost entirely by Roman authors, commenting either on the Celts in continental Europe before their invasion of Britain, or as an army of occupation thereafter. The poet Virgil, in his *Aeneid*, says of the Celts that *Virgatis lucent sagulis* (VIII:660) – the accepted translation of which is 'their cloaks are striped and shining'. As there is no word in Latin to convey 'stripes at right-angles producing a checked effect', perhaps 'striped' means loosely that, while 'shining' could be interpreted as 'brightly coloured'. Other contemporary references comment on the Celts' exuberant sense of colour. None of these references would be conclusive without the evidence of bog burials of the period with their examples of tattooed skin decoration in chequered motifs, and the depiction of captive Celtic warriors wearing chequered trews (*triubhas*).

Last century, close to the Roman Antonine Wall near Falkirk, excavations brought to light an earthenware pot containing over 1,900 silver coins. From the heads of the Roman emperors stamped on the coins and other circumstances of the find, it was possible to date the cache to the middle of the 3rd century AD. Stuffed into the mouth of the pot to act as a seal was a small piece of woollen cloth, preserved for over 1,600 years by the dryness of the soil. After careful cleaning, a simple two-colour check pattern was revealed with a sophisticated twill construction using a herring-bone weave. One archeologist involved in the find suggested that a Pictish raider had buried his loot with a chunk of plaid to keep the silver in marketable condition, only to be prevented by unknown chance from retrieving his haul.

The check pattern was achieved by separately spinning the brown and off-white wool of the primitive, skewbald Soay-type sheep of the period, and producing the two-colour weave with no added dyestuffs. In a way, this pattern is the 'mother and father' of all known tartans, although many would argue that it does not comprise a tartan at all. But this 'dogtooth' check is also the 'shepherd' check – worn as a tartan by those of that name – and no less a tartan than the 'Rob Roy' worn by the Chief of the Clan Gregor, where the white square has been artificially dyed red and the dark brown changed to black. Yet in all the rummaging among the Romans there is no sign of Celts in kilts – merely Roman soldiers in such. At the end of the 18th century the redoubtable Sir John Sinclair of Ulbster, Bart., who raised the Caithness Fencible Regiment, clothed his men in trews with full-frontal sporrans. His contention was that the ancient tribes wore, not the kilt, but these 'trousers and hose all in one piece' – the true garb of Old Gaul.

Nothing in the chronicles of the Pictish period, or the figures portrayed in great detail on Pictish monumental art forms – standing stones and Celtic cross slabs – shows any image of the kilt which we see depicted in Highland portraits from the first half of the 18th century. What clearly emerges is a costume developing from Pictish times of full leggings or trews, topped by a form of surcoat of woven linen (that is, as worn by the warrior caste and nobility important enough to be commemorated on monuments). The mostly unrecorded common people would have used animal skins

Left: 'Piece of a poor man's plaid', c. 235 AD, found near the Roman Wall at Falkirk in the 19th century.

Right: Sir John Sinclair of Ulbster, Bart., by Raeburn, emphasizing his conviction that the trews were the true 'garb of old Gaul'.

Left: Intricately carved Pictish monumental stone from Hilton of Cadboll in Ross-shire, showing mounted hunters at the chase, a lady riding side-saddle and the enigmatic crescent with trumpet spirals, all in a 'knotted' border, (c.A.D. 800)

Right: 18th-century engraving showing soldiers of the 1st Highland Regiment with their 'belted plaids'.

right through until the medieval period. Until then, the sheep population and size of animal were both small. Sheep were more valued then for their milk and, in any event, only produced a third of the usable fleece which the infamous Blackface/ Cheviot cross-breeds were to yield when they were grazed on 'land cleared of Man' after 1800.

Observers began making meaningful comments on Scottish dress from the time of the celebrated saga of King Magnus of Norway. He returned from an expedition to Scotland in 1093 in the costume of those western lands: apparently a cloak or plaid swathed around the shoulders, and a very brief linen shirt or smock (often hooded) which seemed to be called the *leine*. Magnus was dubbed *Barfaet* by his people, which has been politely translated as 'barelegged' by those less familiar with the bawdy nicknames which the Vikings gave each other.

This type of costume – and the style of wearing it, which left the loins unfettered in case of the need for a rapid retreat – is mentioned in numerous reliable accounts by travellers throughout Scotland and Ireland from a thousand years ago. Many of the narrators were quite fascinated by the brevity of the dress:

From the middle of the thigh to the foot they have no covering for the leg.
John Major, 1470

They were naked except their dyed shirts and a sort of light covering made of wool of many colours.
Jean de Beaugue, 1556

Next the skin they wear a short linnen shirt; they wear it short that it may not incumber them when running or travelling.
Gordon of Straloch, 1641

Their plads are worn short that the indecency is plain to be seen . . .

Quite clearly, the 'Wyld Scots' were unlike anything these observers had seen before, and their descriptions vividly convey a general picture of a lifestyle and mode of dress which remained largely unchanged for centuries. In Lowland Scotland, apart from the uplands of Galloway, that change occurred early in the medieval period. North of the Highland Line, which stretched from the southern tip of Loch Lomond across to Perth and skirted the eastern coastal plains up to Inverness and beyond, there were no intrusive influences in certain areas until well into the 1700s.

Incomers often referred to the Highland Scots, or the language they spoke, as *Irish*. Until around 1300, Scottish Gaelic was probably no more than a dialect of the mainstream Irish Gaelic, but by 1600 it had become as separate as Spanish from Italian. Dress styles more or less kept pace with the

language divergence; for example, the Irish *leine croich* remained a common term in descriptions of Scottish clothing until the 17th century. What is not always understood is that this shirt was dyed with *croich* or crocus, producing not only the saffron yellow hue but a herbal antiseptic of great benefit to a warrior in battle. The saffron dyestuff was imported from Ireland as well as ready-dyed linen, and was undoubtedly an expensive item. By the 16th century the *leine croich*, the yellow 'war coat', had become almost a prerogative of local war-lords. Its quaint survival today is in the form of the 'yellow jersey' worn by the frontrunner in the Tour de France and other cycle races.

Over the centuries, some of the descriptions of dress refer to the coarseness of the woollen 'plaid' or 'mantle', possibly woven from goat and cattle hair yarn, and worn over the linen shirt or smock. Eventually the plaid (spelled *plaide* in Gaelic and pronounced with an 'a' as in 'badger', and with a very soft and hesitant -ger at the end) developed into the main item of dress for all Highlanders — and for many country folk in the Lowlands when the winds blew chill.

For the laird (often on horseback) and the tacksmen, or middle management of the clan, trews would be worn under a plaid which could be belted around the waist. Worn as it would be by the average clansman, the lower 50 cm (20 inches) of a 5.5 m (6 yd) length of plaiding were drape-pleated to form a kilt, with the surplus tucked under the belt and fastened on the shoulder with a metal or bone pin. The correct Gaelic terms were *feilidh-Mor* (the 'great wrap') or *breacan an feilidh* (the 'tartan wrap'). Pronounced 'fail-y', *feilidh* comes from an ancient Indo-European root that gives us 'folded' in modern English, *falden* in Old English, and *falten* in German. The French *plié* features the 'p/ph' interchange for the Gaelic 'f' — which brings us full circle to the English synonym for fold: pleat, or plait.

Some of the finest examples of the belted plaid as worn may be seen in portraits of Highland lairds, who would obviously be painted in 'full fig'. What they actually wore around the house is unlikely to have been recorded, any more than the Chief of the Clan Macarore would wish to be preserved for posterity dressed in a much-loved but battered tweed jacket and food-stained tie. After all, portraits only show us what the subject, or the artist working to his commission, want us to see. Yet there are portraits where the artist has produced unflattering images of sitters who seem positively villainous; the 1604 portrait of the ruthless Black Duncan Campbell of Glenorchy is a case in point. Ruthless men tend to succeed in life by inspiring fear in those around them, and a grim portrait presented 'warts and all' was part of the strategy.

The prolific artist Richard Waitt painted a number of excellent portraits of Highland lairds. These provide an insight into contemporary costume, but raise question-marks over the tartans depicted. Around 1704, Waitt painted a Sutherland laird, Lord Duffus, in a perfectly rendered belted plaid, but in a tartan unlike any of the Sutherland tartans known today. It is quite likely that Waitt, no doubt aided by apprentices, produced a large number of 'baseplate' portraits in Highland dress, leaving the face and a few intimate details blank until the time came to paint an actual sitter. It does not seem to have mattered to the dozen or so lairds of the Clan Grant, painted by Waitt before 1714, that they were all shown wearing different plaid patterns. Separate Waitt portraits of two of the chief's henchmen, however, show them wearing the same tartan sett. The supposed portrait of Alastair Grant Mor, Champion to the Chief, appears in at least four different locations in Scotland, all bearing slightly dissimilar features and ascribed to various sitters.

From such sources we can glean a handful of clues about tartans, but nothing definitive enough

Left: James Moray of Abercairney in the full dress of a 'brae Laird' around 1750, in a tartan unlike any other 'Murray'.

Above: 'Black Duncan' Campbell of Glenorchy in 1619, forebear of the Earls of Breadalbane.

They would not have been languishing in irons dressed as they are in Morier's painting.

One clear-cut case of artistic licence is to be found in the otherwise masterly painting by King George IV's Draughtsman, Denis Dighton, of the 'MacGregor Escort to the Honours of Scotland in 1822'. This shows the Chief, Major-General Sir Evan MacGregor, Bart., with his clansmen, and the tartan has been painstakingly reproduced. The costume worn by Sir Evan in the painting is preserved in the collection of the current Chief. But instead of the high tartan collar shown in the painting, the actual jacket has a collar of dark green velvet with intricate leafwork embroidery in gold wire – recorded in the artist's own book of sketches, made in meticulous detail on the occasion in 1822. In the face of such evidence, it is clear that *nothing* can be taken for granted. This is especially true of the innumorable pieces of tartan cloth, lovingly preserved in the archives of this family and that, each supposedly a 'genuine' piece of Bonnie Prince Charlie's plaid, acquired by a forebear from the boy wonder himself. When analysed, the wool in the relic usually turns out to be coloured with aniline dyestuffs unknown before 1856. 'Evidence', in short, is not necessarily fact.

Ono word in particular should never be used in connection with tartan patterns: 'authentic', the dictionary definition of which is 'having an undisputed origin'. In this sense the totally incorrect tartan, designed for the Clan MacSporran in 1976 by a gentleman whose name and address are both known, is 'authentic'. But a tartan pattern which has played and continues to play a crucial role in Scotland's social and military history is not 'authentic'. This is despite the fact that we have samples from the days when it was known as the 'Government Tartan' in official publications, with precise specifications of pattern and colours. But we do not know why, when, and by whom it originated, and so this historic tartan is not 'authentic' in the literal sense of the word.

It was after the Act of Union in 1707, when many traditions and interests of Scotland seemed in jeopardy, that tartan began to be worn as a sign of Scottishness. A century and a half before, Lowland Scotland had benefited from the education forced on even the poorest by the Calvinist Kirk of the Scottish Reformation. But it also suffered out of measure from the harsh prejudice against music, song, dance, dramatic art, and colours other than black, white, and grey, imposed on Scotland's national culture by that ayatollah of the 16th century, John Knox. The savage suppression of Highland tribal identity by an apprehensive Government in London, after the Jacobite Risings in the 18th century, led to the prohibition of tartan and Highland dress for 37 years.

to convince a jury on the subject. A good example is the famous picture 'Episode from the Scotch Rebellion' by David Morier, a Swiss artist respected for his accuracy. This depicts the Atholl Brigade of the Highland Army at Culloden. The Highlanders in the picture are shown wearing such a bizarre mixture of tartan patterns that anyone would be excused for deducing that there was no such thing as a clan tartan. But it seems most likely that Morier, though a witness of the battle as 'war artist' to the Hanoverian Commander-in-Chief, added the details to his original sketches some time later. He is thought to have used Jacobite prisoners, clad in a mixture of complete and orderly costume in which they were dressed to have their 'picture taken'.

By the time the ban was lifted in 1782, times were changing. The prowess of the Highland regiments in fighting Britain's battles around the world was leading to a restoration of Scottish national pride. When the Stuart threat evaporated with Bonnie Prince Charlie's death in 1788, this national pride was preserved from any official taint of treason. At the same time, Europe's flourishing Romantic Movement was discovering new heroes in Celtic myth and folklore to rival the well-worn icons of classical Greece and Rome.

The first half of the 19th century produced a wide range of creative antiquarians who cheerfully invented many traditions still held dear. Apart from tartan patterns said to have been 'laid down when God was a boy', the bagpipe acquired a lineage far outstripping reality – with the embroidered claim that bagpipes were 'banned by law after Culloden', which is false. James Macpherson invented the 'authentic' Celtic poetry of Ossian which delighted and inspired many European leaders, including Napoleon Bonaparte. And the 'legitimate' grandsons of Bonnie Prince Charlie, renamed the Sobieski Stuarts to emphasize their

royal Polish grandma, rewrote the history of tartans and Highland dress so convincingly that even the most learned experts today cannot be absolutely sure what is fact and what is fiction.

The kilt as known today, with knife pleats and using about 6–7 m (7–8 yds) of single-width cloth, did not evolve until the second half of the last century. Before this, a series of drape and box-pleated kilt developments had themselves evolved from the great belted plaid. By the mid-18th century it was no longer practical to sew together two loom-widths of cloth, making a vast garment worn like a cross between a Roman toga and an Indian sari. With fewer Highlanders obliged to sleep rough in the heather in their plaids, kilt and plaid became separate as tartans proliferated.

Below: 'Episode from the Scotch Rebellion' by David Morier, shows the Atholl Brigade confronting Barrell's Regt. at Culloden.

Right: Peter MacDonald, virtually the last full-time, handloom weaver, producing fine tartan cloth to 18th-century settings.

Today there are over 2,500 tartan setts on record in various archives, but no completely definitive list – and new tartans are invented week by week. More books on tartans appear every year, but they only add to the errors which have been immortalized in print since the first attempts to codify and illustrate tartans in the 1830s. Such mistakes have themselves become faithfully incorporated into much of the archival material now available, which only helps muddy the waters more.

For example, one American Professor of Linguis-tics, applying his passion for scholarship to the subject of tartans, 'discovered' a reference to a 'Border' pattern in an old list of tartan patterns. His find was immediately published as the tartan traditionally worn by folk from the Border country between England and Scotland, an area steeped in history but one where tartans were not thought to have been worn. This was hailed by many as an exciting new discovery – but the pattern in queston, sad to say, was no more than that used by 19th century manufacturing weavers for the borders of blankets and plaids. There are about 100 'district tartans' in existence today (including the 'Border') and most of them have been created over the last 20 years.

Some of the latter are, in fact, variations of tweed patterns to which manufacturers have given place-names quite at random ('Glen This' and 'Glen That'). Others, naively presumed to be traditional district patterns, were originally designed for members of the Royal Family or peers with Scottish as well as English dignities – Prince of Wales and Duke of Rothesay; Duke of York and Earl of Inverness; Duke of Kent and Earl of St Andrews, and the like. (The latter became one of Marks & Spencer's best-selling tartan skirt patterns, while one of the setts which could be worn by the Prince of Wales was given a colour change to become the *Welsh* 'national tartan'.)

One of the most enduring myths about tartans, cherished by many, is that every colour and line in every pattern is endowed with deep historical significance. A typical belief is that all red patterns were originally 'battle tartans', designed so that blood would not show – an obvious crib from the red coats of the British Army, or the red-painted gun decks of HMS *Victory*. In more recent times the obsession with using 'symbolic' colours, more specifically with the design of flags, has sunk deep into tartan lore. Thus the Ohio Tartan, produced to commemorate the Scottish connections with that American State, was designed in the 1980s 'in the traditional manner': with all the colours possessing a wealth of symbolic meaning. Green stood for the fields and prairies, dark blue for oil, red for iron ore deposits, light blue for the rivers and streams, yellow for the largest onion farm in the world, and white for the snow. But this is purely a modern fancy, with no evidence at all to show that it had anything to do with the design of 'traditional' clan tartans.

It comes as a surprise to find that there is no public body which regulates, or even records, all patterns of tartan. It is widely presumed (and so affirmed in books) that the Court of Lord Lyon, King of Arms, keeps a record of every tartan. But in fact no more than five per cent of all known patterns *are* so recorded, in either the Lyon Court Books or the Public Register of All Arms and Bearings. Such recording is usually at the request of the chief of a clan associated with a tartan, or in cases where a tartan sett requires definition as an essential element of Arms which have been matriculated at the Lyon Court.

Then again, copies of some tartan patterns are lodged at Her Majesty's Design Registry in Manchester to afford protection under the Patent Acts. Such patterns must be 'new and original' – but in practice virtually nothing can be done to monitor such registrations until they are challenged. In theory, the Royal Stewart tartan could be registered as a new pattern – but in the first court action brought to prevent anyone else from weaving or selling it, its existence for many years 'in the public domain' would certainly be cited as a defence. It happens that 'Royal Stewart' is, after the ubiquitous 'Black Watch', the most popular tartan pattern in the world despite the fact that 'by right' it should only be worn by the Monarch's immediate family and by the Pipers of Royal Regiments. King George V is said to have stated that 'Royal Stewart' was his Family Tartan, and so should be worn only by his Family – which, in his case as King-Emperor, happened to comprise all the peoples of the British Empire . . .

Many books and manuals have been written on the 'rules' and 'etiquette' for wearing which tartan when and how. But a basic principle, one which certainly determined the original Highland dress, has become *de rigeur* for displaying Scottishness. Unless you are a member of a regiment, there are no regimented rules. Wear the tartan connected with your maternal or any other family line, or merely one which you feel is appropriate to your origins in Scotland. If you are not Scottish, you can wear whatever tartan you like, but remember – if you wear a tartan of the Campbells, they are the folk with whom you must fight should war break out once more.

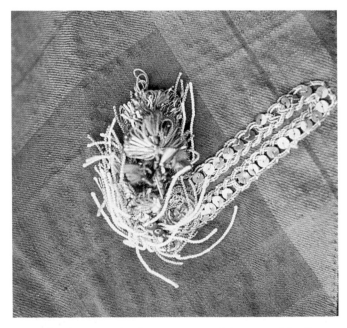

Detail of a 1790 jacket of the Royal Company of Archers, showing the lighter tones of the 'Government (or Black Watch) tartan' in the 18th century.

Tartans

NOTE   'SETT' – the arrangement of lines and bands of colour in one full repeat of a tartan pattern.
'WILSONS' – Messrs Wm Wilson of Bannockburn, Tartan cloth manufacturers from around 1770.
'H.S.L. – The Highland Society of London whose Collection was begun in 1816.
'COCKBURN' – General Cockburn started his Collection in 1810.
'SMITH 1850' – Authenticated Tartans of the Clans & Families of Scotland' by W. & A. Smith.
'TRADE' – applied to tartan designed for commercial sale and not commissioned for that name.
'ROCK & WHEEL'– early type of soft cloth, using wheel-spun weft yarn and spindled ('rock') warp.

*Left: BROWN
Designed in the 1930s for
the Browns of Colston,
and first recorded in the
Collection of John
MacGregor Hastie.*

*Below left: BUCHANAN
This is the symmetrical
version of the clan tartan,
recorded by James Logan
in 1831. The better-
known asymmetrical
version probably arose
from an illustrative error.*

*Below: CURRIE
The 'Old Lord of the Isles'
sett (called the
'Hunting'), with the
addition of the double
gold lines authorized by
MacDonald of the Isles in
1822 for Clan Mhurrich.*

49

Left: CAMERON of ERRACHT
A 'dress' version of the tartan designed on a MacDonald base, for the 79th Regt. (The Cameron Volunteers) in 1793. Possibly dating from the late 19th century.

Below left: CAMPBELL of ARDMADDIE
First illustrated in the 1749 portrait of John Campbell of Ardmaddie, this is one of a number of red setts not now acknowledged by the Campbell chief.

Below: CLARK
People of this surname have been misled into wearing the 'Clergy' or 'Priest' tartans, while this old sett exists for the name (first recorded in Wilsons 1819 Key Pattern Book).

Left: CRAIG
A sett created in the 1950s for a common Scots surname, and designed to evoke the lines and fissures of Scotland's rocky crags.

Below: DRUMMOND
This is the earliest known, reliably 'Drummond' tartan, despite being 'Perthshire Rock and Wheel' in the late 18th century. The Earls of Perth were chiefs of the clan.

Left: DUNDEE
18th-century sett. It appeared in Wilsons 1819 Pattern Book, acquiring its name by selling well in that city. It was revived in the 1950s, but is shown here in Wilson's original dye colours.

Right: FIFE
Two trade tartans were designed for the marriage of Queen Victoria's granddaughter Louise (1889). She and her husband were created Duke and Duchess of Fife, 'Duke' sett has red lines, 'Duchess' blue.

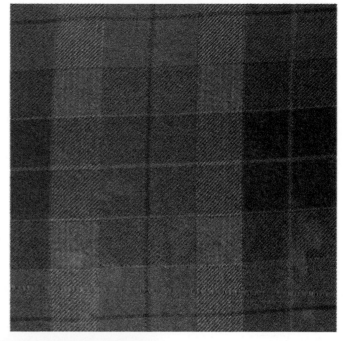

Above Left: MULL
Not a true 'district'
tartan. Also titled 'Glen
Lyon' or (pattern) 'No 53'
by Wilsons in their Key
Pattern Book of 1819.

Above: RED MAR
Now officially adopted by
the Chief of Clan Mar,
this was the sett of a plaid
said to be the last to be
woven in Glenbuchat, in
Mar, before the '45
Rising.

Left: GLASGOW
18th-century 'Rock and
Wheel' sett which
appears in Wilsons 1797
manuscript notebook. It
was so named because it
was popular in that city.
An incorrect version is
currently available.

Left: GRANT of MONYMUSK Similar to 'Old Huntly'. Recorded in Cockburn 1810.

Right: GORDON of ABERGELDIE
An 18th-century sett first illustrated in the portrait of Rachel Gordon of Abergeldie.

Far left: GUNN Recorded in Wilsons 1819 Key Pattern Book, the blue/green/black base is the same for Mackays and Sutherlands.

Left: GRANT Hunting First recorded in Wilsons 1819 Key Pattern Book, when the most usual 'Grant' of later years was called 'New Bruce'.

Below: HUNTER This 18th-century sett, recorded by Wilsons (1819), bears no relation to the commonly retailed modern Hunter pattern.

Left: LUMSDEN of KINTORE
A plaid at Pitcaple Castle, with the stitched inscription, 'Margaret Lumsden, Boghead of Kintore, 1797', was faithfully reproduced in natural dyes for David Lumsden of Cushnie in 1990.

Right: LENNOX
This could be an old 'district' sett, but is taken from the 16th-century portrait of Lady Margaret Douglas, wife of Matthew Stewart, Earl of Lennox.

Left: INDO-SCOTTISH TARTAN
An example of the clan-based tartan patterns introduced to the Madras cotton weavers by Scots officials of the British East India Company in the 18th century.

Below left: MacNAB
This sett – worn by the Chief in Raeburn's 18th-century portrait – is probably much older than the Black Watch variant used for the clan, and was regarded by Wilsons as the more genuine.

Below: MURRAY of OCHTERTYRE
From the portrait of Helen, the laird's daughter, in 1750. The pattern is a Red/Black version of 'Murray', 'Black Watch' or 'Fraser', to all of which she had connections.

*Left: MacDONALD of
GLENALADALE
One of the setts
discovered in Prince
Edward Island in the
1960s among surviving
plaids of the family of
Alex MacDonald of
Glenaladale who
migrated to Canada in
1773.*

*Right: MacARTHUR of
MILTON
This sett, in a Wilson's
1832/3 swatch book, is
more akin to the Black
Watch/Campbell than the
common – MacDonald-
based – clan pattern.
Worn by the current
'Chief apparent'.*

Left:.MORAY of
ABERCAIRNEY
Taken from the portrait of
James, 14th Laird, about
1735, the sett has visual
similarities to other
Perthshire patterns but
not to those of Clan
Murray.

Below left: McIAIN of
ARDNAMURCHAN
This sett, for a Clan
Donald branch also
known as 'MacKeane', is
often called – in error –
'McDonald of Glencoe'.
The tartan for the
MacQueens of Clan
Donald is a variation.

Below: MacSPORRAN
Designed 'professionally'
in the 1970s for the Clan
MacSporran Society, but
later realized to be a
duplication of the Clan
MacArthur sett. One of
the pitfalls of invented
tradition.

*Above: MacGREGOR of
DEESIDE
An old sett, probably of
'district' origin, reputedly
adopted by the clan
branch which fought for
the Gordons on Deeside
in the 16th century and
settled there.*

*Left: MacDUFF
It is intriguing that the
oldest sett for the clan,
associated with Royalty
for centuries, should be a
basic form of the old
'Royal' tartan (later
'Royal Stuart').*

Left: MacCOLL
The family are said to be of old MacDonald stock, and the sett has the MacDonald 'motif'.

Right: MacDONALD of KINGSBURGH
Verified by a well-documented fragment of a tartan waistcoat given in 1746 to 'Bonnie' Prince Charlie by the Kingsburgh laird whose son married Flora MacDonald.

Left: MENZIES
This is probably the
oldest of the Menzies
setts and, curiously, is
almost the same as the
'Dress Sinclair' which it
predates.

Above left: OHIO
Form of 'district' sett,
using a modern
convention of symbolic
colours. It was designed
in the 1980s and
subsequently promoted
as the 'official' tartan for
the State of Ohio in the
United States.

Above: ROXBURGH
Possibly a 'district'
pattern, this sett comes
from a mid-19th-century
book of silk swatches. It
shares features with the
tartan for the
Roxburghshire-based
Clan Kerr.

Above: ROBERTSON of
STRUAN
A specimen of this tartan
is in the H.S.L. (1816)
annotated by this name.
It seems to bear no
relation to any other
Robertson tartan.

Below: WILSON
A classic 18th-
century pattern
designed or adopted
by Scotland's premier
tartan manufacturer
– William Wilson – in
1775, in honour of his
wife Janet.

John Murray, 4th Earl of Dunmore (1732–1809) by Sir Joshua Reynolds.

The restraint of Highland Dress

After the Battle of Culloden on 16 April, 1746, the Duke of Cumberland earned the reputation of 'Butcher' by his savage treatment of survivors of the conflict. In perspective, it has to be remembered that the whole of Scotland was divided in its loyalties, with the majority *opposed* to the Catholic Jacobite Cause, with brother facing brother, and son facing father, across the battle lines. With the aim of 'more effectually securing the peace of the Highlands in Scotland', an Act of Parliament was hastily introduced, which primarily prohibited the carrying of arms by 'such Persons who have lately raised and carried on a most wicked and audacious Rebellion against his Majesty, in favour of a Popish Pretender'. But it further decreed:

Anno Regni
GEORGII II REGIS
In the Nineteenth Year of the Reign of our Sovereign Lord George the Second by the Grace of God, of Great Britain, France and Ireland, King, Defender of the Faith, Etc.
(CAP.XXXIX, Sec. XVII, 1746)

An Act for the more effectual disarming the Highlands in Scotland; and for the more effectually securing the Peace of the said Highlands; and for restraining the Use of the Highland Dress.

From and after the first day of August one thousand seven hundred and fourty-seven, no Man or Boy within that part of Great Britain called Scotland, other than such as shall be employed as Officers and Soldiers in his Majesty's Forces, shall, on any Pretence whatsoever, wear or put on the Clothes commonly called Highland Clothes (that is to say) the Plaid, Philibeg or Little Kilt, Trowse, Shoulder Belts, or any part whatsoever of what peculiarly belongs to the Highland Garb; and that no Tartan or party-coloured Plaid or Stuff shall be used for Great Coats, or for Upper Coats; and that if any such Person shall presume, after the said first day of August, to wear or put on the aforesaid Garments, or any Part of them, very such person so offending, being thereof convicted by the Oath of one or more credible Witness or Witnesses before any court of Justiciary, or any one or more Justices of the Peace for the State of Stewartry, or Judge Ordinary of the Place where such Offence shall be committed, shall suffer Imprisonment, without Bail, during the Space of six Months, and no longer, and being convicted for a second offence before a Court of Justiciary, or at the Circuits, shall be liable to be transported to any of his Majesty's Plantations beyond the Seas, there to remain for the Space of seven Years.

There was an immediate sense of alarm from many far-sighted people throughout Britain, who understood the need to disarm the rebels but doubted the wisdom of humiliating an entire people (including those who had supported the Government) by depriving them of their unique dress, so undermining their self-respect and confidence. Sir Walter Scott remarked later that 'there was a knowledge of mankind in the Prohibition, since it divested the Highlanders of a dress which was closely associated with their habits of clanship and of war'. Influential lobbying must have had an effect, because further legislation was introduced in 1747 and 1748, which extended the deadline when the 'restraining the Use of Highland dress' provision would be introduced until 'the First Day of August one thousand seven hundred and forty-nine'. But it prohibited quite specifically 'the Plaid, Philibeg or Little Kilt' as from Christmas Day, 1748! The use of tartan in other items of dress was obviously a lesser offence. In the Act of 1748, the original penalties imposed in the legislation of 1746 (imprisonment for the first offence and transportation to the American Plantations for the second) were replaced by being 'delivered to serve His Majesty as a soldier' principally in North America. Beneath this apparent softening of attitudes lies an offical fear of the growing French power in the Americas, and the need for more soldiers to supplement those absorbed by the confrontation in Europe and India.

Lairds and Ladies in Tartan

It is obvious that the Act 'Restraining the Highland Dress' was subject to patchy prosecution, depending on the diligence of local magistrates and the Hanoverian patrols. The Act did, however, exclude females and specifically 'Landowners or the sons of Landowners', a point which is scarcely appreciated. In fact, not a single man or boy of political or social importance was arrested for wearing tartan. The poor Highlander, pursued by the patrols, was bearing the brunt of Governmental disfavour along with those active rebel gentlemen who had been executed or exiled.

Enforcement of the Acts

In the Highlands, the Redcoats, including Government Highlanders, were tied down for many years in patrolling the mountains and apprehending tartan-clad rebels. Army proposals that a bounty of £5 be paid, were not implemented, but initially the Act was severely enforced after 1748. Magistrates themselves were prosecuted if they were suspected of leniency, and one soldier was sentenced to 600 lashes for apparently 'turning a blind eye'. At the

12-year-old Helen Murray of Ochtertyre around 1753. The pattern of the silk, tartan dress seems unusual, but is either of the virtually identical (by sett) Fraser, Black Watch or Murray tartans, rendered only in red and black. Her grandmother was a Fraser, and her father wore 'Black Watch' tartan as a Highland officer in the Government service.

other extreme, a civilian tried for murder in 1750 was acquitted on his plea that the victim was dressed in a tartan plaid!

Drummond-Norie quotes a report from a Captain John Beckwith on duty at Strontian in Ardnamurchan, dated 26 May, 1752. On that day the corporal in command of one of his patrols had taken up a man by the name of Cameron, servant to a Mrs Jane Cameron, who had a piece of tartan wrapped round him like a philibeg. The prisoner was sent to the Sheriff Substitute at Fort William who confined him.

A man of the name of Mac A Guir or MacGregor, from Breadalbane, in the year 1750, was acquitted on his proving that his 'kilt' was stitched up in the middle.

'Three soldiers, who were returning to Glensheil, after been to Laggan for their pay, captured John McIntosh for wearing a tartan jacket and philibeg. They determined to take him as a prisoner to Laggan and brought him seven miles on the way hither, to within two miles of Invergarry, where they were beset by many women, who offered a guinea for the prisoner's release. The soldiers refused to take the bribe, and about twenty of the women accompanied them further on to a very thick wood, out of which six men suddenly started and pounced upon their arms before they could use them. The women joined heartily in the fray. The soldiers were disarmed, and forced to take an oath

not to attempt anything against the prisoner, who was set free. When Captain Molesworth was informed of this affair, he sent out a party of sixteen men who captured Macintosh, Sanders MacDonald, who was most active in the rescue, and four women who assisted in it.'

Another report from a Captain Trapaud, dated 25 June, 1752, records the taking up of a certain William Cameron by the Glenmorriston party for wearing the Highland dress. For this, he was sentenced by the Sheriff of Inverness-shire to six months' imprisonment.

A Sutherland man named MacKay was seized in Inverness and charged with wearing the Highland dress. He pleaded ignorance and the fact that he had no other clothing. However, he was sentenced to six months' imprisonment — barely two hours elapsing between his arrest and the sentence. He had a 'short tartan coat upon him and a highland plaid party colloured wrapt lously about him'.

Charles Fraser-Mackintosh expressed an interesting opinion that, in one sense, the diskilting statute did good 'because it gave rise to and originated the formation of societies and clubs exclusively connected with the Highlands, the people and their language, which has tended so much to foster the ancient spirit'. He reproduced a letter, dated June 1748, from William Fraser, a member of a respectable Ross-shire family, to Bailie John Mackintosh of Inverness:

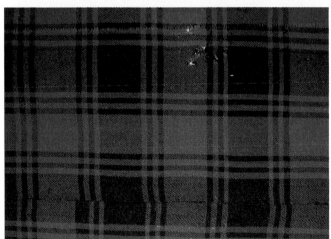

Above: Sheriff Charles Campbell of Lochlane, near Crieff, wearing one of the expensive red plaids favoured by the landed gentry after the tartan, kilt and plaids were banned for 'common' men and boys north of the Highland Line.

Left: Detail of a similar sett worn in 18th-century Campbell portraits but not acknowledged as a Campbell Clan tartan today.

I'll be fond to have from you the Disarming Act for the Highland dress with amendments lately made by Parliament, how soon it comes to hand. Please give the bearer 3 yards and a half of good blew cloth for a great coat, with furniture.

Do not forget to send good buttons, and as much coarse cloth as will make another to cover me when I attend the fishing. . . . As we cannot appear in our country habit any more, may send me some swatches of your cloths and fresees, and acquaint the prices . . . .

A document endorsed as follows: 'Invry, 27 September 1758 – Appoints Peter Campbell, Officer, to put the within John McLeran in gaol, therein to remain till liberated in due course of law. (Signed) John Richardson' states:

John McLeran of the Parish of Ardchattan, aged about 20 years, was brought before me by Lieutenant John Campbell, being apprehended for wearing a Philibeg (kilt), and convicted of the same by his own confession: Therefore, in terms of the Act of Parliament, I delivered him over to the said Lieutenant John Campbell to serve His Majesty as a soldier in America, after reading to him the 2nd and 6th sections of the Act against mutiny and desertion.

Certified at Ardmady, 26th Sept 1758 (signed) Co. Campbell, J.P.

John MacKay of Durness in the County of Sutherland had occasion to go to Inverness on business. His clan had taken up arms on behalf of the Government. Living in a remote part of the country, he was unaware of the prohibition of the dress, till he reached Inverness, where he was apprehended, and locked up in jail. Notwithstanding his declaration that he never heard of the Unclothing Act, and that he belonged to a loyal clan, it was only on the strong protest of his chief, Lord Reay, that he was liberated.

Repeal

When war with France finally erupted in North America in 1757, Prime Minister William Pitt shrewdly chose to commission new Highland regiments to counter the threat, and despite the outcry over the 'arming of former rebels', his strategy proved remarkably successful. Privately, he referred to the Highlanders in the same dispassionate way as General James Wolfe, who said 'No harm if they fall!'. With the accession in 1760 of a less 'Germanic' Monarch, George III, the political climate in the Highlands was changing. The Jacobite threat had evaporated after the hard-core had been executed, transported, or had migrated. With the Highland regiments already legendary and an invaluable element in British foreign policy, a liberalization of the repressive laws of the post-Culloden period took place. Finally, on 17 June, 1782, the Marquis of Graham, one of the leading lights of the recently formed Highland Society of London, rose in Parliament to move 'That the clause of the 19th Year of George II which prohibits the wearing of the Scotch Highland dress, be repealed.' Reports show that the motion was seconded by the brother of the late General Fraser, the same clan chief who had raised the Fighting Frasers for King George.

On 1 July, 1782, the Act Repealing the ban on tartan and Highland Dress, received the Royal Assent, and it became lawful to wear them again. In the North of Scotland, a solemn but joyous proclamation was made.

By the last decade of the 18th century, the Fencible (Territorial) Regiments were adopting bizarre variations of Highland dress, borrowing freely from Continental styles.

Listen Men
This is bringing before all the Sons of the Gael, that
the King and Parliament of Britain have for ever
abolished the Act against the Highland Dress; which
came down to the Clans from the beginning of the
world to the year 1746. This must bring great joy to
every Highland Heart. You are no longer bound
down to the unmanly dress of the Lowlander. This
is declaring to every Man, young and old, simple and
gentle, that they may after this put on and wear the
Truis, the Little Kilt, the Coat, and the Striped Hose,
as also the Belted Plaid, without fear of the Law of
the Realm or the spite of enemies.

After the Repeal, a period of 'gluttony after the
fast' took place, to which excesses the world is still
subject from time to time. At the end of the 18th
century, the fencible (territorial) regiments were
devising bizarre variants of the original – and by
necessity, practical Highland garb. Sporrans and
bonnets, in particular, adopted a style more suited
to comic opera. By comparison, civilian Highland
dress was restrained, although Sir Harry Lauder's
parodies did the dress poor service. Today, tartan
and its accompanying dress form has survived the
tartan fever of George IV's visit to Edinburgh,
Victoria and Albert's cult of Balmorality and to
become a national symbol.

Above: The 'Piccadilly
Highlander', a faithful
image of the expatriate
Scot in Edwardian
times enjoying a break
at a Highland Ball in
London.

Left: Sir Harry
Lauder became rich by
lampooning the kilted
Scotsman on stage, and
reinforced the maudlin
Victorian image of
Scotland.

The Clans

Agnew

This small Lowland clan is an example of a family name which is probably not, in fact, related to its popularly accepted origins. It has been suggested by the Professor of Celtic Studies at Dublin University that the Agnews were one of the original Ulster tribes from which great clans like the MacDonalds and the MacDougalls stem, through the native Celtic mother of Somerled, the half-Norse, half-Celtic King of the Isles in the 12th century. There is certainly an Irish sept or clan called O'Gneeve or O'Gnive, who were hereditary bards to the Clannaboy O'Neils, and who Anglicized their name to Agnew.

Early spellings of the Agnew name in Scotland had echoes of the Irish form: Agnev (1436), Aggnew (1512), and Agnewe (1610), strengthening the arguments that the name is quite different from that of the Norman family which came from the Château d'Agneaux in the valley of the Vire, and who were first recorded in Scotland at Liddesdale in 1190, when William des Aigneu was granted Lochnaw Castle between Randolph Soullis and Jedburgh Abbey.

The Agnews of Lochnaw were created Hereditary Sheriffs of Galloway by King David II in 1363, an office held by the family until the abolition of Hereditable Jurisdictions in 1747. Andrew, Constable of Lochnaw, was appointed Sheriff of Wigtown in 1451, another hereditary post held for many generations. The 8th Sheriff, Sir Patrick, Member of Parliament for Wigtounshire, was created a Baronet of Nova Scotia in 1629. The 4th Baronet, Sir James, married Lady Mary Montgomerie, by whom he produced 21 children.

Many Agnews, descended from Irish emigrants to North America and Australasia, stem from a 'Scotch–Irish' branch of the family which went to Ulster around 1610 and received land grants in the fateful Protestant 'Plantation of Ulster' by King James VI and I.

The 10th Baronet and his wife, Sir Fulque and Lady Swazie, served on the academic staff of a number of university colleges in Africa. The present chief succeeded on the death of his father, while serving in the Royal Highland Fusiliers. He developed an abiding interest in heraldry during his school-days, and when he left the Army in 1981 was appointed Unicorn Pursuivant at the Court of the Lord Lyon. He was subsequently appointed Rothesay Herald.

Lochnaw Castle today is run as a (very superior) guest house by an Agnew trust. Until Sir Crispin Agnew became Chief, the clan – in keeping with most Lowland families – had no tartan, but he designed a simple sett in the late 1970s in response to appeals from clan members.

Anstruther

The Anstruthers are descendants of the Norman family of Malherbe, whose branch of that family held lands at Candel in Dorset during the 11th century. They appear in Scotland a century later, holding the lands of Anstruther in Fife. At the time of his death in 1153, William de Candela is recorded as holding the Barony of Anstruther, but it was his grandson Henry who seems to have been the first to adopt the territorial designation 'de Ainestrother' as a surname. The 'Henry de Anstrother or Aynestrothere' who rendered homage to Edward I of England in 1298 was probably his son or grandson.

The descendants of David Anstruther, who is recorded in the 16th century as an officer in the Scots Guard or *Garde Ecossaise* of the King of France, was created Baron Anstrude in the French peerage and his descendants still hold that title today. Sir James Anstruther, a favourite of James VI & I, was appointed Hereditary Grand Carver: an ancient office still held by the Anstruthers. In 1595 he was also appointed Master of the Royal Household.

The Anstruther Laird at the time of Cromwell, Sir Phillip, had seven sons, three of whom were knighted and two created Baronets of Nova Scotia: Sir Robert Anstruther of Balcaskie and Sir James Anstruther of Airdrie. The 4th Baronet of Airdrie inherited the Carmichael estates in Lanarkshire in 1817 and assumed the surname of Carmichael-Anstruther. His only son was shot dead by a fellow-pupil at Eton and was succeeded by his uncle. The compound surname disqualifies the descendants of this senior line of the family from being recognized as chiefs. The chiefship today has devolved upon the holder of the other Baronetcy, Sir Ralph Anstruther of Balcaskie, 7th Baronet, KCVO, MC, DL, who is Treasurer and Equerry to Her Majesty, Queen Elizabeth the Queen Mother. There is no clan tartan.

Arbuthnott

The Arbuthnott surname is of territorial origin, from the baronial lands of 'Aberbothenoth' in the valley of the Bervie Water in Kincardineshire. In the reign of William the Lyon (1165–1214) Hugh de Swinton was variously described as *Dominus* or *Thanus* – Lord – of 'Aberbuthenoth', having obtained those lands from Walter Olifard (*see* Oliphant), son of the Sheriff of the Mearns.

The name underwent a couple of modifications, as 'Aberbutennauth' (1241) and 'Abirbuthenoth' (1282), before reaching an approximation of today's spelling with 'Phillip Arbuthnet of Arbuthnet', who gave a charter to the Carmelite friars of Aberdeen in 1355. He was the first to be described as 'Arbuthnet/Arbuthnot of That Ilk'. The Chief of the Name and Arms today is the 16th Viscount of Arbuthnott, a title created in 1642, and he still lives on the original lands held by the family since the 12th century. The subsidiary title of the Chief in Scotland is Baron Inverbervie.

The family motto is *Laus Deo* ('Praise be to God'), and the clansman's crest badge is a peacock's head. There is a long-standing family connection with the Royal Highland Regiment – The Black Watch – of which the Arbuthnotts have produced a number of Colonels of the Regiment. The father of the present chief rose above that rank to become Major-General, The Viscount of Arbuthnott. The tartan of the regiment is worn by the family, there being no pattern otherwise associated with the name.

Armstrong

This name tends to be pronounced 'Armstrang' in the turbulent Border country, which was often called the Debatable Lands because it was so much in dispute between England and Scotland. Armstrong families were to be found on both sides of the Border by the 1300s, and their forebears would have peopled the area long before that Border existed.

Like many Scottish names, this one is reputed to have been acquired as a 'canting' or punning reference to some past deed. In this case, it was earned by the armourer to a long distant Scottish monarch scooping his royal master up on to his own saddle when the king's horse had been killed under him in battle. Despite being called Fairbairn, he was called 'Armstrong' thereafter and rewarded with lands on which the clan's fortunes were built.

These lands originally centred on Mangerston in Liddesdale, which became the seat of the chief's line. The success of the clan as breeders of men and of horses saw the acquisition of more lands and a reputation as redoubtable irregular cavalry in an age of constant skirmish and affray. The Armstrongs were described as 'for ay riding' – synonymous with raiding – and were said in 1528 to have been able to put 3,000 horsemen into the field. Their lifestyle was every bit as colourful as the Highland clans, as many Armstrong nicknames suggest: Kinmont Willie, 'Meikle' Sim, Davy 'the lady', 'Stowlugs' Jock, Christie's Will, Davie 'Hang-tail' – even 'Ill Will' . . .

Armstrongs tended to face death with no less flair. The Chieftain of the Gilnockie branch had, by

Armstrong crest badge

his exploits, attracted the disapproving attention of King James V, as he found to his cost when he rode out to greet and pay homage to his sovereign in 1530. The teenage King had ridden into the Border country with a strong force, determined to prove that he was no royal wimp by making an example of troublemakers. On the King's orders 'Black Jock' Armstrong, better known to ballad and folklore as 'Johnnie', was seized with all 40 of his followers and they were strung up on the nearest trees. As Johnnie waited his turn, he contemptuously dismissed the royal boy who had broken the implicit code of honour which should have prevailed at such a meeting. He spoke his own epitaph: 'I was but a fool to seek grace at a graceless face, but had I known you would have taken me this day, I would have lived in the Borders despite King Harry [Henry VIII of England] and you both.'

When the last Chief, Archie Armstrong, was executed as an outlaw in 1610, the lands of Mangerston passed into the hands of the Armstrongs' great rivals, the Scotts. Since then there has been no chief, though there may well be modern claimants to the title. Armstrongs have continued to make their name around the world but none more so than astronaut Neil, who went around the world many times before becoming the first man to set foot on the Moon in the *Apollo 11* mission of July 1969. A story that he left a piece of the Armstrong tartan on the lunar surface is nonsense, and Neil Armstrong himself has repudiated this up-to-date example of 'invented tradition'.

Barclay

The Barclays of Scotland claim kinship with the great Norman family which took its name from the lands of Berkeley Castle in Gloucestershire. The name means 'birch-lea', the clearing in the birchwoods.

John de Berchelai is reputed to have arrived in Scotland with the 'first wave' of Norman knights around 1069, and he is the founder of the Scottish dynasty. His three sons Walter, Alexander, and Richard begat the three major branches of the family, respectively Gartly, Towie-Barclay, and Ardrossan. Sir Walter Berkelai og Gartly held the high office of Chamberlain of Scotland in 1165, but the chiefship passed to the Towie-Barclay branch when the last of the male Barclays of Gartly died in 1456.

Andrew Barclay, kinsman of a 16th-century Laird of Towie, went to Europe as a mercenary and was the forebear of Field Marshal, Prince Michael Barclay de Tolly, Commander-in-Chief of the Tsar's armies at the outset of Napoleon's Russian cam-

Barclay crest badge

paign in 1812. 'Captain Barclay', who became Laird of Urie in 1797, was a famous soldier and sportsman who once walked 1,609 km (1,000 miles) in 1,000 consecutive hours. One of his other pastimes was the claiming of dormant earldoms. In the last 40 years of his life, he tried and failed to become successively Earl of Airth, then Strathearn, and finally Menteith. An Edinburgh merchant who fitted out privateers for the sea war against Holland (1665–67) was created a Baronet of Nova Scotia in 1668 as Sir Robert Barclay of Pierston, Bart., a title that has survived through 14 generations.

The Barclay name lent itself to many variations before surnames became regularized. A note in the Kirk Registers of St Andrews observes 'A witness named Barclay is mentioned four times, and on each occasion his name is spelt in a different way: Barthlhlat, Barclaytht, Bartclaytht, and Barclaitht. Judging by the clerk's attempt to take down his name, this witness probably lisped.'

The Barclays possessed considerable lands in both Aberdeenshire and Banffshire, and were hereditary sheriffs of the latter county. The Chief today is Peter Barclay of That Ilk.

Bisset

The Bissets are the remnant of a great Scottish-Norman dynasty, tilted by circumstance in favour of the females of the clan. As a result the surname is not very common today, but several Bisset heiresses have played important roles in the histories of prominent Highland families.

The Chisholms are a case in point. Alexander, son of the 13th-century de Chisholme chief who was 'Justiciar of the North', married the Wayland heiress who brought to the Chisholms the vast landholdings in five counties which she had herself inherited from the Bisset heiress to the Aird. The Frasers of Lovat also inherited extensive lands, on which they still live, through the female line of the Bissets of the Aird who had founded the great Priory of Beauly in 1231.

Beauly Priory, founded in 1231 by the Bissets of the Aird, who provided the ancestress for a number of Highland clans.

The first Bissets in Scotland are said to have been the 'Biseys', who were among the young Normans of good family whom William the Lyon (1165–1214) brought back to Scotland in 1174 after his captivity in France and England. Around 1198, Henricus de Byset witnessed a charter of William the Lyon – the first appearance of the name in Scotland. But it was his son John who obtained the grant of those lands in the north, sometime after 1205. This became the dowry, enabling successive heiresses to form marriage alliances with some of the newly developing clans.

The power of the Bissets came to an abrupt end in 1242 when Walter Byset, Lord of Aboyne, came off worst in a tournament at Haddington, near Edinburgh. His opponent had been the young Earl of Atholl, and in a fit of jealous rage Walter burned down the house in which the Earl was sleeping. Some indication of the favour in which the Bysets were held by King Alexander II (1214–49) may be judged by the punishment for the crime. Walter, his nephew John (the founder of Beauly Priory) and other prominent menfolk of the family escaped with their lives but were banished from Scotland. Their lands and property were divided among those unmarried daughters of the family, who did not go into exile with their parents. This literally emasculated the clan and ensured that its name was no longer associated with power and wealth. The blood feud seems to have followed the Bisset men overseas, for in January 1252 a pardon was granted to Adam, nephew of the incinerated Earl of Atholl, for slaying some of the Byset men who had fled to Ireland.

There have been some curious renderings of the Bisset name since the Middle Ages – 'Beceit', 'Basok', 'Bissed', and the like. There is even a suggestion that the French composer Bizet (whose actual family surname was Leopold) was 'of the Clan'. Apart from *Carmen*, it is argued, one of Bizet's major works was *The Fair Maid of Perth*. (There is, in fact, a record in Scotland of the name, spelled the same way, in 1686.)

There is no recognized Bisset chief at present, but the senior branch of the clan are the Bissets of Lessendrum in Aberdeenshire. The surname is beginning to flourish once more in that county, and in Morayshire. A tartan for the name was designed in the 1970s by Miss Elizabeth Bisset. The motto of the crest badge is *Abscissa virescit*.

Left: The great keep of Borthwick Castle, built by the first Lord Borthwick in 1430. It was restored by the family in 1902 and is still inhabited.

Right: Kilmarnock Castle, seat of the Boyd family who were Earls of Kilmarnock after 1661. The 5th Earl was beheaded after the '45, and the estates confiscated.

Borthwick

This small but prominent Border clan is represented today by Major The Lord Borthwick, whose father had sold his Mull estates and set about the restoration of Borthwick Castle in Selkirkshire (1430), which was completed in 1902. The family let the Castle after 1911 and moved to Crookston, a Borthwick home of even earlier vintage dating from the mid-14th century.

The 'lands of Borthwic and Thoftcotys' were chartered to William Borthwic in 1410 by Robert, Duke of Albany, Governor of Scotland while the young King James I was held captive in England. 'William of Borthik' was one of the Scottish nobles exchanged as hostages for the King when he was released in 1424. The Borthwick peerage created in 1452 has lain dormant since the death in 1910 of the last Lord Borthwick (not the current Chief's father). As the senior cadet line had failed for want

of an heir, it was left for Major Harry Borthwick to produce irrefutable evidence that he was the heir, in the direct male line of a younger son of the baron, 17 generations ago. (This evidence emerged only recently.)

The Borthwick surname was well known in Edinburgh in the 16th and 17th centuries, as families had spread northwards up the east coast from the 14th century. William Borthwyk is recorded as a baillie of Aberdeen in 1398, and Patrick Borthwik as a burgess of the town in 1400. In 1502 David Borthik from St Andrews was elected Procurator in the University of Orleans in France. In the 16th century, Sir John Borthwick prudently fled the country when a charge of heresy was brought against him. He was condemned and burned at the stake – in effigy – after his departure.

The chief is the Rt. Hon. The Lord Borthwick of Borthwick. The clansman's crest badge is a moor's head and the motto is *Qui conducit*. There is a Borthwick tartan designed this century, echoing traditional Border cloth and colouring.

Boyd

Some doubt surrounds the origin of the Boyd surname, but it most likely stems from Simon, nephew of Walter FitzAlan, the first High Steward of Scotland. Simon was renowned for his yellow hair, leading the the Gaelic nickname *Buidhe*. His descendants were well established in Ayrshire long before Robert Boyd distinguished himself in the battle of Largs against the Norsemen in 1263. Duncan Boyd was hanged in 1306 for supporting Robert the Bruce, and the first feudal Baron of Kilmarnock was Sir Robert Boyd, one of the Scots commanders at Bannockburn in 1314.

Five generations later, another Robert became the 1st Lord Boyd, excelling himself even by the standards of the day by kidnapping the infant King James III, declaring himself sole Governor of the Realm of Scotland, and arranging for his son Thomas, the Master of Boyd, to be created Earl of

Arran in 1467 and to marry the Princess Mary, the young King's sister. They all fled to Burgundy in 1469 when Regent Robert's power-base collapsed, but the son of the Princess and the Earl returned to Scotland with his mother after his father's death in France. In 1484, restored to his grandfather's titles as the 2nd Lord Boyd, the boy was murdered in a feud with the Montgomeries. It was not until 1546 that the 4th Lord Boyd was able to avenge his forebear's murder with an organized slaughter of many of the Montgomerie gentry.

The 10th Lord Boyd found favour with the restored King Charles II, and was created Earl of Kilmarnock in 1661. His grandson voted for the Act of Union in 1707, and raised 500 men in support of George I during the Jacobite Rising of 1715. His son William, the 4th Earl, was a general in the army of Prince Charles Edward in the 1745–46 Rising, but was captured at Culloden, found guilty of treason, and sentenced to be beheaded on Tower Hill. When required to kneel and place his head on the block, he drew a tartan cap from the pocket of his tailcoat and placed it deliberately on his head. 'If I must die,' he is alleged to have said, 'I will at least die a Scotchman.'

His son James, Lord Boyd, had fought on the Government side at Culloden but was still not allowed to resume his father's forfeited Earldom. For all that, he succeeded his staunchly Jacobite great-aunt Mary, Countess of Atholl, who had raised her men for Prince Charlie in '45, when she died childless in 1758. He needed little persuasion to change his name to Hay, and thereupon became 15th Earl of Erroll and Hereditary Lord High Constable of Scotland (see Hay). In the latter role, he officiated at the coronation of King George III in 1761, causing widespread embarrassment by forgetting to remove his cap when the monarch entered – perhaps subconsciously recalling his father's resort to headgear in moments of crisis.

The family had a patchy relationship with luck. The 16th Earl, having inadvertently disclosed a secret entrusted to him by the Prime Minister, felt it his duty to commit suicide. His brother succeeded as 17th Earl of Erroll and his son, the 18th Earl, was created 1st Baron Kilmarnock, marrying the natural daughter of King William IV and Mrs Jordan. Thereafter the family's luck held good until the 19th Earl's great-grandson was murdered by a jealous husband in Kenya in 1941. The ancient Earldom passed to Josslyn Hay's daughter Diana, who became Countess of Erroll. The title 'Baron Kilmarnock' – entailed only to male heirs – passed to the Earl's brother, who immediately resumed the name of Boyd.

If the titles had not been attainted in 1746, the present Chief of the Clan Boyd would be 13th Earl of Kilmarnock and 22nd Lord Boyd. He prefers the Stewart tartan to the more recent 'Boyd' sett, because of his descent from the namefather of the Royal House of Stewart. The Boyd clansman's crest badge is 'A Right Hand Raised in Benediction', and the family motto is *Con Fido*.

Boyle

The Scottish Boyles and their Irish cousins were originally Normans who came from Beauville near Caen. When they first arrived in England in the train of William the Conqueror, they were described as 'De Boyville', a surname which suffered from the medieval convention of interchanging 'U' and 'V'. As early as 1170, the name is recorded as 'Boiuil'. By the 1360s, it was appearing as 'Boyll' and 'Boyuill', first appearing in its current form in 1482. Even so it was still being written 'Boyl', 'Boile', and 'Boyll' in the 1500s, as 'Boyell' and 'Boylle' in the 1600s, and 'Boill' as late as 1721. The

Kelburn Castle, in Ayrshire, seat of the Boyle family who have held the lands since the 12th century, and were made Earls of Glasgow in 1703.

brilliant lawyer who was ennobled as Earl of Glasgow for his subtle drafting of the Act of Union in 1707 (and who, some say, dispensed the £20,000 in bribes provided by Queen Anne to ensure that the Union was approved in Scotland) was David *Boyle*.

The family has held the seat of Kelburn Castle from the 13th century until present times, and the courtesy title of the Earl's eldest son is nowadays 'Viscount Kelburn'. A family talent for the law became interspersed with a love of the sea in the 18th and 19th centuries, with the eldest son of the

4th Earl becoming a naval officer; his brother, the 5th Earl, a Commander, RN; his half-brother the 6th Earl, Lord Clerk Register of Scotland; the 7th and 8th Earls both Captains, RN; and the 9th holder of the title somewhat extravagantly styled Rear-Admiral, the Earl of Glasgow. As a serving naval officer, he was present at the Dunkirk evacuations and the sinking of the German battleship *Bismarck*.

His son, Patrick Boyle, succeeded on the death of the Admiral in 1984, becoming 10th Earl of Glasgow, Viscount of Kelburn, Lord Boyle of Kelburn, Stewartoun, Cumbrae, Finnick, Largs and Dalry in the Peerage of Scotland, and Baron Fairlie of Fairlie in the Peerage of the United Kingdom. As Chief of the Whole Name and Arms of Boyle in Scotland he insists, however, that the Boyles are not a clan 'but a family that has been here for a very long time'. His Lordship (professionally a highly respected film director) was responsible for a controversial documentary film of the first International Gathering of the Clans, held in Scotland in 1977. He neither wears nor possesses a kilt and recognizes no Boyle tartan — but he does possess the sacred kiwi feather cloak of a Maori high chief, of which no more than four are believed to be in existence. This is a relic of the family's strong connections with 19th-century New Zealand. The family's 'crest badge' is a two-headed eagle with the family motto *Dominus Providebit* ('The Lord Will Provide').

Brodie

The Brodie clan is one of the very oldest in Scotland. Indeed, its origins are still not properly known. The clan has been said to stem from the ancient Pictish kings of northern Scotland, one of whom, Brude, received St Columba at Inverness during the saint's great ministry in the later 6th century. Another Brude, perhaps a descendant of the first chief, defeated a great army of Angles under King Ecgfrith of Northumbria at the battle of Nechtansmere (near Dunnichen in Aberdeenshire) in 685. When Kenneth MacAlpin (843–860) became the first king of a united Scotland north of the Firth of Forth and Firth of Clyde, he seems to have let the Pictish royal family continue to live near Inverness, possibly in Moray, and the Brodie family has been associated with Moray ever since.

By the early 12th century, the Kingdom of Scotland occupied more or less the territory of Scotland today. The first great king of Scots of that century was David I (1124–53). His reign was troubled by risings, especially in the north, and a number of Moray families opposed him. They were moved out of Moray to other districts further south, but the Brodies escaped the exile and they re-mained there, 'keeping their heads down', on and around land on which, in the 16th century, the present Brodie Castle was begun. The family's prudence over the centuries has resulted in the fact that a male direct descendant of the ancient clan, still surnamed Brodie, lives in Brodie Castle today.

In 1645 Brodie Castle was attacked during the great Civil War, and most of the family documents were destroyed. Yet it is known that Malcolm Brodie was thane or lord of Brodie in the time of Alexander III (1249–86), and that in 1311 his son Michael Brodie was given a charter raising him to a barony by King Robert the Bruce (1306–29). Alexander Brodie of Brodie (1617–79) was in 1649 appointed a Lord of Session, and soon afterwards was one of the commissioners sent by Scotland to Holland to discuss with Charles, Prince of Wales (son of the recently executed Charles I) on what terms the exiled prince should be accepted as King of Scotland.

There have been several branches of Clan Brodie. One of them produced the distinguished 19th-century surgeon, Sir Benjamin Brodie (1783–1862), who became surgeon to George IV, William IV, and Queen Victoria.

The chief is Ninian Brodie of Brodie and there is a Brodie tartan.

Above: Brodie Castle in Morayshire, built in 1609 on lands held by the Brodies since the 14th century and now managed by the National Trust.

Bruce

The Bruces were originally Normans, from the Cherbourg peninsula. The father of the clan's founder was Sir Robert de Bruis (or Brus) who came to England with William the Conqueror in 1066 and died in 1094. His son, Robert de Brus (1078–1141) was a close companion of David I (1124–53) before and during that King's reign, and received many favours including rich lands in Annandale, of which Brus was created Lord.

The 4th Lord of Annandale, another Robert de Brus (died 1245), married a niece of William the Lyon, King of Scotland 1165–1214. It was this marriage which formed the basis of the later claim by the de Brus, or Bruce, family to the throne of Scotland. The first Bruce to claim the throne was Robert, the 5th Lord of Annandale (1210–95). But it was another claimant, John Baliol, whom Edward I of England chose to succeed Margaret, the Maid of Norway, child-queen of Scotland from 1286 to 1290.

In order to avoid swearing fealty to Baliol, thus permitting the Bruce family to sustain its claim to the throne, the 5th Lord of Annandale resigned his title to his son. Robert Bruce, the 6th Lord of Annandale (1253–1304), was created 1st Earl of Carrick. He chose to fight for Edward I in the latter's struggle with Baliol and his son Robert also took the English side for a time.

This Bruce – the 2nd Earl of Carrick and 7th Lord of Annandale – was the renowned Robert the Bruce, the greatest figure in Scottish history: the national leader whose dogged persistence won Scotland's independence from English rule. Born in 1274, he succeeded his father, the 6th Lord, in 1304. He was shocked out of his initial support for Edward I by the barbarous treatment of William Wallace, the first great leader of Scotland's struggle for independence. (Wallace was the man for whom the English invented the traitor's ghastly death by hanging, drawing and quartering.) Taking up the Bruce claim, he had himself crowned King of Scotland, as Robert I, in 1306.

The aged Edward I set out for Scotland to settle accounts with Bruce but died on the way, in 1307. Aided beyond measure by the ineffective rule of the new English King, Edward II, the Scottish independence movement gathered momentum under Bruce's bold and imaginative leadership. Bruce's crowning victory was the shattering defeat inflicted on the English in the Battle of Bannockburn (24 June, 1314). Although the English still refused to recognize Scotland's independence, it was nevertheless a fact, and all subsequent English attempts to avenge Bannockburn were beaten off.

King Robert the Bruce lived to see Scottish independence finally accepted by the English, in the Treaty of Northampton of 1328. Robert died the following year at Cardross, and was buried at Dunfermline Abbey. He was succeeded by his son, King David II (1329–71). The daughter of Robert the Bruce, Marjorie, married Walter FitzAlan, Great Steward of Scotland, and their son became King Robert II in 1371: the first of the Steward/Stewart/Stuart ruling dynasty of Scotland.

The Bruce family, however, did not die out with the Stuart dynasty. Thomas Bruce aided his kinsman King Robert II to quell a rising in Kyle and was rewarded with lands in Clackmannan, founding the Bruce of Clackmannan branch. His son, Robert Bruce of Clackmannan, had three sons. One was James Bruce, Chancellor of Scotland and Bishop of Dunkeld. The second was Edward Bruce, who married the heir to the Airth and Stenhouse estates; their descendants hold the present baronetcy of Stenhouse. And the third son, Robert, was ancestor of the Earls of Elgin and Kincardine whose family name is still Bruce. The present chief is Andrew Bruce, Earl of Elgin and Kincardine K.T.

Robert the Bruce, the greatest figure in Scottish history.

Buchan

The lands of Buchan in Aberdeenshire gave their name to the early lairds who were invested with them, such as William de Buchan (1298). The name itself stems from the ancient Pictish Mormaers of Buchan. The earldom which crystallized from Buchan's Pictish past became one of the most important in Scotland. It passed by marriage to the Comyn family, and was held briefly by members of the Stewart Royal Family between 1382 and 1470.

Sir Thomas de Boghan, who did homage to King Edward I of England in 1296, is described on his seal as *S' Thomae de Bvcan*, but the name underwent fewer variations than most ('Buchthaine', 'Buquhan', 'Bowchane', and the like). The clan lost influence with the demise of the earldom, and is a small but justifiably proud family today. The novelist and historian John Buchan — whose superb life of Montrose, today lamentably out of print, remains a model for biographs — was created Baron Tweedsmuir on being appointed Governor-General of Canada. He died in Canada during his term of office in 1940.

Buchan crest badge

Above: The Bullers of Buchan, part of the coastal landscape which forms the eastern boundary of the ancient principality and clan territory.

The chiefship devolved upon the Buchans of 'Achmakwy', an old barony near Ellon in Aberdeenshire held today by the present Chief, Captain David Buchan of Auchmacoy. The clansman's crest badge is a sunflower and the family motto is *Non inferiora secutus* ('Not Having Followed Mean Pursuits'). The Buchan tartan is shared with Clan Cumming but was originally the Glenorchy district pattern, although the Buchans have no apparent connection with that region.

Buchanan

The first Chief of the Clan Buchanan, Anselan O'Kyan, was a scion of an Irish royal family. About the time that Canute the Great became King of England (1016), this Irish warrior crossed the sea to Argyll to fight for Malcolm II, King of Scots, against the Vikings then occupying large tracts of the western islands and mainland of Scotland.

The grateful King rewarded Anselan O'Kyan with lands in the Lennox, to the east of Loch Lomond, known as *buth chanain* (which means 'canon's seat') from which the name 'Buchanan' derives. The clan held on to much of this territory up to the late 17th century, when after the death of the 22nd chief it had to be sold to pay debts. The clan also had lands elsewhere, and over the centuries it divided into a number of branches.

Buchanans distinguished themselves fighting for King Robert the Bruce in his heroic struggle for Scottish independence in the early 14th century. A hundred years later, in furtherance of the 'Auld Alliance' between Scotland and France, Buchanans helped the French in their efforts to recover territory lost to England after Henry V's victory at Agincourt, during the Hundred Years War. At the battle of Beaugé in March 1421, the English were defeated by French and Scottish troops in one of the few English reverses before the successes of Joan of Arc in 1429. The English had been led by Thomas, Duke of Clarence, the brother of Henry V, and it is believed that Clarence was killed by Alexander Buchanan.

By far the most famous of the Buchanans was a man of more peaceful pursuits, George Buchanan (1506–82), a leading Scottish religious reformer and one of the foremost Latin scholars of 16th-century Europe. Buchanan was educated at St Andrews (in the age when Scotland had three universities to England's two) and then at Paris. He spent many years running risks with his championing of the new cause of Protestantism – imprisoned in St Andrews Castle in the 1530s, escaping to France where he taught at Bordeaux (one of his pupils was Montaigne, later to become one of the great essayists of literature), then moving to Coimbra in Portugal where he was arrested by the Inquisition for heresy. His life was spared and he returned to Scotland in the 1560s where he was appointed Latin tutor to Mary, Queen of Scots, despite his determined Protestant views. Buchanan was elected Moderator of the General Assembly in 1567, and two years after Mary's flight to England (1568) he was appointed tutor to the young King James VI and Keeper of the Privy Seal.

Opinions vary as to Buchanan's influence on the young King. He certainly overworked the boy, thrashed him when he made mistakes, and seems also to have taught James to hold women in contempt. Buchanan wrote plays, verse, and political and religious tracts, among them *De Jure Regni* (1579): a cogent argument that monarchs exist only by the will of, and for the good of, the people. Perhaps, after all, Buchanan's influence on the King may be measured by the obstinacy with which James held to the view that kings ruled by Divine Right and were answerable only to God!

Clan Buchanan may have lost its lands and have no chief, but it does have the oldest clan society in Scotland. It was founded in Glasgow in 1725 – not solely to perpetuate the memory of the Buchanans but also to help the poor, particularly to assist boys at school, university, and in suitable work training. Buchanan tartans are acknowledged.

Buchanan crest badge

Left: Loch Lomond in the Lennox.

Burnett

This name derives from the Saxon *Beornheard* – 'brave warrior' – which became 'Burnet' in Scotland and 'Bernard' in England. Alexander Burnett served King Robert the Bruce (1306–29), for which he was granted land in the Forest of Drum and the Barony of Tulliboyl in the Sheriffdom of Kincardine, when these lands were confiscated from the Comyns.

In the main hall of the Burnett Castle of Crathes (now in the care of the National Trust for Scotland) can be seen the bejewelled ivory 'Horn of Leys', said to have been presented to Laird Alexander by the Bruce as a symbol of his Barony and its lands. The first 'Laird of Leys' was John Burnett, in 1446. Sir Robert Burnett of Leys, the 7th Baronet (who named his son Robert Horn) served in the Royal Scots Fusiliers and was taken prisoner with the army of General Burgoyne at the Battle of Saratoga (1777) in the American War of Independence. The present Dingwall Pursuivant at the Court of the Lord Lyon is Charles Burnett.

The Chief today is James Burnett of Leys, whose mother was the only surviving child of Major-General Sir James Burnett of Leys, the 13th Baronet. The General's brother succeeded to the title, which became dormant when he died without heirs in 1959.

There are two clan tartans: 'Burnett' and 'Burnett of Leys (Dress)', the latter being preferred by the chief. The clansman's crest badge is 'A Hand Pruning a Grape Vine', and the family motto is *Virescit vulnere virtus* – 'Virtue Flourishes from a Wound'.

The bejewelled, ivory 'Horn of Leys', presented to Alexander Burnett of Leys by Robert the Bruce as the symbol of his barony lands.

Cameron

One of the most famous of the Scottish clans, the Camerons take their name from the Gaelic nickname *Camshron* ('wry-nose'), an unflattering description of an early chief. Some historians accept a connection between the Camerons and the MacDuffs.

Clan Cameron has always been associated with the Lochaber region, particularly around Loch Lochy and, later, Loch Eil. The first recorded Cameron Chief was Donald Dhu, mentioned in a document of about 1410–11, and he is reckoned the 11th Chief. A Sir Robert de Cameron, Sheriff of Atholl in 1296, may have been an earlier chief; Sir John de Cameron, a signatory of the Declaration of Arbroath in 1320, may have been another. But by the 15th century, the Camerons were definitely occupying lands in Lochaber and were vassals of the MacDonalds of the Isles.

There were two main branches of the clan, stemming from the two sons of Donald Dhu: Allan, the 12th Chief, and Ewen. Allan was Constable of Strone Castle, and his brother became the ancestor of the Camerons of Strone, from whom the Camerons of Lochiel descend. Allan's son Ewen became the 13th Chief and was the first to call himself 'Cameron of Lochiel'; his territory was created a Barony in 1528. Since then, the chief of the Camerons of Lochiel has been regarded as chief of the whole clan. Ewen's grandson, also called Ewen, founded the branch known as the 'Camerons of Erracht'.

The 17th Chief of the Camerons, Sir Ewen Cameron of Lochiel, was born in 1629 and lived to be 90 years old. He was knighted in 1680, and fought in Claverhouse's army at the Battle of Killiecrankie in 1689. Sir Ewen was too old to fight in the first Jacobite Rising of 1715, but he sent his son John to lead Clan Cameron under the Earl of Mar, who commanded the army of James Edward Stewart, the 'Old Pretender'.

John's son Donald, the 19th Chief, known as 'Gentle Lochiel', joined Bonnie Prince Charlie in the second Jacobite Rising of 1745–46, escaped to France after the defeat of the Highlanders at Culloden, and died there as an exile in 1748. His cousin Donald Cameron, 7th Chief of the Camerons of Erracht, had been Lochiel's second-in-command at Culloden but chose to defy the Government occupation and remain in his homeland; he wandered the Highlands as a fugitive, often in disguise, for three years after Culloden. In the aftermath of the Jacobite defeat the Cameron lands were all forfeited, but were restored in the 1780s. It was Donald's son Allan who raised the 79th Regiment the Cameron Highlanders, who fought their first campaign in Flanders in the 1794–95 action against Revolutionary France.

Campbell

The most powerful of the Highland clans, the Campbells played a major role in Scottish national affairs over a long period. The clan claims descent from the very earliest kings of Ireland, and thus from the first kings of Dalriada in western Scotland (roughly the region of modern-day Argyll). This led them also to claim kinship with Somerled, the half-Scot/half-Norse ruler of the Western Isles and many parts of the mainland, who was killed in battle with the Scots in 1164.

The first Campbells in Argyll were probably the family of Duncan MacDuibhne, who lived in the reign of Alexander II (1214–49). He was a Chief in Lochawe who rejoiced in the nickname of *Cambeul* ('Crooked Mouth'). His son (or grandson), Sir Colin Campbell of Lochawe, was knighted in about 1280. In 1292 he was one of the 12 lords of the Argyll region whose territories were linked to create a new Sheriffdom of Argyll.

By the time he was killed soon afterwards in a feud, he had already come to be known as *Cailean Mor*, 'Colin the Great', and the chiefs of Clan Campbell ever since have had among their titles the Gaelic honorific *MacCailean Mor* – 'Son of Colin the Great'. This Colin the Great was the founder of the Campbells of Argyll, with his principal seat, Innischonaill Castle, on an island in Loch Awe. Later, towards the end of the 15th century, the Argyll Campbells moved their power-base to Loch Fyne, where their seat was, and still is, Inverary.

Sir Colin's immediate descendants supported Robert the Bruce, and one of Bruce's sisters, Mary,

was married to Neil Campbell of Lochawe. From then on the Campbells flourished increasingly by supporting the Crown. From the later 15th century, they began to exert influence on a widening scale and continued to do so for centuries. For a time the Campbells acted on behalf of the Royal Government in the west, just as the Gordons did in the eastern Highlands (*see* Gordon).

Colin, the 2nd Lord Campbell, was created 1st Earl of Argyll in 1457, appointed Master of the Royal Household in the 1460s (an office that later became a hereditary one for the Campbells), and

Cameron crest badge

Left: Kilchurn Castle on Loch Awe. Begun by Sir Colin Campbell of Glenorchy and extended after his death in 1475 by Sir Duncan, it dominated a number of strategic routes through Argyll.

Lord Chancellor in 1483. He married the daughter and heiress of John Stewart, Lord of Lorne, which greatly extended his territory and his power by the time he died in 1493. His son Archibald, the 2nd Earl, fell at Flodden Field in 1513 along with King James IV and most of the Scottish nobility engaged. Colin Campbell, the 3rd Earl, became Warden of the Marches between Scotland and England, and in 1528 was made Lord Justice General of Scotland (though he did not live more than a few months to enjoy it).

His son Archibald, the 4th Earl of Argyll, was Justiciary of Scotland and one of the very first magnates of Scotland to adopt and promote the Protestant Reformation. When he died in 1558, the 5th Earl took the side of Mary, Queen of Scots in her struggle with the Scottish Parliament and the Regent, the Earl of Moray. When Moray was murdered in 1570, Argyll became one of the Lieutenants of Scotland governing the country during the minority of Mary's son, James VI; but he was not made Regent when Moray's successor Lennox died in 1571. When he died without issue in 1575 the Earldom passed to his brother Colin as

Campbell of Breadalbane crest badge

Below: Castle Campbell, in the hills overlooking Dollar, was known as Castle Gloume when it was acquired by the Earl of Argyll in the 15th century.

Campbell crest badge   *Campbell of Cawdor crest badge*

6th Earl; he became Lord Chancellor in 1579.

By the time of Archibald Campbell, 7th Earl (1584–1638), the Campbells were Scotland's paramount clan: almost a kingdom within a kingdom. Their chiefs bid for the highest offices in the land as a matter of right, while no effort was spared to extend the Campbell domination by force or by law. No clan was ever more successful at buying up the debts of weaker neighbours. 'The Campbells', writes John Buchan in *Montrose*, 'had a knack of winning by bow and spear, then holding for all time by seal and parchment.' Thanks to the sea trade brought in by its long coast, Clan Campbell was also the richest clan in Scotland bar none. With Campbell raiding parties cowing the clan's weaker neighbours as far east as Badenoch, Lochaber, and the Braes of Angus, the Campbells were also the most hated.

Archibald Campbell, 8th Earl of Argyll from 1638 to 61, was a leader of the Covenanters in their resistance to Charles I. He was compelled the King to bow to the demands of Covenant and Parliament in 1641, yet in true Campbell style accepted the new title of 1st Marquis bestowed during the King's visit to Scotland in 1641 (one of many knighthoods and titles, none refused, with which the King vainly hoped to make the rebellious nobility of Scotland his loyal supporters). Though no soldier himself, Argyll threw the immense resources of Clan Campbell into the Covenanting cause during the Great Civil War – only to see that power broken, and the Campbell lands plundered by exulting enemy clansmen only too eager to get some of their own back, during Montrose's amazing winter campaign of 1644–45.

After Montrose's defeat at Philiphaugh, Argyll

John Campbell of Ardmaddie, Principal Cushier for the Royal Bank of Scotland, painted by Wm. Mossman in 1749. Known in the Highlands as Cambeul a' Bhanca ('Campbell of the Bank').

Ordered as it was by King William, the massacre encouraged much Highland support for the cause of the exiled Stewart King James in what now became known as the Jacobite cause. But the Campbells continued to prosper as Government adherents. The 10th Earl received a Dukedom in 1701; two subsequent Dukes of Argyll became Field Marshals in the British Army; the 9th Duke married Princess Louise, daughter of Queen Victoria, and became Governor-General of Canada.

Of the several branches of Clan Campbell, two of the most important were those of Breadalbane and Cawdor. The Breadalbane Campbells stem from Colin of Glenorchy, son of Duncan Campbell of Lochawe, the 1st Lord, who obtained Glenorchy when the MacGregors were driven off it. One of their earliest seats was Kilchurn Castle on Loch Awe. This branch became Earls of Breadalbane in 1677. The Cawdor Campbells stem from an act of dynastic piracy on the part of the 2nd Earl of Argyll. In 1499 he kidnapped the infant daughter of the Thane of Cawdor a few weeks after the latter's death, and ten years or so later married her to his third son, Sir John Campbell. This made the Campbells Lords of Cawdor, and in 1827, the 10th Lord of Cawdor became 1st Earl of Cawdor. Both earldoms, Breadalbane and Cawdor, still exist.

Carmichael

This clan name is of territorial origin, from the baronial lands of Carmichell [sic] in Lanarkshire. Robert 'de Carmitely' is the first (and badly transcribed) Carmichael on record, around 1220; but by 1410, when William de Carmychale appeared as a witness to a charter, they were regarded as 'of That Ilk'.

John Carmichael, in recognition of the contribution of the Scots who fought the English on behalf of the King of France, was made Bishop of Orleans, and is remembered in French ecclesiastical records as 'Jean de St Michel'. A variation of the name recorded in 1497 was 'Kermychell', and the Dutch descendants of a Carmichael mercenary who was fighting in Holland only a few generations later are still called 'Kermiggelt' to this day. The West Highland names of 'Macgillemicheill', 'McIlmichell', 'McIlvechal', and 'McMichael', were often anglicized to 'Carmichael' (for Mitchell) and are not connected with the Lanarkshire families.

The present chief inherited the chiefship through the female line, from his cousin Sir Windham Carmichael-Anstruther, in 1980. There is a Carmichael tartan and a clansman's crest badge of an 'Armed Arm, Embowed, holding a Broken Spear'. This alludes to an incident at the Battle of Beaugé

shared the widespread contempt earned by the Covenanters for betraying and handing over Charles I to the tender mercies of the English Parliamentarians. He sought to dominate the young King Charles II when the latter attempted a Royalist comeback in 1650, placing the Crown of Scotland on the King's head during the coronation at Scone, then made a pact with Cromwell after the latter's defeat of the Scots at Dunbar and Worcester. For this he was not forgiven at the Restoration in 1660, and was executed at Edinburgh in 1661.

Though the Marquessate of Argyll was forfeited on the conviction and execution of the 8th Earl, the other Campbell honours were restored to his son, the 9th Earl. He was the last Argyll to oppose the Crown, in 1685, supporting the Protestant Duke of Monmouth in his bid to oust the Catholic James II, Charles II's brother and successor. Argyll was captured and executed and his seat at Inverary (though subsequently rebuilt) was razed to the ground.

It was under the 10th Earl, who backed William of Orange in 1688–89, that the Campbells earned lasting infamy for their role in the notorious Massacre of Glencoe (13 February, 1692). The treacherous attack on his hosts, the Glencoe MacDonalds, by Captain Robert Campbell and his troops, violated every ancient tenet of hospitality.

in 1421 when Sir John de Carmichael unhorsed the brother of the English King Henry V, so demoralizing the English forces. The clan motto is *Tout Jour Prest* ('Always Ready').

Carnegie

In the reign of King David II (1329–70), a grant of the baronial lands of Carnegy was made to John de Balinhard, who adopted the land-name as his own. These 'Carnegies of That Ilk' died out in the 16th century, when the chiefship passed to the Carnegies of Kinnaird near Brechin.

Sir David Carnegie, High Sheriff of Forfar, was created Lord Carnegie in 1616 and Earl of Southesk in 1633, the latter creation being one of many resulting from Charles I's state visit to Scotland for his coronation as King of that realm. Katherine, daughter of the 2nd Earl, married the 11th Earl of Erroll in 1658 and is the heroine of the bawdy ballad *The Countess of Erroll*, wherein she berates her impotent husband, and which gave rise to the local proverb 'Carnegie mares cannot live on Hay'.

James, the 5th Earl, was the hero of another song, *The Piper o'Dundee*. He fought as a Jacobite under MacDonnell of Glengarry in the 1715 Rising, and the clan today wears the Glengarry sett with the white overcheck rendered in yellow (probably an error which crept into the weaving, when a faded off-white was perceived as yellow). By contrast with the bravery of most of the Carnegies at the Battle of Sheriffmuir in 1715, the Laird of Phinhaven was celebrated as the 'best flier from the battlefield'.

The most famous Carnegie is undoubtedly the son of the Dunfermline linen weaver, Andrew Carnegie, who emigrated to Pittsburg in 1842 and worked his way up through the iron and steel industries to become one of the richest men in the world. In his lifetime he gave away more than 350 million dollars, endowing libraries and universities in Britain and North America.

The present Chief of the Carnegies is the Earl of Southesk, and the clansman's crest badge is a 'Winged Thunderbolt'; the clan motto is 'Dread God'.

Cathcart

Rainaldus de Kethcart appears to be the first of the name in Scotland – a name taken from the title of baronial lands in Renfrewshire. Sir Alan was made Baron Cathcart by James III (1460–88), and the family has served successive monarchs ever since,

both as diplomats (a number were ambassadors to Russia) and as soldiers. The 8th Baron fought for the Government at Sheriffmuir in 1715 but died *en route* to North America in 1740, having been appointed Commander-in-Chief of all British forces there. His great-grandson finally succeeded in filling the post a century and a quarter later, when he became Governor-General of all British North America – Canada. The Governor's brother, General Sir George Cathcart, fell at the Battle of Inkerman (1854) in the Crimean War.

Today the surname is somewhat rare, with only 41 listed in the nearest major conurbation (Glasgow). The present Chief is Major-General Alan Cathcart – Baron Cathcart in Scotland, Baron Greenock and 6th Earl of Cathcart in the Peerage of the United Kingdom. The clansman's crest badge is a 'Hand Grasping a Crescent', and the motto 'I Hope to Speed'. There is no tartan for the name.

Charteris

At the Battle of Culloden in 1746, a troop of horse in Prince Charles Edward's Lifeguards was commanded by David, Lord Elcho, *de jure* 6th Earl of Wemyss. When he was attainted after the Jacobite defeat, the Earldom fell to his brother Francis, who had adopted the name of Charteris. This had been the name of his grandmother, to whose estates he was heir.

It is said that the name stems from Thomas de Longueville in the reign of Robert the Bruce, who 'chartered' to him the lands of Kinfauns near Perth. He adopted the name of Charteris, and many of that name were subsequently Lord Provosts of the City of Perth. The surname actually derives from Chartres in France, although the early Latin version of it was 'Carnoto'. Robert and William de Chartres rendered homage to Edward I of England in 1296, and the records of succeeding centuries show limited variations on the name ('Charterhous', 'Charteouris', 'Chartrews', 'Chairteris', etc.).

The Charteris of Amisfield branch, which married into the Earldom of Wemyss and later the Earldom of March, acquired lands in Peeblesshire. The Chief today is the 12th Earl of Wemyss and March. The clansman's crest badge is a 'Hand Holding a Dagger', and the motto 'This is our Charter'. There is no tartan for the name.

Chattan

The surname 'Gillechattan' derives from those who were followers of St Catain, who was commemorated in Bute, Gigha, and Colonsay. In 1291 an heiress married the 6th Chief of MacKintosh, around whose emerging clan gathered a number of smaller clans, forming the Clan Chattan federation. This included the MacPhersons, Farquharsons of Invercauld, MacThomases of Finegand, McBains of Kinchyle, MacLeans of Dochgarroch, Queens of Conisborough, McGillivrays of Dunmaglas, and the Davidsons. Until the 18th century Clan Chattan was a powerful force in and around the Badenoch region in the Spey Valley.

The present Chief is Mackintosh of Clan Chattan, and there is a Chattan tartan. The crest badge of a rampant wildcat and the motto 'Touch not the Cat Bot [without] a Glove' both play on the similarity of the ferocity of the wildcat and the name of St Catain.

Below left: Kingussie, in the heartland of the Clan Chattan federation.

Above: A silk, tartan dress from around 1832, in the Clan Chattan tartan.

Chisholm

The Chisholms were almost certainly of Norman descent. They appeared in Scotland in Roxburghshire, in the Border district to which a number of Norman families were invited by some of the Scottish kings in the 11th and 12th centuries; their original family name was de Cheseholm. The Ragman Roll, a list of Scottish nobles and landowners who recognized the right of Edward I to be King of Scotland after the deposition of John Baliol, contains mentions of the family for the year 1296.

The Chisholms were established in the Highlands by 1359, when Sir Robert Chisholm, the grandson of Sir Robert Lauder, succeeded Lauder as Constable of Urquhart Castle on Loch Ness. This honour was followed by his appointment as Sheriff of Inverness. Sir Robert Chisholm also acquired lands further north, in Moray and Nairn. His son Alexander married the heiress to the Erchless lands west of Loch Ness, and the Clan Chisholm became powerful in that region.

The family's history is relatively undramatic, but Chisholms fought gallantly in support of the Jacobites in the risings of 1715 and 1745–46. Before then, the clan chief had become known simply as 'The Chisholm'. He was not the only clan chief to be distinguished by the definite article, but in the 19th century one of the chiefs did manufacture the claim that only three people in the world were entitled to the simple use of 'The': the Pope, the King, and The Chisholm. In quarters where the Papacy was not popular, this phrase was rendered as 'The Devil, the King, and The Chisholm'.

The chief is Alastair Chisolm of Chisolm.

Chisholm crest badge

Below: Glen Affric, in the Clan Chisholm homelands of Strathglass, focusses on Loch Benevean and the smaller Loch Affric.

Cochrane

The 'Fighting Cochranes' take their name from the lands of Coueran, or Cochran, near Paisley in Renfrewshire. William de Coughran rendered homage to Edward I of England in 1296. The direct male line died out with the heiress to the last Cochrane of That Ilk, but her husband adopted the name and arms of Cochrane. Their son William became Baron Cochrane of Dundonald in 1647, and Earl of Dundonald in 1669.

Of the Cochrane Chiefs, the most famous was undoubtedly Thomas, the 10th Earl. As a serving Naval officer and Member of Parliament, he was expelled from both Parliament and the Royal Navy for attacking the corruption and abuses which

riddled the Admiralty of his day. After being found guilty on a trumped-up charge of fraud, he was stripped of his knighthood and imprisoned. Having thereby lost the chance of ever gaining promotion to Admiral in the Royal Navy, he decided to market his nautical skills abroad, ending up as one of the most celebrated multi-national admirals of all time. Between 1818 and 1828 he fought successively – and successfully – for the independence of Chile, Brazil, Peru, and Greece. Money and honours were showered upon Cochrane (including the Brazilian Marquisate of Maranhao) and he returned to Britain a popular hero, having been Admiral in the navies of four countries. Even then it took four more years, during which time he succeeded to the Earldom of Dundonald, before a curmudgeonly establishment acknowledged its errors. In 1832 his knighthood was restored and he was promoted Rear-Admiral,

Royal Navy, dying in 1860 and being buried in Westminster Abbey.

The present Cochrane Chief is Iain, 15th Earl of Dundonald; the clansman's crest badge shows a passing horse, with the motto *Virtute et Labore* ('By Virtue and Labour').

At one stage the Cochrane tartan was incorrectly recorded in the Lyon Court Books by a typing error that resulted in some confusion among the cloth manufacturers. It is based on an old Lochaber sett which itself gave rise to the Clan Donald. The mistake seems to have been caused by the apparent connection between the MacEacharns of that clan, anglicized to MacCochran and so on to Cochrane. (In the *Garde Ecossaise* or Scots Guard of the King of France, the Cochrane mercenaries were recorded as 'Colqueran'.)

Colquhoun

The origins of this ancient clan, whose name is sometimes pronounced 'Co'hoon', are obscure. The Colquhouns may derive from an Norman immigrant family in the Lennox, perhaps Dunbartonshire, or they may have much older beginnings, from a succession of Celtic priests who were the custodians of the crozier of St Kessog, who had lived on Monk's Island in Loch Lomond. In fact the name 'Colquhoun' comes from the territory of that name west of Loch Lomond. In the reign of the Scots King Alexander II (1214–49) the head of the family, Humphrey Kilpatrick, was granted these lands by Malcolm, Earl of Lennox. In 1368 Sir Robert Colquhoun married the Fair Maid of Luss, heiress to nearby lands in Glen Luss, and since then the clan name has properly been Colquhoun of Luss.

The Colquhouns have had a long, interesting, and sometimes violent history. Colquhouns supported King Robert the Bruce and also backed the early Stewart kings. Sir John Colquhoun of Luss, the Fair Maid's grandson, was Governor of Dunbarton Castle in the reign of James I (1406–37). His grandson, also Sir John (or Iain), was Great Chamberlain of Scotland for part of the reign of James III (1460–88). He was killed by a cannon ball at the siege of Dunbar in 1478.

In 1589, the 16th Chief, Humphrey Colquhoun, became involved in a local scandal which had a horrifying sequel. Fancying the wife of the nearby Chief of Clan MacFarlane, he was caught *in flagrante delicto* with her and fled to his castle at Bannachra, which the MacFarlanes set on fire. In a scuffle, Colquhoun was killed. The cuckolded chief then avenged himself on his wife by having Colquhoun's private parts cut off and served to her for dinner. 'That is your share. You will understand yourself what it is.'

Humphrey's successor, Alasdair, also met a violent end. In 1602 the MacGregors raided the Colquhouns in Glen Luss, killing two clansmen, injuring others, and carrying off hundreds of livestock. The Colquhoun women appealed to King

Colquhoun crest badge

Left: The Abbey of 1169 in Paisley, where the lands of Cochran spawned the Clan Cochrane.

James VI for redress, displaying the bloodstained shirts of the killed and wounded men. The King responded by granting the Colquhouns leave to pursue the MacGregors 'with fire and sword'. But the MacGregors retaliated by laying a deadly ambush. In a bloody engagement in Glen Fruin, the Colquhouns were overwhelmed and their chief was killed. When King James heard of the massacre he ordered that the entire MacGregor clan be outlawed (see p.134).

The Colquhouns thereafter had a more peaceful history on the whole, and some of the family were prominent in public affairs. Widely known as the 'Black Cock of the West', Sir John Colquhoun (c.1620–1676) was a member of the first Restoration Parliament after the return of Charles II in 1660. Sir James Colquhoun, the 25th Chief, fought at the Battle of Dettingen in 1743. The 31st Chief, Sir Iain, was Lord High Commissioner to the General Assembly of the Church of Scotland and Chairman of the National Trust of Scotland.

Cranstoun

The earliest mention of this name is during the reign of William the Lyon (1165–1214), when Elfric de Cranston was witness to a charter of Holyrood. The township of Cran gave its name to the baronial lands of the first Cranston, who was described as *dominus eodem* or 'Lord of That Ilk'. Other medieval variants on the name included Andrew de Cranstoun, sometime before 1338; Thomas of Creinstoun, Ambassador for James II, King of Scots, in 1449; and William of Cramnstoiun, one of the conservators of the truce between Scotland and England in 1451. The 1st Lord Cranstoun was created in 1609, but the title died out with the 11th Lord in 1813.

The current Chief is Lieutenant-Colonel Alastair Cranstoun of That Ilk, MC, who was Military Attaché in Lisbon and Vienna after World War II.

The clansman's crest badge is a stork, with the motto 'Thou Shalt Want Before I Shall Want' – said to have been the philosophy motivating many early Cranstouns setting off on clan raids. The Cranstoun tartan was first illustrated in the *Vestiarius Scoticum*, published in 1842.

Crawford

The family name of the Earls of Crawford and Balcarres is Lindsay, and it has been aptly described as 'ane surname of renown'. The present Clan Chief of the Lindsays is the 29th Earl of Crawford and 12th Earl of Balcarres, and the Crawford Earldom dates back nearly 600 years.

The name of Lindsay is of Norman origin: from Baldric de Lindesay, first mentioned in 1086, the year of England's Domesday Survey. He owned lands in Lincolnshire as well as Normandy. His

Crawford crest badge

Lindsay crest badge

Below left: Glen Luss, which leads into Loch Lomond, where the Clan Colquhoun have

held lands since the 13th century. The present chief is the 32nd Laird of Luss.

grandson Walter Lindsay was a close friend of King David I of Scotland (1124–53) and acquired the lands of Crawford in Lanarkshire; he was also a member of the King's Council. Over the next two centuries or so, the Lindsays increased their land-holdings, including the acquisition of the district of Glenesk in Angus. In 1398 King Robert III (1390–1406) created Sir David Lindsay, the Clan Chief, Earl of Crawford. David Lindsay had already married the King's half-sister Katherine, and in 1403 he became Admiral of Scotland. In time the Earls of Crawford became the Premier Earls of Scotland, and have remained so.

The Crawfords, however, were unable to resist the temptation to get involved in the protracted quarrels between the early Stewart Kings and their leading nobles, particularly the immensely powerful Douglas family. The 3rd Earl of Crawford, David Lindsay, had been regarded as an upholder of the great legal changes which James I has sought to introduce. But as soon as the King was murdered in 1437 and was succeeded by his six-year-old son, many of the nobles, instead of supporting the boy King and helping to govern for him, used the power vacuum to further their own interests. Crawford was no exception; he 'turned thief himself and pocketed the customs duties levied at the port of Dundee'. Crawford was finally killed in 1446, in a clash between his family and the Ogilvies.

David Crawford's son Alexander, the 4th Earl, rejoiced in the colourful nicknames of 'Auld Beardie' and the 'Tiger Earl'. He joined another Douglas-led revolt against King James II (1437–60) in the 1450s, but was defeated by the Earl of Huntly at Brechin in 1452. Though attainted and disgraced, Crawford was shortly afterwards pardoned and restored. If this was an attempt to split the Lindsays from the Douglases, it was successful. 'Auld Beardie's' son, the 5th Earl, supported the Crown in a long and distinguished career during which he became Admiral of Scotland, Master of the Household, Lord Chamberlain, finally (1488) being created Duke of Montrose by James III (1460–88). But in that year, the King fought and lost the Battle of Sauchieburn against a group of rebellious nobles and their men. Crawford had given the King a fine grey charger on which to ride into or from the battle. Though the King chose the latter, he was murdered after taking refuge in the nearby house of a miller. Crawford gave loyal support to the dead King's successor, James IV (1488–1513), until his own death in 1495 when the Dukedom of Montrose lapsed.

Other Lindsays of interest include David Lindsay of the Mount (1490–1567), a relative of the 9th Earl of Crawford. He became a celebrated Scottish poet and playwright, and was for a time a close friend of King James V (1513–42) and Master of the Royal Household. Robert Lindsay of Pitscottie (c. 1500–65) wrote a celebrated history of Scotland from 1437 to the year of his death. David Lindsay, 10th Earl of Crawford, was one of the gang who helped Lord Darnley, husband of Mary, Queen of Scots, to murder her Italian secretary David Rizzio in 1566.

Sir David Lindsay, a son of the 9th Earl of Crawford, married his cousin Helen, a daughter of the 10th Earl. He inherited a Lindsay tower-house castle at Edzell, and in 1580 added a quadrangle of apartments to it. He later became a judge, received a peerage as Lord Edzell, and further improved Edzell Castle by adding a spacious pleasaunce, a stone-walled garden with a bath-house tower and a summerhouse, and one of the most famous castle gardens in western Europe. Edzell Castle is today cared for by the Scottish Development Department.

In the Great Civil War, the Lindsays supported the Covenant against Charles I, gaining the Lindsay Earldom of Balcarres in the process. Alexander Lindsay, the 1st Earl of Balcarres, led the Covenant cavalry into two defeats at the hands of Montrose in 1645, at Alford on the Don (2 August) and at Kilsyth (15 August), before the subsequent overthrow of Montrose at Philiphaugh on 13 September.

The Lindsays have long been associated with the arts. The 29th Earl of Crawford was Chairman of the Royal Fine Art Commission, Chairman of the Trustees of the National Galleries of Scotland, and Chairman of the National Trust.

Crichton

This family takes its name from the baronial lands of Kreitton in Midlothian, which indicates how the name should be pronounced. Turstan de Crectune is the first on record, witnessing the great charter of David I to Holyrood in 1128.

In 1439, Sir William Crichton became Chancellor to the nine-year-old King James II. In the following year, after the death of his old rival the 5th Earl of Douglas, Sir William organized the 'Black Dinner' at Edinburgh Castle to which the new Earl (all of 16 years old) and his younger brother were invited as guests of honour. In the presence of the stunned

Charles Crichton of that Ilk (on the left), chief of the clan, with Sir Nicholas Fairbairn M.P. at Monzie, Perthshire.

boy-King, the two young Douglases were bundled out of the dining chamber with their meal barely digested and were summarily executed in the courtyard below.

Robert de Crichtoun is recorded as one of the conservators of the truce between Scotland and England in 1451, and it was probably his son, Sir Robert Crichton of Sanquhar, who became 1st Lord Crichton of Sanquhar in 1488. The 9th Baron Crichton became Viscount of Air (Ayr) in 1622 and Earl of Dumfries in 1633; but these honours passed out of the family through the marriage of Elizabeth, only child of the 6th Earl, to the eldest son of the 1st Marquess of Bute.

The present chief, who was born Charles Maitland-Makgill-Crichton, descends through the line of the Crichton Viscounts of Frendraught. There was no Crichton tartan historically, but Charles Crichton of That Ilk, as he is now known, has designed a pattern. The clansman's crest badge is a Griffon, and the motto 'God Sends Grace'.

Cumming

Known for much of its history as Comyn, Clan Cumming was of Norman origin. It was derived from de Comines, the name of one of the knights who accompanied Duke William of Normandy to England in 1066 and settled there. His grandson William came to Scotland in the reign of King David I (1124–53), was given land in Roxburghshire, and eventually became Chancellor of Scotland. (According to another tradition the clan stems from a Celtic saint, Cumin, who was Abbot of Iona in the mid-7th century.) It has also been suggested that the name derives from the herb; bundles of cummin do appear on the coat-of-arms.

The nephew of William de Comines, Richard, married the grand-daughter of Donald Bane – King Donald III of Scotland (1093–97), the second son of Duncan I (1034–40). The de Comines, then known as Comyn, became a powerful clan. In the early 13th century, as a result of good marriages, they were the holders of three earldoms: Menteith, Angus, and Buchan. One of their acquisitions was the Lordship of Badenoch, a grant from King Alexander II to William Comyn, Earl of Menteith.

Alexander III (1249–86) was tragically killed at Burntisland when his horse threw him down a steep cliff. His heir was a little girl of four, Margaret, 'The Maid of Norway', daughter of Alexander III's daughter and her husband, King Eric of Norway. A council of six Guardians of Scotland was appointed to govern the country during her minority. Two of these were Comyns, both direct descendants of Duncan I: Alexander Comyn, Earl of Buchan, and 'Black John', Lord of Badenoch.

Four years later, in 1290, Margaret died on her way home to Scotland, and for two years Scotland had no ruler. Apart from the Comyns there were at least four other claimants, and all six claims were more or less as good as each other. One was John Baliol, whose sister Marjory married Black Comyn, and another was Robert Bruce, grandfather of the great Bruce.

The Scottish lords, in some cases to their subsequent and eternal regret, invited King Edward I of England to decide who should succeed the Maid of Norway on the Scottish throne. He agreed on condition that whomever he chose must recognize him as overlord of Scotland. The lords were not in much of a position to resist, and they accepted Edward's choice of Baliol. This choice was not at all in Scotland's interests. Baliol, the weakest and most ineffectual of all the claimants, could be relied upon to do what he was told by Edward, who delighted in humbling him. This went on for four years until even the pliant Baliol had had enough, broke his oath of allegiance to Edward, and came to terms with France – the beginning of the 'Auld Alliance' between Scotland and France against England.

Baliol was deposed, Edward took over the Kingdom, and appointed Anglo–Norman officials to run it. A Scottish resistance movement emerged, and the English had much trouble keeping control. All the claimants took sides, the Comyns included, changed them from time to time, and followed their own interests rather than Scotland's. By 1306, Robert Bruce and his son had both died and the grandson Robert, having for a time fought with Edward, finally decided to go all out to win the Scottish throne for himself and drive the English out of Scotland altogether.

Meanwhile (1304) Black Comyn's son, Red Comyn, Lord of Badenoch, having fought against Edward, now went over to his side. He and young Robert Bruce had been enemies for some time, and it is possible that Comyn's defection to Edward's cause helped influence Bruce to go in the opposite direction. In 1306 Bruce made an effort to win Comyn to his side, inviting Comyn to a meeting in church at Dumfries. But there they quarrelled, Bruce drew a dagger, and stabbed Comyn to death in the church. It was a serious crime, for which Bruce was excommunicated. Red Comyn's son was defeated in a skirmish with Bruce and fled to support the English cause, dying in battle at Bannockburn. It was the end of the Badenoch line of the Comyns, and the Comyns were never as influential or powerful again. Yet they were not entirely finished.

Although Bruce helped bring about the fall of the

Cumming crest badge

Badenoch Comyns, other branches of the family survived and some have continued to the present, with the family name changing to Cumming. The Cummings of Altyre near Forres, descended from Black Comyn's brother Robert, became powerful in Moray. In the 19th century the family assumed the name Gordon-Cumming, after an inheritance from the Gordons of Gordonstoun. One of the clan was the celebrated explorer and big game hunter, Roualeyn Gordon-Cumming. Another was Sir William Gordon-Cumming, 4th Baronet, who in 1890 was accused of cheating at baccarat in a game which included, among others, the Prince of Wales (afterwards Edward VII), and who sued for slander, causing something of a royal scandal.

The clan's motto is *Courage*.

Cunningham crest badge

Cunningham

According to one tradition, the Cunningham clan takes its name from the district in Ayrshire where a certain Wernibald was granted land by Hugh de Morville, Constable of Scotland, in about 1140. Another tradition suggests that the clan descends from Malcolm, son of Freskin, the Flemish noble who was also the ancestor of Clan Sutherland (*see page 177*).

In the great Battle of Largs (1263), where the Scottish King Alexander III routed the Norseman, Harvey de Cunningham fought for the King and was rewarded with confirmation of his land, with the additional grant of the nearby estate of Kilmaurs. Hugh de Cunningham was granted the estate of Lamburghton by Robert the Bruce in 1321, presumably for services rendered since the Battle of Bannockburn (1314). Hugh's great-grandson Sir William Cunningham acquired further territory and was created Lord Kilmaurs in about 1462. He was advanced to the Earldom of Glencairn in 1488, but was killed the same year in the Battle of Sauchieburn.

William, 3rd Earl of Glencairn, fought for James V at the Battle of Solway Moss but was captured by the English. His son Alexander Cunningham is said to have been a personal friend of the 'Moses of Scotland', the Protestant reformer John Knox. The 8th Earl, William Cunningham, was appointed Lord Justice General in 1646, and after the Restoration of Charles II in 1660, he became Chancellor of Scotland. His descendant, the 14th Earl, was a friend of Robert Burns, Scotland's national poet, and his son the 15th Earl was the last Earl of Glencairn. Maxwellton House, birthplace of Robert Burns' Annie Laurie includes part of the Earl's ancient stronghold.

The Cunningham family has had several branches, some of whom spelled the name differently – Cuninghame, Cunynghame, and even Coningham. These achieved a unique 'triple' in the Middle East theatre during World War II, when in the autumn of 1941, the British Mediterranean Fleet was commanded by the brilliant Admiral Sir Andrew Cunningham (afterwards First Sea Lord and Admiral of the Fleet Lord Cunningham of Hyndhope), the 8th Army was commanded by his brother Lieutenant-General Sir Alan Cunningham, and the Western Desert Air Force was commanded by Air Vice-Marshal Arthur Coningham. By a further coincidence, Admiral Sir Andrew Cunningham was succeeded as First Sea Lord by another Cunningham, though no relation: Admiral Sir John Cunningham.

Three branches of the Cunningham family have received Baronetcies: those of Milncraig, Corsehill, and Robertland.

Currie

The Curries of Balilone are also known as the MacMhuirrich and are not to be confused with the surname 'Currie' which is a variant of 'Corrie', from the parish of that name in Dumfriesshire. Today the Curries of Balilone use the anglicized version of the Gaelic patronymic *Mhuirrich*. They are the descendants of one of the oldest families of warrior poets in the western world, who for almost 500 years were hereditary bards to the Lords of the Isles.

The namefather of the MacMhuirrich was Muiredach O'Daly, a member of the most famous bardic family in the Celtic world, and of the Irish royal blood. In 1213 he was highly respected as the King's Poet at the court of Cathal Crodhearg of Connaught. Unfortunately, he was forced to flee to Scotland after making an enemy of the powerful chief of the O'Donnels, whose steward had arrogantly demanded money from the Muiredach for some service that the Royal Bard considered should have been his 'by grace and favour'. He had cleft the hapless steward with a blow of his battleaxe, then expressed his surprise at the ensuing fuss in an extempore poem ('. . . he was merely a churl'). True to their traditional calling, the Curries of Balilone seem to have a genetic flair for verse and violence.

Shortly afterwards, the Bard arrived in Islay at the court of Donald, Lord of the Isles and grandson of Somerled, the Celtic–Norse founder of the Kingdom of Innesgall. The addition of the famed Bard to his court brought Donald additional prestige, and the two became great friends. Donald became the founder and namefather of Clan Donald, and Muiredach of the MacMhuirrichs: the contracted Scots Gaelic patronymic *mac Mhuireadhaigh*, 'son of Muiredach'.

The hereditary bard took precedence in the high chief's household and ranked immediately after the royal family. In war he was the chief's right arm, responsible for summoning the clan to arms in the days before the 'fiery cross'. His war chants and firebrand poetry reminded the warriors of the clan's past glories, and exhorted them to victory. In peacetime, the bard was the authority on all matters of clan history, genealogy, and heraldry, and wielded extraordinary power and influence.

Like many Scots, the Curries of Balilone claim descent from as far back as the 126th King of Ireland known as 'Niall of the Nine Hostages', who died in AD 403. Irish royal lineages are broadly accepted as accurate to this point. But the Curries also claim a further 250 years of authenticated lineage to 'Conn of the Hundred Battles', who died in AD 157. Even allowing for some very casual grafting to the family tree, the Currie/MacMhuirrich genealogy is formidable. The family is often confused with the Clan Vurich/MacFurichs; these are associated with Clan Macpherson's descent from Muriach, Chief of the 12th century Clan Chattan federation of which the Macphersons still form a key part.

Some vassal clans which served the Lordship of the Isles before its annexation by the Stewart kings in 1493 claim the 'right' to tartans from that connection. The Currie variant of the old 'Lord of the Isles' tartan was granted by the 2nd Lord MacDonald, as direct descendant of the last Lord of the Isles, in 1822. It was confirmed by the present Lord MacDonald in 1976 to the most recent of a long line of chiefs, Colonel William McMurdo Currie, 22nd Laird of Balilone and the 30th Chief of Clan MacMhuirrich. In 1959 a bond of allegiance, signed by over 400 West Highland members of Clan Currie, was presented to 'Colonel Bill' as their acknowledged Chief.

Davidson

The Davidsons form one of the main branches of Clan Chattan, the great clan confederation. Clan Davidson was originally named Clan Dhai, so named from David *Dhu* or *Dubh* ('Black David'), son of Muriach of Kingussie, 4th Chief of Clan Chattan. From David Dhu were descended the MacDhais, or David-sons, of Invernahavon.

In 1396, the MacDhais took on the Macphersons in a great clan battle at Perth. Thirty clansmen from each side fought it out on the Inch of Perth in the presence of King Robert II, who called an end to the battle when only 12 men were still left alive. Only one of these was a MacDhai.

The Davidsons had several branches. In the first years of the 18th century Alexander Davidson of Davidson in Cromarty married a Miss Bayne of Tulloch, near Dingwall. In the middle of the century he bought the Tulloch estate from his father-in-law, including its castle – but to do this he had to sell Clan Davidson's Invernahavon lands.

Davidson crest badge

Below: 14th-century Threave Castle, built on an island in the River Dee by the 3rd Earl of Douglas.

Douglas

For a time the Douglases were the most powerful

family in Scotland after the Stewart royal family, which they hated. The Douglases helped kings to get thrones; they used them, abused them, and often betrayed them – yet never aspired to be kings themselves.

The name of Douglas is a territorial one, from Lanarkshire, and the first on record was William de Douglas in the last quarter of the 12th century. His eldest son Archibald had two sons, William and Andrew; the latter was the ancestor of the Douglases, Earls of Morton. William's son William the Hardy, 1st Lord of Douglas (d.1298), was the founder of the two great branches of the Douglas family: the Black Douglases and the Red Douglases.

Sir William's eldest son was 'The Good Sir James' Douglas, closest friend and chief captain of King Robert the Bruce. When Sir James Douglas died in 1330, the estates went to his brother Hugh because the son of Sir James, Archibald 'the Grim', was illegitimate. These estates incorporated lands in Galloway, Annandale, Ettrick, Lauderdale, Eskdale, and Teviotdale. After Hugh they passed to his nephew Sir William, who in 1357 was created 1st Earl of Douglas, and also became Earl of Mar through marriage: he was the first of the Black Douglases. When he died in 1384, he was succeeded as 2nd Earl by his son Sir James, who was killed at the Battle of Otterburn in 1388. But the 1st Earl also had an illegitimate son, George, who was created 1st Earl of Angus and died in 1403; he was the first of the Red Douglases.

When the 2nd Earl of Douglas died, his title passed to Archibald the Grim, who died in 1400. He was succeeded by his son Archibald, the 4th Earl, who had married a daughter of King Robert III (1390–1406) and been created Duc de Touraine in France; he was killed at the Battle of Verneuil in France in 1424. The 5th Earl, also Archibald, was the 4th Earl's son. He was imprisoned by James I in 1430, then released, and when James I was murdered in 1437, became Regent during the minority of James II. The 5th Earl Douglas died of the plague in 1439 and was succeeded as 6th Earl by his 18-year-old son William; he was murdered in 1440 by a faction controlling the young King, the Crichtons and the Livingstons. The Douglas Earldom now passed back to the 6th Earl's great-uncle, James 'the Gross', brother of Archibald the Grim. He was not only hugely obese but idle, and did nothing to curb the excesses of the Crichton/Livingston faction.

By the end of the 14th century, the Douglases had become all powerful in the Lowlands. During the long rule of the Duke of Albany, brother of Robert III and uncle of James I (1406–37), the Douglases were a constant source of trouble because of their loathing of the Stewarts.

When the 7th Earl Douglas, James the Gross, died in 1443, he was followed by his son William, who was determined to break the Crichton/Livingston faction. He set about it, however, by making a pact with the Earl of Crawford and MacDonald, Lord of the Isles, whereby they would divide Scotland between themselves and replace James II with a candidate of their choice. The King handled the crisis by offering Douglas a safe conduct to attend discussions, then stabbing Douglas when he came.

The royally-murdered 8th Earl Douglas was succeeded by his brother James, who was Bishop of Aberdeen. On becoming the 9th Earl Douglas, he abandoned clerical principles along with his robes and collected a force of angry Douglas retainers, with which he sacked Stirling. The King riposted by leading an army against Castle Douglas in Dumfriesshire and forcing the Earl to submit. Though James II pardoned Douglas, it was by now clear that a final showdown could not be avoided forever. It came at Arkinholm in 1455 when James II scattered the forces of Douglas and killed two of his brothers, the Earls of Ormond and Moray. Douglas himself escaped but was condemned in his absence, stripped of his titles and lands (thereby making the Stewart dynasty extremely rich) and remained in exile until his death in 1488. It was the end of the Black Douglases.

The story of the Red Douglases was no less colourful. George, 1st Earl of Angus, also married a daughter of King Robert III. His grandson George, the 4th Earl Angus, supported James II against the Black Douglases (George's cousins) and fought beside the King at Arkinholm. For this he was rewarded with some of the Black Douglas land.

Archibald Douglas, the 5th Earl of Angus (nicknamed 'Bell the Cat') led the Scottish lords to defeat King James III at the Battle of Sauchieburn in 1488. The old Earl took no part in the Battle of Flodden in 1513 but two of his three sons were killed there, which may have hastened his own death a few months later. He was succeeded by his grandson Archibald, the 6th Earl, who married the widow of King James IV: Margaret Tudor, daughter of Henry VII of England. They had no sons, but their daughter Margaret married Matthew, 4th Earl of Lennox, and *their* son was Henry Stewart, Lord Darnley, future consort of Mary, Queen of Scots.

When the 6th Earl of Douglas died, the title passed to another branch of the family. The 11th Earl of Douglas was advanced to become Marquess of Douglas in 1633, and the 3rd Marquess was created 1st Duke of Douglas in 1703. When he died without issue, the Douglas titles passed to the Dukes of Hamilton (*see* Hamilton).

The chiefship is vacant as the potential claimants retain compound surnames, unacceptable by the rules of clan succession. The clansman's motto is *Jamais arrière* ('Never behind').

Drummond

Clan Drummond takes its name from the territory of Drymen in the Lennox, east of Loch Lomond. The original title of the clan chief was *An Drumanach Mor*, or 'The Great Man of Drymen'.

An early ancestor of the clan was Malcolm of Drummond, who held an official position in the Lennox in the 1220s. His elder son, also Malcolm, was captured at the siege of Dunbar in 1296 and appears to have been a prisoner of the English King Edward I. His son Malcolm fought with Bruce in the war of independence and is said to have been responsible for scattering caltrops (bunches of upturned spikes, broadcast for crippling enemy horses) at the Battle of Bannockburn in 1314, so helping to carry the day for the Scots.

Malcolm Drummond was given lands in Porth shire as a reward and the present Chief of the Drummonds, the Earl of Perth, still lives at Stobhall which was part of that gift. Robert the Bruce's son, King David II (1329–71) married Margaret, daugh-ter of Malcolm Drummond of Bannockburn fame. Robert III (1390–1406) married Annabella, daughter of John Drummond of Stobhall, and their third son was King James I of Scotland (1406–37). This may have been one of the reasons why James, on his return from a long exile in England, set up the seat of his reign at Perth, the principal town in Drummond country.

The Drummonds remained loyal to Scotland's Stewart kings. In 1488, Sir John Drummond received a barony. The 4th Baron became 1st Earl of Perth in 1605, and the 4th Earl was a founder-knight of the revived Order of the Thistle in 1687.

Sir William Drummond, a cousin of the 4th Earl of Perth, was for a time Commander-in-Chief of the army in Scotland during the reign of Charles II (1660–85). During the Republican Commonwealth (1649–59), Drummond had spent some years in Russia, where he had gained the rank of Lieutenant-General and become Military Governor of Smolensk. He later became 1st Viscount Strathallan. One of his descendants, the 4th Viscount Strathallan, was killed at Culloden in 1746. He was the ancestor of the present Earl of Perth.

Drummond crest badge

Left: Drummond Castle, where Margaret Drummond – secret Queen of James IV – and her two sisters were poisoned in 1502.

Dunbar

The 11th-century Earl Gospatric, who claimed descent back through the Kings of Scotland to Kenneth MacAlpin, was given the important Earldom of Dunbar by King Malcolm Canmore in 1072. Gospatric's descendents held the Earldom until it was forfeited in 1435. The title was revived for the Home family in 1603, but lapsed again in 1611. The Dunbars acquired the lands of Glenkens and Mochrum in 1368, and the Mochrum branch is the chiefly line today.

A branch of the Dunbars in Caithness descends from the Westfield line of the family. The son of the 7th Earl – who fought in the Scottish army against the Norsemen at the Battle of Largs in 1263 – was succeeded by his son, Patrick 'Blackbeard'. He assumed the title 'Earl of March' because his Earldom commanded the March, or border, with England. His Countess held Dunbar against the English forces of Edward I in 1296.

The Dunbar/March Earldom was confiscated in 1435 by King James I, who thought that the Dunbars had become too powerful. But John Dunbar, cousin of the last Earl of March, had been created Earl of Moray in 1372 by King Robert II, whose daughter Marjorie he had married. His grandson, the 4th Earl of Moray, was murdered in 1429, leaving only a son by a 'handfast' marriage, who could not inherit the title. The son of *that* son married the heiress to the Mochrum Dunbars, eventually producing the 1st Baronet of Nova Scotia in 1677.

The Chief today is, therefore, Sir Jean Dunbar of Mochrum, 13th Baronet, who was a Sergeant in the United States Army in World War II, and was for a while personal jockey to that celebrated American philanthropist and entrepreneur Alphonse Capone. The chief resides in Florida.

Dundas

The Dundases are one of Scotland's oldest historical families, and they played a major role in the legal and political affairs of the nation. It was once said

The romantic, sea-girt ruins of Dunbar Castle, which was once a powerful fortress commanding the most important harbour on Scotland's south eastern seaboard.

that 'any Prime Minister can raise a man to the House of Lords, but it takes seven centuries of Scottish history to make a Dundas of Dundas'.

The lands of Dundas are first recorded when they were chartered to Helias, son of Uchtred, probably in the reign of Malcolm IV (1153–65). Helias was a grandson of one Gospatric, almost certainly a scion of the great Earldoms of Northumberland and Dunbar. The early arms of the Dundases bore the Lyon Rampant, an indication of the connection. Serle de Dundas rendered homage to Edward I of England in 1296, and the first recorded 'Dundas of That Ilk' was one of the conservators of the three years' truce between Scotland and England in 1484.

The most celebrated of the name was a descendant of the Dundas of Dundas branch, via the Dundas of Arniston Baronets. He was Henry Dundas, an astute lawyer who was nicknamed 'Henry IX' because of his enormous power on the English political scene in the second half of the 18th century. (This was before Bonnie Prince Charlie died as titular 'King Charles III' in 1788 and his brother became titular 'King Henry IX'.) In 1784, as Pitt the Younger's Secretary of State for Scotland, Henry Dundas introduced the Bill restoring the estates forfeited after the Jacobite Rising of 1745–46. Dundas was also remembered for arranging that the sons of many Scottish families of his acquaintance obtained key posts in the East India Company, which controlled and administered British India until the Great Bengal Mutiny of 1857. In 1805, Dundas was impeached for 'gross malversation [sic] and breach of duty' as Treasurer of the Navy, and retired to his vast estate in Perthshire.

The Chief today is Sir David Dundas of Dundas, Bart. There is a Dundas tartan; the clansman's crest badge is a 'Lion's Head in Bush of Oak', with the motto *Essayez* ('Strive').

Durie

The small clan of Durie derives its surname from the lands of Durie in the Parish of Scoonie, in Fife. About the year 1260, Duncan 'de Durry' is recorded as witnessing a charter by Malise, Earl of Stratherne. John 'Dury' was a priest at St Andrews in 1464; Walter 'Doray' was one of the brethren at the Priory of Cupar, Fife, in 1500.

Another cleric, Andrew Durie or Dury who died in 1558, became Bishop of Galloway, but according to John Knox, 16th-century Scotland's most prominent Bible fundamentalist and Church reformer, was so notorious 'for his filthiness, that he was sometimes called Abbot Stottikin'. John Durie, a native of Edinburgh, was author of *The Reformed librarie keeper*, published in London in 1650 – the first British treatise on library management.

The chiefship of the Durie family lay dormant until 1988, when Lord Lyon, King of Arms, recognized Lieutenant Colonel Ramond Durie of Durie as Chief of the Name and Arms of Durie. As yet there is no specific Durie tartan.

Elliott

The Elliotts are a Border clan from Roxburghshire, probably from Redheugh where the family still has a seat today. Their early history is obscure and no Elliotts appear to have distinguished themselves until the 17th century. Gilbert Elliott acquired land at Stobs in Roxburghshire in the 1630s, and his eldest son, William, was Member of Parliament for Roxburghshire in the 1640s. Gilbert's third son, Gavin Elliott, was the ancestor of the earls of Minto.

William Elliott's eldest son Gilbert, also MP for Roxburghshire, was knighted by Charles II while the King was in exile, and in 1666 was created a baronet. Sir Gilbert's great-grandson, George Augustus Elliott (1717–90) was a younger brother of the 4th Baronet. This George Elliott became a general in the army. He won immortal fame as Governor of Gibraltar and commander of the British forces defending the Rock in the 'Great Siege' of 1779–82, beating off French and Spanish land and sea attacks. Elliott was created 1st Baron Heathfield in 1787, and died in 1790.

Gavin Elliott's descendants included Sir Gilbert Elliott, who was Governor-General of Bengal from 1807 to 1812 and was then created 1st Earl of Minto. His great-grandson, Gilbert John (1845–1914), became Governor-General of Canada (1898–1904), then Viceroy of India from 1905 to 1910.

The chief is Mrs Margaret Elliott of that Ilk.

Elliott crest badge

Below: Today's 'Common Riding' processions are held annually in the Border country to confirm boundaries which were in constant dispute by clans like the Elliotts.

Erskine

The Erskines come from a family headed by Henry de Erskine in Renfrewshire, first recorded in the reign of Alexander II (1214–49). They fought for Robert the Bruce in the Scottish war of independence. In the 1430s the head of the family, Sir Robert, inherited the title Earl of Mar, but his son Thomas was deprived of it in 1457, ten years later receiving a barony as Lord Erskine.

The 5th Lord Erskine was made guardian of the infant Mary, Queen of Scots, when her father James V (1513–42) died soon after the defeat of the Scots by the English in the Battle of Solway Moss. Erskine eventually sent Mary to France into the protection of the French King Henry II. This Lord Erskine had been a close friend of James V; his daughter Margaret had been one of the King's mistresses (probably his favourite). She became the mother of James Stewart, Earl of Moray, Mary's half-brother and Regent of Scotland after Mary's deposition. One of Lord Erskine's sons, Alexander, was the ancestor of the earls of Kellie.

Lord Erskine died in the early 1550s. His son John, the 5th Lord (also confirmed as Earl of Mar) was made guardian of James, the infant son of Queen Mary and her husband, Lord Darnley. Mary was captured at Carberry Hill in 1567 and taken to Loch Leven Castle, held by her half-brother Moray, where the chatelaine was Margaret Erskine. It was not a comfortable imprisonment. Margaret Erskine thought she should have been Queen because her lover, James V, had planned to defy a Papal ruling that they should not be married.

At the end of July 1567, the infant James was crowned King James VI. At the ceremony Mar had to hold the crown above the baby's head because it was too heavy to be worn. As Regent, Moray governed Scotland well until he was assassinated at Linlithgow by one of the Hamiltons (1572). Moray was succeeded as Regent by the Earl of Lennox, grandfather of James VI, but Lennox was killed the next year at the siege of Stirling Castle. Mar was chosen to follow Lennox, but he died the next year, and his brother Alexander became guardian of the King.

When in 1715 James Edward, the Old Pretender, made his bid for the British throne, he wrote from France to John Erskine, Earl of Mar, inviting him to raise the clans and start the war against the Hanoverian King George I and his Government. Mar had been one of the original signatories to the Treaty of Union in 1706 which became the Act of Union in 1707, and had also been made Secretary of State for Scotland, but he had begun to regret the Union. He gathered an army and took Perth without

Above: Braemar Castle, built in 1628 by the 7th Lord Erskine, was captured by Farquharsons in 1689.

Erskine crest badge

much resistance, but was then worsted in an engagement at Sheriffmuir and withdrew. Other Jacobites were defeated at Preston, across the Border in England. Although the Pretender came to Peterhead and stayed a few weeks in Scotland, he saw that his cause was lost and sailed for France. With him went Mar, who was stripped of his titles and estates in exile (see page 154).

The chief is the Earl of Mar and Kellie.

Farquharson

One of the confederation of clans known collectively as Clan Chattan, the Farquharsons descend from Farquhar, the fourth son of Alexander Ciar (or Shaw) of Rothiemurchus on the Spey. Farquhar's son Donald married Isabel Stewart, the heiress to

Invercauld, and their son was Finlay Mor, killed in the Battle of Pinkie Cleugh in 1547.

Farquharsons fought with Montrose for King Charles I in the Civil War. In the war between William III and the followers of the exiled James II – the Jacobites – the Farquharsons joined the army of John Graham of Claverhouse, Viscount Dundee, who defeated Government forces at Killiecrankie in 1689 but who was killed on the battlefield.

In the Jacobite Risings of the 18th century, the Farquharsons achieved a unique if somewhat depressing 'double'. In 1715, John Farquharson of Invercauld joined the Clan Chattan forces on the Jacobite side, but was captured at the Battle of Preston. Thirty years later, in the 'Forty-Five', the Farquharsons rallied to Bonnie Prince Charlie – and Francis Farquharson, of the Monaltrie branch,

was captured at the Battle of Culloden.

The chief is Captain Alwynne Farquharson of Invercauld.

Farquharson crest badge

Below: The Auld Brig O' Dee, not far east of Invercauld, the seat of the chief of the Clan Farquharson, whose neighbours are the Royal Family at the Balmoral Estate.

Fergusson

It is possible that the Fergussons were descended from Fergus of Dalriada, an Irish chief who, in the 6th century, settled in Kintyre and brought to Scotland the Stone of Scone, which eventually became the Scottish Coronation Stone. There are several Fergusson families. They may all have the same beginnings, or they may not all be related, but the Fergussons of Kilkerran in Ayrshire are, and have been, recognized as chiefs of the Fergussons. The name Kilkerran is said to stem from St Ciaran, one of the earliest Irish missionary saints to land in Scotland. The first Fergusson of Kilkerran was John Fergusson, who died in about 1483.

The principal Fergusson families were those of Kilmundy, Craigdarroch, Raith, Dunfallandy, and Kilkerran. One of the Fergussons was a signatory of the famous Declaration of Arbroath in 1320, Scotland's most celebrated document. This was a letter to Pope John XXII, in which the signatories insisted on recognition of Scotland's independence.

One of the later Fergussons was Sir James Fergusson of Kilkerran (1688–1759). He was the 2nd Baronet and a famous lawyer, a Lord Justiciary with the title Lord Kilkerran. The 6th and 7th Baronets were both Governors-General of New Zealand (1873–75 and 1924–30 respectively), and the 7th Baronet's third son, later Lord Ballantrae, was also Governor-General of New Zealand from 1962 to 1967. The chief is Sir Charles Fergusson of Kilkerran, Bt.

Fletcher

The small group of families which settled at Achallader in Argyll in the 11th century carried the Gaelic patronymic surname *mac an fhleistar* – 'son of the flighter', or fletcher. (The Old French name for the craftsman who made the carefully balanced, feathered flights and attached them to the arrow shafts was *flechier*.)

The small Clan Fletcher handed down the traditional oral charter to its lands, in which the Fletchers declared that they '. . . were the first to raise smoke and boil water in Glen Orchy'. One of the clan's families settled just over the hills to the west, in Glen Lyon. These Fletchers established a special relationship as arrowmakers to the MacGregors, at a time when that clan was landless and much persecuted by the powerful Clan Campbell.

It was Black Duncan Campbell of Glenorchy who had 'beheddit the Chief of MacGregor with his ain hands' who tricked the unsuspecting Fletcher Chief out of the Glenorchy lands at Achallader before 1600. For a century or so, the Fletchers suffered the indignity of being tenants on their own lands. But by the Jacobite Rising of 1715, they were being led into battle by Gillespie the 9th Chief, who had purchased the estate of Dunans in Cowal, where he incorporated the great door from Achallader into his new home.

Andrew Fletcher of Saltoun (1653–1716) was a long-term opponent of the enforced Union between Scotland and England in 1707 – a crusading Member of Parliament, a philosopher, and a charismatic orator. There is controversy over his relationship with the Clan Fletcher, arising from the wide interchange between the unconnected names 'Fletcher' and 'Flesher' (Old Scots for the trade of butcher). One family in St Andrews, first recorded

Above:
Ferguson crest badge

Below:
Fletcher crest badge

as 'Flesher' in 1537, evolved as follows: Fletchour (1539), Fleschar (1541), Fleschor (1522), Flescheoir and Fleschour (1563), Flescher (1589), Fleger (1609), Fledger (1612), and Flager (1627). Consequently many Fletchers were undoubtedly recorded as Fleshers, with their descendants living under that name today, while many Fleshers equally became Fletchers.

The Dunans estate passed with the last Fletcher heiress, Harriet, to the Cuddon family of Norfolk, and the principal representative of the family today is Lt. Col. Archibald Cuddon-Fletcher, a former battalion commander in the Scots Guards. The direct line from the last chief died out in 1911 in North America, where many Fletchers had been forced to migrate after the Clearances of the 19th century. A chief for the clan today has yet to be found. There are two tartans for the name.

Forbes

The name of Forbes comes from territory on Donside in Aberdeenshire. John de Forbes, in the reign of King Alexander II (1214–49), was the father or grandfather of Alexander de Forbes, who was killed defending Urquhart Castle on Loch Ness against the English forces of Edward I. Alexander's descendant Sir John Forbes, who lived in the late 14th and early 15th centuries, had several sons, and from these descended four branches of the family: Forbes of Pitsligo, Culloden, Waterton, and Foveran. John's eldest son Alexander was created Lord Forbes in about 1442. The title – Scotland's premier barony – is still in existence, and the present holder is the 22nd Lord Forbes.

Perhaps the most celebrated of the whole family was Duncan Forbes (1685–1747), a brilliant lawyer who, though sympathetic to the Jacobite cause, tried hard to prevent violence and revolt. During the administration of Sir Robert Walpole, Britain's 'first prime minster' (1721–42), the government of Scotland was left largely to the Duke of Argyll and to Duncan Forbes, Lord Advocate (1725–37) and later President of the Court of Session (1737–47).

Forbes was apparently taken by surprise by the second Jacobite Rising. He strove to persuade a number of clan chiefs, such as the MacDonald of Sleat, the MacLean, and also old Lord Lovat, the Chief of Clan Fraser, to keep out of the struggle. When the rising collapsed after Culloden, Forbes tried desperately to dissuade the English government, particularly the Duke of Cumberland, from rounding up and proscribing the survivors and their families. After an interview in which Forbes begged him to show mercy, 'Butcher' Cumberland dismissed Forbes as 'that old woman who spoke to me of humanity'.

The chief is the Lord Forbes K.B.E.

Forsyth

This clan surname could either come from a place formerly of that name or from the Gaelic *fear sith*, 'peacemaker'. There may even be two separate groups of Forsyth families, unconnected with each other, as in the case of the Highland and Lowland Shaws (*see* Shaw). A Robert of 'Fauside' swore allegiance to Edward I of England in 1296, and a number of persons described as 'de' or 'of Forsith' appear in records thereafter. Yet there seems to be no place of that name. The Arms of a number of Forsyth families appear in 16th-century manuscripts at Falkland Palace, in connection with monarchs of the Royal House of Stewart.

Alexander Forsyth, a clergyman and inventor, patented his principle for detonating firearms which led to the introduction of the percussion cap. He was given a pension by the British Government after it was discovered that he had refused to sell his secret to Napoleon. Thomas Forsyth was knighted for his diplomatic work during the Indian Mutiny of 1857, and for averting a war in Burma in 1875.

The descendant of a Falkland laird from the early 1600s, Alastair Forsyth, who restored Ethie Castle in Fife, was recognized as Chief of the clan in the 1970s. This was after a *Gilfine* or voting deputation of nine armigerous (bearing Coats of Arms) gentlemen and ladies of the clan supported his petition, together with more than 2,000 Forsyths from around the world. The clansman's crest badge is a winged mythical animal with the motto *Instaurator ruinae* ('Repairer of Ruin'). There is an approved 'Forsyth' tartan.

Left: Forbes crest badge
Right: Forsyth crest badge

Fraser

The Frasers were of French origin, and de Fréselières appeared in southern Scotland in the 1160s. There were three names, Simon, Udard, and Gilbert, but their relationship is not known. A Ralph de Fréselière was a knight of Richard Plantagenet, son of King Henry II (1154–1189), who became Richard I in 1189.

In the 13th century, some of the Frasers settled in Moray and one of the family, William Fraser, was Bishop of St Andrews in the 1280s. He was one of the six Guardians of Margaret, the 'Maid of Norway', granddaughter and heiress to King Alexander III (1249–86). When she died on her way home to Scotland from Norway in 1290, this Bishop Fraser wrote to King Edward I of England inviting him to arbitrate in the various squabbles among the Scottish lords as to who should succeed her. In doing so Fraser presented the English King, probably quite unwittingly, with the ideal chance to plant a puppet king on the Scottish throne, and so effectively annexe Scotland and add it to his Kingdom of England and Wales.

King Edward's choice was the weak and pliant John Baliol, but after he was deposed in 1296, Edward's attempt to rule Scotland directly sparked off the war of independence in which another Fraser, Sir Simon Fraser of Tweeddale, joined the army of William Wallace. Caught and condemned by the English King in 1306, Sir Simon Fraser was hanged, drawn, and quartered. This was the hideous new death penalty devised by the English for the 'rebellious' Scots.

A relative of Sir Simon's, Sir Alexander Fraser, was one of Robert the Bruce's right-hand-men at Bannockburn in 1314, and he subsequently became Lord Chamberlain. He was the ancestor of the Frasers of Philorth, who eventually became Lords Saltoun. The latter are recognized today by the Lord Lyon as Chiefs of the Whole Name and Arms of Fraser.

The Chief of Clan Fraser today is Flora Marjory Fraser, The Lady Saltoun (in her own right), 20th Saltoun of Abernethy. Lady Saltoun is married to Captain Alexander Ramsay of Mar, great-grandson of Queen Victoria.

The clansman's crest badge is a 'Flowering Strawberry (*Fraise*) Plant', with the motto 'All My Hope is in God'. There are 11 Fraser tartans – *not* including 'Fraser of Lovat', which should only be worn by Frasers of that branch.

Castle Fraser, Aberdeenshire, built *around 1588 and a clan stronghold till 1921.*

Fraser of Lovat

Hugh Fraser, descendant of King Robert the Bruce's Lord Chamberlain, Sir Alexander Fraser, was created 1st Lord Lovat in the 1450s. In the early 18th century, the 11th Lord Lovat (*c.* 1667–1747), known as 'The Fox', sided with the Hanoverian Government in the Jacobite Rising in 1715. After capturing Inverness Castle for George I, he became involved in a lengthy and complex legal battle with the Government over his representation in Parliament as Lord Lovat. This he eventually won, but it seems to have soured him in his dealings with London. When Bonnie Prince Charlie landed at Moidart and raised the Royal Standard at Glenfinnan in 1745, Lovat joined him. When the Rising collapsed after the disastrous Battle of Culloden, some of the rebel lords were tried and executed. Among them was Lord Lovat, by now about 80 years old. He was taken to the Tower of London and beheaded on Tower Hill in 1747 – the last peer to suffer this form of execution in Britain.

Lovat's son, Simon Fraser, fought at Culloden. Though attainted and deprived of his estates, he was later pardoned and restored. In the Seven

105

Years War (1756–63) he raised a regiment of 1,600 men in three weeks. Known as the 'Fighting Frasers', it fought with great distinction against the French in Canada – most notably at the Battle of Quebec (1759) which won Canada for Britain. General Wolfe, killed at Quebec in the moment of victory, is said to have died in the arms of a sergeant of Fraser's Highlanders. Simon Fraser took his reconstituted regiment into the American War of Independence, having increased its strength by recruiting in Scotland, and the regiment acquitted itself bravely throughout that conflict. On the death of General Fraser's half-brother in 1815, the male line passed to Thomas Fraser (descended from the second son of the 4th Lord Lovat) who became the 14th Baron Lovat; his great-grandson is the chief today.

The Frasers of Lovat are today regarded as a clan in their own right, with Lord Lovat recognized as the chief – *not* a mere chieftain of Clan Fraser, but of a 'Considerable Family'. That is to say, a family sufficiently numerous to be regarded as being a clan in its own right. The present Chief of the Frasers of Lovat is the famous World War II Commando leader, Brigadier Simon Fraser, DSO, MC, TD, Légion d'honneur, Croix de Guerre, and Order of Suvorov (Soviet Union), 17th Lord Lovat and, by his Highland designation, 22nd *Mac Shimi* ('Son of Simon').

The clansman's crest badge is 'A Buck's Head, Roaring' with the motto *Je Suis Prest* ('I am Ready').

There is *one* specific 'Fraser of Lovat' tartan. The Lovat Frasers may wear any of the other 11 'Fraser' tartans, but the reverse does not apply.

Above: A Fraser's Highlander can be seen attending the dying General Wolfe at the Battle of Quebec, 1759.

Fraser of Lovat crest badge

Gayre

Some authorities trace this surname to the Domesday manor of Gayre in Cornwall, where a family of that name flourished before 1200. A junior branch is said to have fled northwards and finally settled in Scotland.

A Gaelic word suggests a surname stemming from a physical description: *gearr*, meaning 'short' or 'stocky'. In Norse (possibly more applicable to Sutherland surnames which are not obviously Celtic) *geirr* means 'spear' – or, in practical terms, a man who is handy with one. It is an old Norse personal name. A noted pirate in the north-east was referred to as *Mac Iain Giorr*, while Ewin McVean Gair, in Urquhart in 1613, was fined for sheltering outlawed MacGregors. Thomas Gaire, 'a chapman that carries a wallet through the countrie', was made Councillor of Cromarty in 1669, and Iain Dubh Gearr MacGregor was the composer of the famous 'Reel of Tulloch'.

The present Chief of Clan Gayre is a noted ethnologist and international heraldic authority: Lieutenant-Colonel Robert Gayre of Gayre and Nigg, who has transferred the *duthus* or clanland to Minard Castle in Argyll, where the clan library and other archival material are now located. The clansman's crest badge is a 'Golden Coronet', and at least five Gayre tartans are recorded.

Gordon crest badge

Left: Loch Fyne in Argyll on the shores of which stands Minard Castle, the present seat of the Chief of Clan Gayre.

Gordon

The origins of the Gordons are not absolutely clear, but they probably stem from an Anglo–Norman family which settled in Berwickshire in the 12th century. It has been suggested that the name comes from the district where they settled, which incorporated a fortified hill, *gor-dun*, which is Celtic for 'great hill fort'. A Richard de Gordon figures in a document of the mid-12th century.

The Gordons moved from the Lowlands into the Highlands sometime in the later 13th century. Sir Adam of Gordon was an associate of John of Badenoch, the 'Red Comyn', who opposed Robert the Bruce's claim to the throne, and was stabbed by Bruce in the chapel at Dumfries in 1306 (*see* Cumming). Disgusted by the crime, Adam of Gordon made overtures to King Edward I of England. These do not seem to have been rejected, but King Edward nevertheless permitted his forces in the Borders to ravage the Gordon lands. This prompted Adam to switch loyalty to Bruce, and although there is no evidence that Adam fought for Bruce at Bannockburn in 1314, he was Scottish Ambassador to the Papacy in 1320 and personally delivered to the Pope the historic Declaration of Arbroath. He also did much to reconcile the Pope with Bruce, who had been excommunicated after murdering the Red Comyn. Bruce rewarded Gordon generously with huge estates; the Strathbogie estate alone was about 310 km² (120 sq miles) in area, and Gordon also received parts of the MacDuff lands. Adam was finally killed fighting the English at the Battle of Halidon Hill in 1333.

Adam's great-great-grandson, Sir Adam, Chief of the Gordons, died in the defeat of another disastrous Scottish invasion of northern England, at Hambledon Hill in 1402. His heiress was his daughter Elizabeth, married to Sir Alexander Seton, whose son became 1st Earl of Huntly (part of the huge Strathbogie estate) in 1447. He adopted the surname of Gordon in place of Seton. The Earldom passed to his son George, who became Clan Chief; Adam, the second of his four sons, married Elizabeth, Countess of Sutherland (*see* Sutherland).

George, 4th Earl of Huntly, became an extremely important and influential nobleman. Indeed, for a long time the Gordons of Huntly acted on behalf of the royal government in the eastern Highlands, as did the Campbells in the west (*see* Campbell). This 4th Earl of Huntly was killed in a skirmish at Corrichie in 1562 between James Stewart, Earl of Moray (the half-brother of Mary, Queen of Scots, and afterwards the Regent Moray), and the staunchly Catholic Gordons, who objected to the accept-

Graham

ance of the Reformation by the Scottish Parliament.

George, the 6th Earl of Huntly, was advanced to the 1st Marquess of Huntly by King James VI in 1599, and died in 1636. His son George, the 2nd Marquess, was an active Royalist in the Civil War and paid for this with his head in 1649.

The Gordon clan had several branches. One of these, the Earldom of Aberdeen, began with the creation of the 1st Earl in 1682. He was Lord Chancellor of Scotland from 1682–84. The 4th Earl of Aberdeen was Prime Minister from 1852 to 1855, and was driven to resign after the scandals about the dreadful conditions endured by the Army in the Crimean War (1854–56). The 7th Earl of Aberdeen was Governor-General of Canada from 1893–98, and was advanced to a Marquessate in 1916.

Colonel William Gordon of Fyvie painted in Rome by Pompeo Batoni in 1766.

The Grahams go back at least to the 12th century, when William de Graham an Anglo-Norman baron who was an associate of King David I (1124–53), was given lands in Dalkeith and Abercorn. One of his sons, John, was ancestor to the famous Marquis of Montrose *(see below)*. John's great-great-great-grandson, Sir John Graham of Dundaff, was William Wallace's right-hand-man in Scotland's fight for freedom against the English, and was killed in the Battle of Falkirk in 1298. His nephew, Sir Patrick Graham of Kincardine, had been killed on the other side two years earlier at the Battle of Dunbar while carrying the banner of John Baliol, the puppet King of Scots.

Sir John's son, Sir David Graham, was the first to acquire lands in the Highlands for the family, including the territory of Montrose. A descendant, Sir Patrick Graham, Chief of the Clan, who had been one of the Guardians of James II (1437–60) during the latter's minority, was created Lord Graham in 1445. Patrick's grandson William, 3rd Lord Graham, was made 1st Earl of Montrose by James IV in 1505, and died fighting beside his King at Flodden in 1513.

One of Patrick's great-uncles was Sir Robert Graham, who killed King James I (1406–37), because James had sent Graham's young nephew to England as a hostage. Sir Robert was hunted down and tortured to death; his nephew remained an English captive in Pontefract Castle for a quarter of a century.

James Graham, 5th Earl and 1st Marquis of Montrose (1612–50) was the brilliant commander who, in a series of remarkable battles (1644–45) defeated seven Covenant armies and briefly reconquered Scotland for Charles I in the Great Civil War. After being defeated at Philiphaugh by Sir David Leslie in 1645, Montrose left Scotland on the King's orders. He returned after the King's execution in 1649 to raise Scotland for Charles II, but was defeated again at Carbisdale, captured, and hanged at Edinburgh in 1650. In an act of savage barbarism, his body was then quartered and displayed at

Graham crest badge

Stirling, Glasgow, Perth and Aberdeen. Charles I had created him Marquis of Montrose in 1644. He is remembered among Scotland's greatest sons, and among the Great Captains of British military history.

Montrose's great-grandson, the 4th Marquis, was created the 1st Duke in 1707. A distant cousin, James Graham of Claverhouse, Viscount Dundee, won the Battle of Killiecrankie in 1689 against the Government forces under Hugh MacKay, but was killed in the moment of victory.

It was largely due to the 3rd Duke of Montrose that the British Government repealed its hated Act of 1767 prohibiting the wearing of Highland dress. The present Duke was for a time a Cabinet Minister of the government of Southern Rhodesia.

Grant

'Grant' simply means 'Great', from the French *grand*. Clan Grant descends from Norman ancestors, though there is also a claim to origins as far back as Kenneth MacAlpin, the first King of Scots.

The Grants settled in north-east Scotland, and are identifiable in the 13th century. There had also been Grants further west, and one of them, Sir Laurence, was Sheriff of Inverness in the mid-13th century. The clan grew steadily in strength and, by the 14th century, was holding lands in Glenmoriston, Stratherrick, and Strathspey. Sir Iain Grant was Sheriff of Inverness in the 1430s, and he enlarged the Strathspey landholding which has been the clan's principal sphere of influence ever since.

In 1694, because the clan supported William III rather than the cause of the exiled James II, the Grant lands were elevated to the status of a 'Regality'. This created almost a state within a state: a form of home rule. The Grant Regality was abolished, along with others, after the collapse of the Jacobite Rising of 1745–46, but the clan continued to dominate local affairs in many directions. The small town of Grantown-on-Spey was rebuilt by the clan chief in the 1760s. The chief is Patrick Grant, the Lord of Strathspey.

Gunn

The Gunns are of Norse origin, probably from a Viking chief called Gunni, mentioned in Norse sagas. They settled in the far north-east of Scotland, near Morven in Caithness, and this remained Gunn territory for a long time. The lands of Clan Gunn adjoined those of the MacKays, and the two clans remained at loggerheads for several generations.

Grant crest badge *Gunn crest badge*

By the 15th century, the Gunns were also deeply involved in clan feuds with the Keiths of Ackergil, and in 1438 the Gunns were overwhelmed in battle against a combined force of Keiths and MacKays at Wick.

In 1464, the two chiefs of the Gunns and the Keiths agreed to meet to settle their differences. Twelve horses from each side were to gather at a chapel near Girginghoe in Caithness, implying one man per horse. The Gunns arrived first, and went into the chapel to pray. When the Keiths arrived, they brought two clansmen on each horse. Fighting broke out and in a short time all 12 Gunns were slain. It was an act of black treachery, which the Gunns did not forgive or forget. Nearly 70 years later, the grandson of the slaughtered Gunn chief succeeded in despatching George Keith, Chief of the Keiths, together with 12 of his men, at Drummoy.

The Gunns also feuded with the earls of Caithness and Sutherland, and supported the Government side against Bonnie Prince Charlie in the Jacobite Rising of 1745. Clan Gunn also claims descent from the Viking Olaf the Black, King of Man and of the Isles, who died in about 1237. The chiefship is vacant today.

Guthrie

Until comparatively recent times, Guthrie Castle was one of the last fortified houses in Scotland still to be standing on Barony lands of the same name and inhabited by a family of that name, after five centuries. In the 1980s, after the death of the Chief who had restored the estate – Colonel Ivar Guthrie of Guthrie – his daughter sold the castle and its contents, and moved away.

The first Guthrie to be recorded in Scotland was the Laird of Guthrie, who was sent to France to escort Sir William Wallace home in 1299. Sir David Guthrie was armour-bearer to King James III after

1460. A Guthrie who became a citizen of Danzig in Poland in the 16th century was recorded, in Polish dialectical form, as 'Dhowzski'.

In more recent times, Samuel Guthrie (1782–1848) was one of the original discoverers of chloroform, and invented percussion priming powder; Sir James Guthrie (1859–1930) was a celebrated painter of the Glasgow School; and Sir William Tyrone Guthrie (1900–71) was the great theatrical director and producer who founded the Tyrone Guthrie Theater in Minneapolis.

An ancient rhyme lists the main branches of the Clan:

> Guthrie o' Guthrie
> and Guthrie o' Gaigie,
> Guthrie o' Taybank
> an' Guthrie o' Craigie.

The present Chief is Madam Rosalind Guthrie of Guthrie. The clansman's crest badge is 'An Arm Brandishing a Sword', with the motto *Sto pro veritate* ('I Stand for Truth').

Haig

The Haigs are a Border clan, first recorded when Petrus del Haga witnessed a deed of sale for two serfs, their sons and daughters, and all their progeny, around 1165. The Haigs came to occupy the lands of Bemersyde on the River Tweed, where the name in its present spelling is first recorded in 1412. Originally pronounced in two syllables as 'Hay-ge', it stems from the Old English *haga* meaning 'enclosure', from the verb *hag*, 'to surround' (*see* HAY).

The celebrated bard known as 'Thomas the Rhymer' (*c.*1210–94) predicted that

> Tyde what may
> Whate're betyde
> Haig shall be Haig
> of Bemersyde

which some may say was proved false when the direct line died out in 1867 and the house and lands were sold off. But the Haigs are still in possession because, in 1921, a grateful nation purchased and then presented Bemersyde to Field Marshal Sir Douglas Haig, Commander-in-Chief of the British forces during World War I. He was also made an earl and gifted £100,000 in cash (easily making him a millionaire by today's values).

The 1st Earl Haig descended from the 17th Laird of Bemersyde, who founded the whisky dynasty. Despite this, the family motto is not 'Don't be

Vague, Ask for Haig', but 'Tyde What May'. The current Chief and 2nd Earl, who succeeded his father in 1928, is the 30th Laird of Bemersyde, the original charter of which is one of his proudest possessions. General Alexander Haig, former NATO Commander in Europe and American Secretary of State under President Reagan, descends from the Field Marshal's uncle.

The 1st Earl wore the version of the Buccleuch tweed or tartan, which he is said to have continued by tradition from his days as Colonel of the King's Own Scottish Borderers, who wore that pattern. Basically 'Black 'n White', it was rejected vehemently by the Haig whisky company during its search for a corporate tartan, for fear of giving aid and succour to one of Haig's great competitors (Whyte and Mackay Distillers manufacture Black

Hamilton

One of Scotland's greatest families, unique for having produced two dukedoms, the Hamiltons were a Lowland family with large estates in the south, who also acquired territories in the Highlands.

The first Hamilton in Scotland was probably the Walter FitzGilbert of Hameldone, recorded as living in Renfrewshire during the last years of the 13th century. He was of Norman descent, related to the powerful d'Umfraville family. Walter FitzGilbert served as Castellan of Bothwell Castle for King Edward I in the Anglo–Scottish war which followed the deposition of King John Baliol in 1296. Sometime in the early years of the 14th century, FitzGilbert changed sides, offered to support Robert the Bruce, and fought with him at Bannockburn in 1314.

FitzGilbert's reward for this service was the Barony of Cadzow, and at this time he took on the name of Hamilton. His son, Sir David FitzWalter of Hamilton, 2nd Lord of Cadzow, sat in the Parliament of David II. While fighting with the King against the English at the Battle of Nevill's Cross in 1340, he was captured and kept in custody by the Archbishop of York until a ransom was paid.

In 1445, the 6th Lord of Cadzow was created a Peer of Scotland as Lord Hamilton. He joined the revolt of the Douglases in 1455 before changing sides and supporting King James II (1437–60). The 1st Lord Hamilton married the King's daughter, Princess Mary, and acquired lands and influence in the Highlands. From this marriage descends the Hamilton Dukedom of Abercorn.

For the next century, the Hamiltons of this line were often the nearest lords presumptive to the throne of Scotland. In 1503, the 2nd Lord Hamilton was created 1st Earl of Arran. His son James Hamilton, 2nd Earl of Arran, was appointed Regent of Scotland when King James V died in 1542, leaving his infant daughter Mary, only a few weeks old, as heiress to the throne.

The 2nd Earl's third son was created Marquess of Hamilton in 1599, and he died in 1604. His son James, the 2nd Marquess, also succeeded his uncle as 4th Earl of Arran, dying in 1624, and his eldest son (also James) was advanced to a dukedom by King Charles I in 1643. He was the ancestor of the present Duke of Hamilton and Brandon, the Premier Peer of Scotland.

The very eminence of the Hamiltons brought about one of the strangest episodes of World War II: the flight of Rudolf Hess, Hitler's deputy, to Scotland in May 1941. Having met the Duke of Hamilton at the Berlin Olympic Games of 1936,

Above: The tombs of both Field Marshal The Earl Haig and Sir Walter Scott lie amid the ruins of the great Abbey at Dryburgh, founded in 1150.

Hamilton crest badge

and White Whisky). The current chief feels that the traditional Border Shepherds' Plaid (black and white, or 'Dog's Tooth Check') is the most appropriate Haig tartan.

Hess had come to the conclusion that because of his position at the head of the Scottish Peerage, Hamilton was a natural potential focus of opposition to Churchill's wartime Government. Hess therefore chose the Duke as the ideal British intermediary for a 'make or break' high-level mission to persuade Britain to make peace on the eve of the German invasion of the Soviet Union. Needless to say, the naive hopes of Hess were soon dashed. The Duke of Hamilton, serving as a Wing Commander in the Royal Air Force, handed his surprise visitor straight over to the Government authorities, and Hess spent the rest of his life in jail.

Hannay

This name was originally 'Ahannay', from the old Celtic-British patronymic *ap Sheanaigh* – the contraction from the pre-*mac* form for 'son', *map*, to *ap*. Other modern variants of the name are 'Hanna' and 'Hannah'.

In 1296, 'Gilbert de Hannethe of the county of Wiggetone' rendered homage to King Edward I; John of Hanna was Shipmaster for King James I in 1424; James Ahannay was the King's Culveriner or

master gunner in 1529; John Ahannay was Baker to Mary, Queen of Scots in 1566. Yet probably the most famous Hannay of all never existed: the fictional hero Richard Hannay, from John Buchan's novels *The Thirty-Nine Steps, Greenmantle*, and others.

The Hannay stronghold in the old Celtic province of Galloway was originally Sorbie Tower, but after centuries of feuding with their most powerful neighbours – the Kennedys and the Dunbars – the Hannays began to lose whatever power and influence they may have had as a small clan. After 1600 they were even outlawed by King James VI for their

behaviour towards the Murrays of Broughton.

Today Sorbie Tower is back in the hands of the Hannays, who have restored it for use by the Clan Society. Other branches of the family are the Hannays of Kingsmuir in Fife; the Hannays of Kirkdale had their seat at Rusco Castle, near Gatehouse of Fleet. The present Chief is Ramsay Hannay of Kirkdale and of that Ilk. The two Hannay tartans were designed by a Councillor Hannay in the 1930s, along with the red and green setts of the 'Galloway' tartan.

Hay

There are several branches of the great Hay clan and three of them are peerages: the Earls of Erroll, the Marquesses of Tweeddale, and the Earls of Kinnoull. The 33rd Chief of the Hays is the 24th Earl of Erroll, Hereditary Lord High Constable and Knight Marischal of Scotland.

The original family was Norman: the de la Hayes from the Cotentin peninsula. The first Hay in Scotland was William de la Haye, Butler of Scotland and 1st Baron of Erroll (created 1178), who was an associate of Kings Malcolm IV (1153–65) and William the Lyon (1165–1214). He became ambassador to England at the end of the century. The 2nd Chief's brother, Robert de la Haye, was ancestor of the Marquesses of Tweeddale, and his son William was ancestor of the Earls of Kinnoull. The 3rd Lord Erroll, Gilbert de la Haye, was Sheriff of Perth and twice acted as co-Regent of Scotland during the minority of Alexander III (1249–86).

His grandson Sir Gilbert, 5th Lord Erroll, was a staunch supporter of King Robert the Bruce, and after the Battle of Bannockburn (1314) was confirmed as Hereditary Constable of Scotland, an office previously held by Bruce's enemy, the Red Comyn. He was also hereditary Commander of the Royal Bodyguard, and this honour cost the deaths of two Hay chiefs in battle, fighting beside their sovereigns. The 6th Lord Erroll was killed at the Battle of Neville's Cross in 1346, at which King David II was captured by the English. William, 4th Earl of Erroll, was killed with King James IV at the Battle of Flodden (1513), where a large number of Hays and their dependants also fell.

Sir Thomas Hay, 7th Lord Erroll, married Elizabeth, daughter of King Robert II (1371–90). Their younger son, Sir Gilbert Hay, was one of the Scottish knights who assisted Joan of Arc in having

The ruins of Slains Castle, originally called the Tower of Bowness, *and held by the Clan Hay from around 1590 until 1920.*

113

King Charles VII of France crowned at Reims in 1429. William, the 9th chief, was created 1st Earl of Erroll in 1452. He had married Beatrix, daughter of James, 7th Earl of Douglas, and eventually co-heiress to her brother William, 9th Earl of Douglas – last of the Black Douglases – who was banished by James II in 1455.

In 1559 George Hay, 7th Earl of Erroll, was appointed Lord Lieutenant of all central Scotland, from Earn to Loch Ness, by Mary, Queen of Scots. His grandson Francis, 9th Earl of Erroll, was involved in Philip II of Spain's plot to bring about the deposition of Elizabeth I of England and her replacement by James VI, as a prelude to the conversion of James to Catholicism and the restoration of the 'Auld Religion' in Scotland. The chief plotters, Erroll, Huntly, and Douglas, were driven abroad for a time, but returned and were reconciled with James VI.

Mary Hay, Countess of Erroll in her own right, was an ardent Jacobite who raised the clan to fight for Bonnie Prince Charlie in the Rising of 1745–46. William, 19th Earl of Erroll and exceptionally popular in Scotland (1823–91) was a maternal grandson of King William IV by his mistress, the actress Mrs Dorothea Jordan.

Josslyn Hay, 22nd Earl of Errol (1901–41) said to have been one of the best-looking men of his day, went out to Kenya in the 1920s, was married twice, and in January 1941 was shot dead in his car near Nairobi. He had been having an affair with Diana, the young wife of Sir Jock Delves Broughton, who was tried for the murder but acquitted; the mystery has never been solved. Diana later married Tom Cholmondeley, 4th Lord Delamere. Erroll's daughter Diana succeeded as Countess and was followed by her son in 1978.

Hay crest badge

Henderson

This surname embraces two Highland clans, and probably a number of smaller ones in the Low-

lands. Originally meaning 'son of Henry' and rendered as 'Henryson', the name took on a 'd' from the Scots pet name for Henry – 'Hendrie'.

There was a clan of the name in Liddesdale in the Borders, so small that it escaped inclusion in the roll of unruly Border clans drawn up for King James VI in 1594. The major family in the Lowlands were the Hendersons of Fordell in Fife; their romantic castle is today owned by Sir Nicholas Fairbairn, the advocate and Member of Parliament.

A branch of Clan Gunn claims the Hendersons as descending from Henry, son of George Gunn, the

15th (or thereabouts) Chief of Clan Gunn and 'Crowner' or Coroner of Caithness. MacHendrie, MacHenry, MacHinery, MacHendrick, and Mac-Kendrick names appear throughout the north-east Highlands and in Glencoe, where they were under the protection of the McIains of Abrach (Mac-Donalds) to whom they became hereditary pipers.

John Henderson of Fordell is the present Chief of the Lowland Name of Henderson. There is a Henderson tartan, which is used by both Hendersons and the Highland MacKendricks. The Gunn Hendersons wear the tartan of that clan.

Above: The dramatic scenery of Glencoe, where the infamous massacre of the MacDonald's took place in 1692. The Highland Hendersons were hereditary pipers to the clan.

Henderson crest badge

115

Home

Home crest badge

Above: Lord Home of the Hirsel, Clan Chief.

The family of Lord Home of the Hirsel, formerly Sir Alec Douglas-Home, British Prime Minister in 1963–64 and before that the 14th Earl of Home, began with Alden, or Aidan de Home, a 12th-century knight who held lands in the district of Home in Berwickshire. One of his descendants, Sir Thomas de Home, married the heiress to Dunglass and had two sons, Alexander and David. Lord Dunglass is still a subsidiary title of the Earls of Home.

The elder of Sir Thomas's sons, Alexander Home, served with Archibald, 4th Earl of Douglas, at the Battle of Hambledon Hill in 1402, when the English defeated the Scots. The two men survived the defeat to serve together again in France during the Hundred Years War; they fought on the French side, and both were killed at the Battle of Verneuil in 1424, one of the last English victories of the war. Alexander Home had three sons, and the eldest, Sir Alexander, continued the family line. He was Scottish ambassador to England in 1459, and created 1st Lord Home in 1473. His son Alexander predeceased him and the title went to a grandson, also Alexander, 2nd Lord Home, whose brother John was the ancestor of the Whiterigs branch of the family.

Alexander, 2nd Lord Home, led the van of the rebel army of Archibald Douglas, 5th Earl of Angus, against King James III at the Battle of Sauchieburn in 1488, in which James was defeated and afterwards murdered. His son Alexander, 3rd Lord Home, supported King James IV (1488–1513). He managed to survive the Battle of Flodden (1513) in which so many of the Scottish nobility perished with their King. But Home was persuaded to intrigue with the English against the Regent Albany, governing Scotland during the minority of James V. For this he was seized, tried for treason and executed.

The 5th Lord Home supported the Reformation in Scotland and stood by the Regent, the Earl of Moray, after the ousting of Mary, Queen of Scots, in 1568. Later, however, with Mary a captive in England, Home changed sides and supported the Queen's friends. His son Alexander, the 6th Lord, became a close friend of King James VI. When James became King of England in 1603, Alexander accompanied the King on his journey to London and was created 1st Earl of Home in 1605. His son James succeeded as 2nd Earl in 1619, but died without issue in 1633. The title passed to a distant cousin, James Home, a descendant of John Home of Whiterigs, who was the ancestor of Lord Home of the Hirsel. The chiefship is vacant.

Hunter

This clan now embraces all those families with a name which occurred widely throughout Britain during the Middle Ages. The name was attached to a prominent official who was huntsman to a royal or noble family. William the Hunter was recorded in a Latin manuscript around 1120 as William Venator (from the Latin verb 'to hunt' which also yielded the word 'venison', originally describing

Hunter crest badge

Below: The Hunterston Brooch, Anglo-Saxon crafting, but Celtic style (A.D. 700).

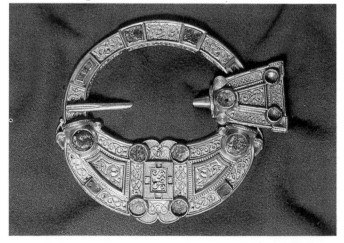

the meat of any animal killed in the hunt).

After arriving in Scotland from Normandy around 1110, the principal family acquired lands in Ayrshire which were called 'Hunterston' thereafter. The Hunters of Hunterston, being the only Hunter family whose head was called historically 'Hunter of That Ilk', successfully contested a claim by the Hunters of Polmood to be the oldest family of that name. Their original charter lands were said to have included the fore-shore and the seabed some distance out from the shore, after an early king granted their seaward boundary as far as their chief could hurl a javelin from the beach.

William and John Hunter were 18th-century surgeons and physicians, whose collections became the cores of two famous museums, respectively the Hunterian in Glasgow and that of the Royal College of Surgeons in London. The 'Hunterston Brooch', discovered on the estate by a shepherd in 1026, dates from about AD 700 and is one of the finest examples of Celtic–Anglian design and craftsmanship.

During this century, the Chiefship passed to the Cochrane-Patrick family and the lands of Hunterston were sold to the Atomic Energy Authority, which then built a nuclear power station complex alongside one of the finest deep-water anchorages in Britain. The current Chief, Neil Hunter of Hunterston, resides in Andorra. The *de facto* 'Commander' of the Clan, and 'Master of Hunterston' is the eldest son, Charles Hunter, Younger of Hunterston, whose father has appointed him 'Clan Administrator'. The lands now comprise some 16 hectares (40 acres) around the 18th-century mansion house and the 15th-century castle.

Other prominent Hunter cadet families (apart from Polmood) are Bonnytoun and Doonholm, Auchterarder and Thurston, and the Hunter-Blairs of Blairquhan. There is a 'Hunter' tartan of 1819, a 'Hunter of Hunterston' designed recently and approved by the chief and the pattern sold commercially as 'Hunter'. The clansman's badge is a hunting dog, with the motto *Cursum perficio*.

Innes

Clan Innes descends from Berowald, a knight of Flanders who was given the lands of Innes in Moray by Malcolm IV (1153–65). It was Berowald's grandson who assumed the name of Innes, as recognized in a charter of 1226 from Alexander II (1214–49). The 9th Chief of Innes, Alexander, added to the clan territory when he married the heiress to the last Lord of Aberchirder.

The 15th Chief, William Innes, had a seat in Scotland's historic Reformation Parliament of

Innes crest badge

1560. By this time there were several branches of the family, mostly in the north of Scotland. The 20th Chief, Robert Innes, was Member of Parliament for Moray; he was made a baronet in 1625. The 6th Baronet and 25th Chief, Sir James Innes, claimed the Dukedom of Roxburghe in 1805 when his kinsman the 4th Duke died without a direct heir. Sir James was eventually successful when the House of Lords decided in his favour in 1812. He added the Roxburghe surname Ker, and was titled James Innes-Ker, 5th Duke of Roxburghe; he died in 1823. The present Duke is the 10th.

Irvine

Irvine, Irving, and Irwin are Old English personal names from *eoforwine*, 'boar friend'. However, the Scottish surname derives from two territorial sources: the Parish of Irving in Dumfriesshire, and the Parish of Irvine in Ayrshire. From either source, 'Irvine' is the more common rendering, and Robert 'de Hirwine' (1226) is the first of the name recorded. The Robert 'de Iruwyn' who witnessed a charter about the year 1260 may be the same person, or his son.

The ancestor of the chiefly family, the Irvines of Drum, was William 'de Irwyne', Clerk of Register for Scotland. He was armour-bearer to King Robert the Bruce, and in 1324 obtained the lands of the Forest of Drum in a free Barony. His descendant, remembered in verse as 'Gude Sir Alexander Irvine, the much renownit Laird of Drum', died at the Battle of Harlaw in 1411.

In Ayrshire Adam Irvine, Burgess of the town of Irvine, was recorded in 1455, but in an Act of 1587 producing a Roll of Clans and Landlords, the Irvines of Boneschaw were apparently regarded as the major family. In Ireland there is sometimes confusion with the name 'Erwin', which is an anglicized form of 'O'Hirwen'. Most Irwins and Irvines in Ulster stem from the notorious 'Plantation' of that province with Scots settlers in the early 17th century.

Some Irvines settled in the Northern Isles, where

the name sometimes appeared as 'Vrowing', 'Vruving', or 'Vrwin'. The American author, Washington Irving, was the son of William Irving of Shapinsay in Orkney. The present Chief of the Clan is C.F. Irvine of Drum.

Jardine

The surname is derived from the French *jardin* or 'garden' or 'orchard'. A Norman knight called du Jardin fought at Hastings in 1066. The first in Scotland was probably Walfredus de Jardine, recorded before 1153 as witness to the charter to the Abbey of Kelso by King David I (1124–53).

In 1296, the name is rendered 'd'Gardino', which was anglicized to 'Orchard', with the seal of the bearer indicating a tree. By the 14th century the 'Jardings' were established at Applegirth, a parish on the River Annan in Dumfriesshire just north of Lockerbie. Not being a major clan, the Jardines of Applegirth were in frequent conflict with their more aggressive neighbours in the Border country: the Armstrongs, Maxwells, and Johnstones. They lost control of one of their earliest strongholds, Spedlins Tower, and their later seat at Jardine Hall has also passed out of their hands.

Alexander Jardine of Applegirth was created a Baronet of Nova Scotia in 1672, and the now expanding and prosperous family began to send its younger sons abroad to seek their fortune. Sir William Jardine (1800–74), the 7th Baronet, grew up under the influence of the botanical discoveries of Sir Jospeh Banks during Captain Cook's voyages to the Pacific, and wrote several books on natural history. His nephew Frank was also drawn to the lure of the islands, marrying the niece of the King of Samoa and opening up north-eastern Australia. The new Australian state became known as Queensland, and seven of its premiers between 1866 and 1903 were fellow Scots. Frank Jardine settled there with his bride, and called one of his properties 'Lockerbie'.

One of the most influential of the Jardines was Dr William Jardine (1784–1843), a surgeon with the East India Company. Around 1827, he began a trading company in Canton, in partnership with James Matheson. The firm of Jardine Matheson was the first to establish a warehouse in Hong Kong, and grew to be the most influential merchant colossus in the Far East.

The present Chief is Sir Alec Jardine of Applegirth, 12th Baronet and 23rd Chief of Clan Jardine. His father once swore that there was not and never would be a Jardine tartan, because of the family's Lowland origins. But pressure from overseas members of the clan brought about his authorizaton of a Jardine sett in the 1970s, and Sir Alec has now designed – by computer – a pattern for his clan. The clansman's crest badge is a 'Spurrowel' (a spinning spur) with the ominous family motto of *Cave Adsum* ('Beware, I am Here') – a motto poached by Sir Walter Scott, in *Ivanhoe*, for the villainous Sir Reginald Front-de-Boeuf.)

Johnstone

This is a Border clan that goes back at least to the 12th century. The clan held territory in or near Annandale, which eventually became a Barony. A John de Johnstoun had a son, Sir Gilbert, who is believed to have lived in the last quarter of the 12th century and the first quarter of the 13th. Gilbert's grandson is mentioned in 1296. Several branches of the clan emerged and all, it seemed, supported the Stewarts for many generations. For centuries, Clan Johnstone was involved in feuding with neighbouring clans, especially the Clan Maxwells, but were often in league with the smaller Clan Elliot (*see* Elliot).

In 1633, Sir James Johnstone was created Lord Johnstone by Charles I, and was later advanced to the Earldom of Hartfell. During the dramatic year of 1644–45 he displayed all the canny flair for survival required of a successful Border family. He was slow to declare for Montrose in 1644, and only swore allegiance to the Royalist cause after the Covenant defeat at Kilsyth in August had left Montrose virtually master of Scotland. Though sentenced to death by the vengeful Covenant leaders after the defeat of Montrose at Philiphaugh, Hartfell was pardoned due to the influence of the Duke of Argyll. After the Restoration, in 1661, his son James was created Earl of Annandale and Hartfell, and he died in 1672. His heir, William Johnstone, was created Marquess of Annandale in 1701.

The title became dormant in 1792, but in the 1980s, Lord Lyon King of Arms recognized Major Perey Hope Johnstone as Johnstone of Annandale and of that Ilk, after the family dropped the compound surname Hope-Johnstone. The chief was acknowledged at the same time as 10th Earl of Annandale and Hartfell. The present chief is his son Patrick Hope Johnstone, chief of the Whole Name and Arms of Johnstone, and 11th Earl of Annandale and Hartfell.

The Aberdeen branch of the Johnstones was represented by the Baronets of Caskieben, who migrated to Alabama in 1887. The 14th baronet is the fourth in line to bear the name Sir Thomas Alexander Johnstone of Caskieben, Bart. – although the United States does not really approve of foreign titles.

Keith

The Keiths were for centuries the hereditary Earls Marischal of Scotland; the first Keith, probably of the early 12th century, was Great Marischal. The Keiths acquired lands in East Lothian and also in Caithness where they feuded with Clan Gunn.

Sir Robert Keith, Great Marischal, distinguished himself in the Battle of Bannockburn (1314). He commanded a force of 500 horsemen with great skill, driving off a large company of English archers that was threatening the Scottish left wing. When the battle was won and the English put to flight, some 60 of Keith's horsemen accompanied Sir James Douglas to Stirling in an attempt to capture the defeated English King Edward II, but he escaped.

Sir William Keith, Great Marischal during the reign of James II (1437–60), was created first Earl Marischal of Scotland. Anne Keith, daughter of the 4th Earl, married James Stuart who was Earl of Moray, Regent of Scotland from 1567 to 1570. Their son George, the 5th Earl (1553–1623), founded Marischal College at Aberdeen University in 1593.

The 7th Earl Marischal, William Keith (1617–61) was Lord Privy Seal to King Charles II for the first year of his reign. William's brother, Sir John Keith, held the family castle at Dunnottar against Cromwell during the Parliamentary campaign in Scotland (1650), and thereby managed to save the Scottish Crown regalia: the Honours of Scotland.

One of the sons of the 9th Earl Marischal, James Francis Edward Keith (1676–1758) served in first the Spanish army, then in the Russian army of Tsar Peter the Great. Keith was a Russian general in Peter's wars against the Turks and the Swedes. He crowned a remarkable career by being made a marshal in the Prussian army and Governor of Berlin by Frederick the Great, King of Prussia (1740–86), being killed in the Battle of Hochkirch during the Seven Years War of 1756–63.

The chief is Michael Keith, 13th Earl of Kintore.

Keith crest badge

Below: Fishermen's cottages on the Banffshire coast of Clan Keith territory.

Kennedy

The founder of Clan Kennedy, Duncan Kennedy of Carrick, was created 1st Earl of Carrick by Malcolm IV (1153–65). His grandson, Roland Kennedy of Carrick, was made chief of the clan in 1256. A descendant, John Kennedy of Dunure in Ayr, was an associate of Kings David II and Robert II; he was granted the lands of Castlys, or Cassilis, also in Ayr.

John's grandson James Kennedy married Mary, daughter of King Robert III (1390–1424). They had two sons, both of whom became distinguished Scottish statesmen. Gilbert, created 1st Lord Kennedy in 1457, was one of the six Regents who governed Scotland during the minority of James III (1460–88). The other son, James Kennedy, became Bishop of Dunkeld and later of St Andrews, and finally Chancellor of Scotland. He is still remembered as one of the greatest of all Scottish statesmen, renowned, in what was a treacherous and self-seeking age, for his singleness of purpose and integrity of character.

There is a story of how Bishop Kennedy persuaded James II not to despair over his bitter wrangles with the Douglas family, which had been joined by other lords and clan chiefs hoping to oust the Stewarts. Kennedy placed in front of the King a bundle of arrows tied with a leather strap. 'Put the bundle on your knee and break it,' Kennedy told the King. James said that it was impossible. The Bishop replied: 'Yes, you can. I'll show you how.' With that he undid the strap, broke the arrows one by one, and piled the bits on the floor. The King got the message at once: he must detach the supporters of Douglas one by one, with promises of rewards. Then he could concentrate on breaking Douglas; and so it fell out. The Douglas threat to the Crown was finally overcome in 1455.

The 3rd Lord Kennedy was made 1st Earl of Cassilis in 1509 by James IV (1488–1513). He fell in battle, with the King and many of the Scottish lords, at Flodden Field in 1513. His grandson, the 3rd Earl of Cassilis, was Lord Treasurer of Scotland from 1554 to 1558. He was poisoned in France while on a mission to arrange the marriage of Mary, Queen of Scots, with the French Dauphin François.

John Kennedy, the 6th Earl, sided with the Scottish Covenant against Charles I in the Great Civil War. A Presbyterian zealot, whose nickname was 'The Solemn', he was forced to flee to Ireland after the defeat of the Covenant at Kilsyth (15 August, 1645) which briefly left Montrose master of Scotland. He was afterwards one of the Covenanting envoys who haggled with the exiled Charles II over the humiliating terms on which the King would be recognized on his throne of Scotland.

In 1831 the 12th Earl of Cassilis was created 1st Marquess of Ailsa by King William IV. The present chief is the Marquess of Ailsa O.B.E.

Kerr

The Kerrs were of Anglo-Norman origin, and first appeared in Roxburghshire in the 12th century. They branched out into many families, the main ones being Kerr of Cessford and Kerr of Ferniehirst. The Marquessate of Lothian is descended from the Cessford Kerrs, and the title was created in 1701. The name Kerr is also found as 'Ker' and 'Carr'.

Right: The Kennedy Castle at Culzean in Ayrshire.

Kennedy crest badge

One of the Kerrs, Andrew, conspired with Lord Darnley and others to murder David Rizzio, Italian secretary to Mary, Queen of Scots. When the gang came to her drawing room one day in 1566 to carry out the deed, Andrew Kerr held a pistol to the Queen's breast while the others cut down the wretched secretary at her feet. Robert Kerr, the 2nd Earl of Lothian (died 1624), committed suicide, in circumstances darkly rumoured to have involved the practice of witchcraft.

Probably the most famous (or notorious) of the Kerrs was Robert Kerr or Carr of the Ferniehirst branch, who became the favourite of King James VI of Scotland and I of England. He was knighted in 1607, created Viscount Rochester and made a Knight of the Garter in 1611, advanced to the Earldom of Somerset in 1613, and made Lord Chamberlain in 1614.

In 1613 he had married Frances, daughter of the 1st Earl of Suffolk and the divorced wife of Robert Devereux, 3rd Earl of Essex, son of the wayward Essex of Elizabeth I's time. Together they plotted to murder Sir Thomas Overbury, an English poet and courtier who had been knighted by James I in 1608. They devised a trumped-up charge against Overbury who was sent to the Tower of London in April 1613, and who was found dead from poison in September. No action was taken for nearly three years but, in 1616, pressure forced the King to allow an official enquiry into the circumstances of Overbury's death. The countess confessed, and the Earl's conviction followed swiftly. They were confined in separate quarters in the Tower until 1624, when they were pardoned.

Kincaid

The lands of Kincaid in the Parish of Campsie, Stirlingshire, are the origin of this surname and the small clan connected with it. Robert 'Kyncade of Kyncade' appears as a witness in records of 1450 and 1451. Six years later, land charters at St Leonards in Edinburgh were witnessed by Patrick and George 'de Kynkad', who were presumably close relatives. David 'de Kyncade' was registered as a baillie in Edinburgh in 1467; Thomas 'Kyncayd of that Ilk' witnessed charters to the collegiate church at Biggar in 1545 and was recorded again in 1550, this time as 'Kincaide'. Other variants of the name in Scotland were 'Kinkaid' (1547) and 'Kynked' (1493). As 'Kinkead' and 'Kincaid', the name became well established in several northern counties of Ulster by the middle of the 17th century, but especially in Antrim and Derry. A branch also settled further south in County Sligo.

The present Chief is Madam Heather Kincaid of Kincaid, and there is a tartan for the name.

Kerr crest badge

Below: Glamis Castle, seat of the Lyon branch of Clan Lamont.

Lamont

The early history of the Lamonts is not clear, but the family first appears in the Cowal region of Argyll in the early 13th century; a lord of Cowal called Ladman, or Lauman, is regarded as the founder of the clan. A John Lamont of Inveryne, owner of Toward Castle, was knighted in 1539.

The Lamonts became well established in Knapdale, but in the 17th century, the clan clashed repeatedly with the formidable and much more powerful Clan Campbell. In 1646 the Campbells invaded the Lamont territory in Argyll between Loch Striven and the Firth of Clyde. Led by Sir Colin Campbell of Ardkinglas, they besieged Toward Castle and attacked the Lamont stronghold at Ascog – despite the fact that Sir James Lamont, the clan chief, was married to Sir Colin's daughter.

In the face of the Campbell onslaught, Sir James Lamont offered to surrender and proposed a treaty by which he would agree to yield Toward Castle and other possessions in return for safe conducts for his family, descendants, and clansmen. No sooner had they agreed to this treaty than the Campbells seized Sir James and imprisoned him in

Lamont crest badge

Dunstaffnage Castle, keeping him there for five years without allowing him ever to change his clothes. The rest of the Lamont family and clans-folk were kept in custody for a week, during which time one or two of the women were killed. Meanwhile the Lamont lands were ravaged and some 3,000 head of cattle stolen.

But the worst of this tale of Campbell perfidy was yet to come. The remaining prisoners were hurried off to the Lamont town of Dunoon. In a churchyard there, more than 100 Lamonts were shot, stabbed, or had their throats cut, while three dozen of the leading Lamont men were hanged from the same tree, cut down while still alive, and hurled into ready-dug pits where they were covered with earth, many being stifled to death. Yet Clan Lamont survived this atrocity and today has branches both in Scotland and overseas, including Australia.

Leask

The name of this small clan comes from the old lands of Leask – now Pitlurg – near Slains in Aberdeenshire. William 'Lask of Lask' granted the Church of St Mary at Ellon a yearly pound of wax from his lands. Thomas 'de Laysk', in the year 1390, was Baillie of the Barony of Findon, and in 1391 witnessed a charter by Henry Sinclair, Earl of Orkney.

Amy 'Lowsk', in 1402, showed commendable mercantile enterprise (alas, only by modern stan-dards) when she was accused of 'being a forestaller' – an old term for cornering the market in a certain range of goods. Umfra 'Laysk of that Ilk' granted a charter of a piece of land called 'Brinthous', in Aberdeen, in 1461. There were migrations of Leasks to Orkney from very early on, and James of 'Lask', described as 'Lawman', is recorded there in 1438. The name is comparatively rare today.

The present Chief is Madam Leask of Leask, who recorded a tartan for the name in the 1970s.

The ancient Principality of the Lennox, embraced much of Loch Lomond in medieval times.

Lennox

The district of old Levanax, consisting today of what is mainly Dunbartonshire, was an important region of Scotland in early times, ruled by one of the Celtic princes known as *Mormaers*. From it, there arose the powerful Earldom of Lennox, which became part of the Royal House of Stewart.

Henry, Lord Darnley, who became King-Consort to Mary, Queen of Scots, was son of the 4th Earl of Lennox, and inherited a place in the succession to the English throne through his Tudor grandmother. Esme Stewart, a favourite of James VI and I, was created Duke of Lennox. The same Dukedom was revived by Charles II to bestow on his illegitimate son by Louise de Kerouaille, whom he had already ennobled as Duchess of Portsmouth.

The name Lennox survives as a more mundane surname from the late Middle Ages, and its bearers

would seem to have been as disreputable as their noble and royal kinsfolk. In 1508 William Lennox or Levinax was accused of 'forethought felony and oppression' – a quaint term to describe a serious and premeditated crime, as opposed to the spur-of-the-moment murder committed by George Lennox at Glenluce in 1526.

Far more respectable were Robert Lenox, a Scots merchant who emigrated to the emergent United States in 1784; and his son John Lenox (1800–90), who founded the Lenox Library – now incorporated into the internationally-renowned New York Public Library.

The Chief of the Clan today is Edward Lennox of that Ilk. There is a Lennox tartan, which is possibly an old regional pattern. It is said to have featured in a contemporary portrait of the Countess of Lennox, Lord Darnley's mother; a portrait last seen in a private collection in Paris around the middle of the 19th century. If genuine, this would date the pattern to at least 1550.

Leslie

In the 12th century a Flanders knight called Bardolf, or Bartholomew, acquired lands in the Leslie region of the Garioch, in Aberdeenshire. In time, his family came to be known as Leslie.

A Sir Andrew de Leslie was one of the signatories of the Declaration of Arbroath which proclaimed Scotland's independence in 1320. By the end of the 14th century, Leslies had infiltrated into the Scottish royal family through judicious marriages. The Leslies had inherited the great Earldom of Ross when the second son of Sir Andrew Leslie married the heiress of that family, and they had widened their landholdings extensively, acquiring Rothes, Fythkill, and Balquhain.

George Leslie, the great-grandson of Sir Andrew, was created Earl of Rothes and John Leslie, the 6th Earl, was made Duke of Rothes in 1680 by Charles II. When he died without male issue, the dukedom ended with him, though the earldom passed to his daughter Margaret, ancestress of the Earls of Rothes today. There are also several cadet branches of the Leslies, which include the family headed by the Earl of Leven and Melville.

One of the most distinguished of the Leslies was Sir Alexander ('Sandy') Leslie, created 1st Earl of Leven in 1641. Born in 1580 (or thereabouts), he became the commanding officer of Scottish mercenaries fighting for King Gustavus Adolphus of Sweden, champion of the Protestant cause in the Thirty Years War (1618–48). Leslie was noted for the strict discipline he imposed on his troops: no looting, no burning, no molesting women, and no refusal of quarter to a beaten enemy trying to surrender. 'Murder', he insisted, 'is no less intolerable in time of war than it is in time of peace'.

Retiring from the German wars with the rank of marshal in Gustavus's army, Alexander Leslie was given command of the national army when the Scottish Covenanters declared war on King Charles I. One of Leslie's officers testified to the awe in which he was held in the Scotland of the late 1630s: 'Such was the wisdome and authoritie

Leslie crest badge

of that old, little, crooked souldier that all, with ane incredible submission, from the beginning to the end, give over themselves go be guided by him, as if he had been Great Solyman.' Leslie led the Scottish army into England during the 'Bishops' War' of 1640, capturing Newcastle and humiliating King Charles I – who nevertheless created Leslie Earl of Leven in the ensuing peace settlement with the Scots. Leven repaid this honour by commanding the Scottish army in alliance with the English Parliamentarian forces at Marston Moor in 1644.

Another fighting Leslie who championed the Covenant cause was David Leslie, the fifth son of Sir Patrick Leslie of Pitcairly in Fife. Though of no direct relationship to Leven, David Leslie served the same military apprenticeship under Gustavus Adolphus in Germany before returning to Scotland to fight for the Covenant. He too fought with the Scots at Marston Moor but is chiefly remembered for ending Montrose's run of victories at Philiphaugh in 1645. Before marching to defeat at David Leslie's hands, Montrose had gallantly vowed that 'though God should rain Leslies from Heaven, he would fight them'. Created Lord Newark by Charles II at the Restoration, David Leslie outlived Leven by 21 years, dying of apoplexy in 1682. The chief is the Earl of Rothes.

Lockhart

A classic example of a family that predates many larger and more famous clans, the Lockharts came from Normandy to settle at 'the Lee' in Lanarkshire in 1272. Their name was originally spelled 'Locard', an Old French personal name, but in 1330 Sir Simon Locard acted as custodian to the keys of the casket containing the heart of King Robert the Bruce, which was then carried to a holy repository in Jerusalem. In typical 'canting' or punning style, the surname was changed to Lockhart to reinforce the family's prestige, with a lockfast heart being added to the knight's coat of arms.

Sir Simon also brought back from the Holy Land the 'Lee Penny': a magic Arabic cure-all stone which the knight received as part of the ransom for an emir he had captured. Sir Walter Scott, whose daughter married John Gibson Lockhart, based his novel *The Talisman* on the incident, and the stone is carefully guarded by the family to this day. It is said to cure sickness in humans, cattle, and horses.

Lockharts have been prominent in every century since they first set foot in Scotland, but like many old families of note they have never been ennobled. They were a famous legal family who both infuriated and pleased their adversaries. Sir William of the Lee fought both for and against King Charles I but was knighted by him, only to end up marrying Cromwell's niece and sitting in his Parliament – none of which prevented him from being made Ambassador to France when Charles II was restored to the throne in 1660. The contentious Sir George Lockhart, of Carnwath, was murdered by a disgruntled litigant in 1685. His son George, a famous Jacobite who opposed the Union with England in 1707 but later became a reluctant Commissioner for it, was arrested for his political views in 1715 but fled to Holland, where he was killed in a duel. The Lockhart lairds were variously involved in the Jacobite risings of 1715 and 1745–46, but confirmed the family's talent for survival. On one occasion, Lockhart of the Lee managed to ride so swiftly from the battlefield to his house that he was able to convince the Government troops, sent to arrest him, that he had never left home.

As well as their own tartan, the Lockharts wear the MacDonald clan sett as their tartan, after a marriage with an 18th-century MacDonald heiress.

Lumsden

This small clan derives its surname from the old manor of the name in the Parish of Coldingham, Berwickshire. The first of the name on record in Scotland were Gillem and Cren 'de Lumisden', witnessing a charter around 1170; Adam and Roger 'de Lummesdene' paid homage to Edward I of England in 1296. The Lumsdens of that Ilk acquired the lands of Blanerne, by Duns in Berwickshire, by a charter of 1329. In the early 15th century, the territorial name of Lumsden was reapplied to new lands in Aberdeenshire.

The muster rolls of the Scots Archer Guard to the King of France around 1498 list the surname variously as 'Lunsten', 'Lumesten', 'Le Musten', 'Lomesdel', and 'Alomesden'. James Lumsden of Innergellie (1598–1660) and his two brothers Robert and William, served under King Gustavus Adolphus of Sweden in the Thirty Years War (1618–48). 'Lumsden's Musketeers' was a regiment raised by James Lumsden. Andrew Lumsden (1720–1801) was Secretary to Bonnie Prince Charlie in 1745.

Over the centuries there has generally been a close association – though no vassal relationship – between the Aberdeenshire branches of the Lumsdens and the Clan Forbes. Some authorities wrongly claim the Lumsdens to be a branch of the Forbes. The other branches of Clan Lumsden are Cushnie, Pitcaple, and Tillycairn. The present chief is Gillem Lumsden of that Ilk and Blanerne.

The clansman's crest badge is 'An Osprey or Sea Eagle Devouring a Salmon', with the motto 'Beware in Time'. There are five acknowledged Lumsden tartans.

MacAlister

The Clan MacAlister descends from the great Somerled, the half-Viking, half-Scottish hero who became King of the Hebrides and Argyll in the 1140s. It was Somerled's grandson Donald of Islay, Lord of the Isles, whose son Alasdair Mor gave his name to Clan MacAlister, which means 'Son of Alasdair' (the Gaelic version of Alexander). Alasdair Mor held land in south Knapdale, with a seat at Tarbert. In 1299 he was killed in a feud with his kinsman Alasdair MacDougall, Lord of Lorne, also a descendant of Somerled.

Apart from its illustrious ancestry, not much is known of Clan MacAlister's history. In 1480 Charles MacAlister was made Steward of Kintyre, which adjoins Knapdale. He belonged to one of the clan branches. Another branch had lands at Loup, and there is a record of a MacAlister chief in 1493. The family makes another brief appearance on record in the reign of James VI (1567–1625). It is known that Alexander MacAlister of Loup fought at the Battle of Killiecrankie in 1689 on the side of Dundee, and that he was present at the Battle of the Boyne in Ireland in 1690, on the side of the exiled James II – James VII of Scotland.

Left: MacAlister crest badge
Right: MacArthur crest badge

MacArthur

The origins of the MacArthurs are obscure but they were certainly *not* descendants of King Arthur, that mythical figure of ancient Britain in the last days of the Romans (who, if he existed at all, was probably a Romano-British cavalry leader who managed to keep at bay the Anglo-Saxons attempting to settle in what is now southern England, towards the end of the 5th century AD). It is more likely that the MacArthurs came from one of the early Campbell families in Argyll.

Arthur, a son of Sir Arthur Campbell, is mentioned in a charter of 1275 as receiving lands in Moidart, Arisaig, and on the islands of Rhum and Eigg. The MacArthurs of Strachur, on Loch Fyne, were the main branch of the clan and appear to have supported Robert the Bruce. Iain MacArthur, Chief of the Clan, described as 'a great prince among his own people', was put to death in 1427 by James I (1406–37). MacArthur's offence was probably that of having given support to Murdoch Stewart, Duke of Albany, Regent of Scotland from 1420 to 1424. Most of the MacArthur lands were forfeited at this time. The clan declined, and some of the members served as castellans of the Earl of Argyll's castle at Innisconnell.

In 1790 John MacArthur, born in 1767, joined the Army and was sent out to the penal colony of New South Wales in Australia, where he pioneered large-scale sheep farming, and also introduced the vine to the colony. He is remembered as one of Australia's 'founding fathers', and also for having inspired the mutiny of January 1808 which deposed William Bligh (of *Bounty* fame).

The greatest MacArthur of the 20th century was a descendant of the clan: American military hero General of the Army Douglas MacArthur. After becoming the youngest American Brigadier-General of World War I and building up the defences of the Philippines between the wars, MacArthur reversed the shattering Japanese conquests of 1941–42 as American Commander in the South-West Pacific. He accepted the surrender of Japan in September 1945, and commanded the United Nations forces which prevented the Communist conquest of South Korea in 1950–51.

The chiefship is vacant.

MacAulay

There are two separate origins of this surname, one Hebridean and the other in the south-west Highlands. The MacAulays of Uig derive from Gunni Olafson, a Norse chieftain who was received hospitably by the MacLeod chief after being expelled from Orkney by its Earl. Gunni was given lands on Lewis, which belonged to Norway until 1266. He had earlier settlements in Ross-shire on the mainland and the name of MacAulay is not uncommon today in the vicinity of Ullapool – which is Norse for 'the homestead of Olaf'. In Gaelic, 'son of Olaf' became *mac Amhlaibh*, which sounds as 'MacAulay' in English. The Uig MacAulays still owe allegiance to Clan MacLeod and its chief, but there has been a centuries-old feud with the Morrisons of Lewis.

Thomas, 1st Baron MacAulay (1800–59), best known for his *Lays of Ancient Rome* and *A History of England*, was a brilliant scholar and essayist whose roots were among the Lewis clan. His father Zachary MacAulay became a leading light in the movement for the abolition of slavery, after a chequered career managing plantations on Jamaica.

The MacAulays of Ardencaple on the mainland were first recorded when 'Duncan *filius (mac)* Auleth' witnessed a charter by Malcom, Earl of Levenax, in 1285. Their lands were in the Lennox, stretching for some 10 km (6 miles) from Cardross to Garelochhead on the eastern shore of the Gareloch. Their name stems from the Gaelic *mac Amhalghaidh*, which is an Old Irish personal name.

'Duncan *filius* Auleth' was probably son of one of the younger sons of the Earl of Lennox at the end of the 12th century – *Amhalghaidh mac Amhalghaidh*. He bore an Old Irish patronymic because of the descent of the Lennox dynasty from the Irish kings of Munster. The MacAulays were always described by their friends as 'not numerous, but of good account'. As cousins of the Earls of Lennox their influence – and landholdings – waxed and waned with the fortunes of the Earldom.

The MacAulay Chief was referred to as 'Aulay Ardincaple of that Ilk' until 1536, when he begins to appear in documents in the full patronymic style. 'Awla McAwla of Ardencapill' is probably more in keeping with the chief's claim to be head of the whole name of MacAulay. He acknowledged, in a bond with the Chief of Clan Gregor of 1592, that he was also of the *siol Alpin* (stemming from the legendary King of the Scots of Dalriada from whom many clans drew claims of antiquity). But while admitting to MacGregor that he was 'of his hous', MacAulay insisted that he must 'haiff his awin libertie of the name M'Cawley as chyffe'. Five years previously, MacAulay had been listed in the 'Roll of Landlordis and Baillies' of 1587 as 'The Laird M'Cawla of Ardincaple', but the Statute of 1594 refers to 'M'Cawlis' in the category of 'many broken men of the surnames of . . .'

The connection with the MacGregors proved damaging for the MacAulays after the *Gregorach* were outlawed in 1604, and their Campbell neighbours in particular were eager to include the Ardincaple clan in the repression of the MacGregors. The Earl of Argyll, Chief of Clan Campbell, was accused of 'Lying at wait for the Laird of Ardincapill upon set purpose to have him slane'.

By the mid-17th century, MacAulays were appearing far from Lennox, a sign that adherence to clan traditions was slackening. John 'M'Kauley', merchant burgess of Edinburgh in 1623, is mentioned as the heir to Thomas 'M'Cauley'. Another Thomas, 'writer to the signet', or lawyer, is recorded as 'Makcaulay' in 1638, 'M'Callow' in 1647 and 'M'Calley' in 1648. Forty years later, George

'Makallay' was heir to Patrick 'M'Kalla', an apothecary in Cupar, Fife.

By the end of the 17th century, the MacAulay lands of Ardincaple were being sold piecemeal to support the extravagance of the lairds who had set up homes in the south, after following in the train of James VI when he became King James I of England. Laird Archibald McAulay sold off the lands on which the town of Helensburgh now stands, together with Faslane, where the British nuclear submarine base is now located. All the clan lands had gone by 1767, when the last chief was forced to sell Ardincaple Castle to settle his debts shortly before he died. The seat of the MacAulays was promptly purchased by the Duke of Argyll, after centuries of attempting to oust the MacAulay chiefs. After it was sold on to Sir James Colquhoun of Luss, an attempt was made in the 1920s to re-purchase the now-ruined castle and the 18th-century house at Ardincaple, but by then the clan had dispersed all over the world. The chiefship today is vacant.

The MacAulay clansman's crest is a 'Spurred Boot', with the motto *Dulce periculum* ('Sweet danger'). There are four recorded tartans for the name.

MacAulay crest badge   *MacBean crest badge*

MacBean

The Highland name MacBean or MacBain (whose subtle Gaelic vowel-sound lies somewhere between the English 'bean' and 'bane') comes from the Gaelic *mac Beathain*, 'sons of Beathan'. The heartland of the clan is at the north-eastern end of Loch Ness, where the MacBeans rub shoulders with their confederates in the Clan Chattan (*see* Chattan): the clans Shaw, MacGillivray, and MacKintosh. The four principal families within the clan are Drummond, Faillie, Kinchyle, and Tomatin, but the

McBains of Kinchyle are the chiefly line.

Aeneas MacBean of Kinchyle, eldest son of the chief, fought in the Jacobite Rising of 1715 in the MacKintosh Regiment. His giant of a younger brother, Gillies mor MacBean, died a hero's death at Culloden. As a major in the Mackintosh Regiment which had had to be called out by the wife of the stay-at-home chief (see Mackintosh), Gillies was seen by a Government officer with his back to a wall, fighting off a horde of Redcoats, 12 of whom he had already killed single-handed. The officer yelled 'Save that brave man!' but Gillies was already mortally wounded, and his opponents ill-inclined to be lenient anyway.

After Culloden a succession of chiefs struggled to keep the MacBean lands together, but Kinchyle finally had to be sold in 1760 and the direct line of the chiefs died out. Sons of the clan, however, continued to earn renown. In November 1857, Private John McBean of the Sutherland Highlanders was awarded the Victoria Cross (one of six 'won before breakfast') for his gallantry at the Relief of Lucknow in the Indian Mutiny. More than a century later, American astronaut Commander Alan Bean carried a swatch of his Clan MacBean tartan to the surface of the Moon during the *Apollo 12* Lunar Mission in November 1969.

In 1959 Hughston McBain, President of the Marshall Field Corporation in Chicago, petitioned Lord Lyon to establish his right to be chief as the senior surviving representative of the Kinchyle line. At least six McBeans and McBains had been transported to the plantations in Virginia, Maryland and South Carolina after the 1715 rising – sparing them and their posterity from the slaughter of 1746, which weeded out the sons of the chiefly line back in Scotland. Hughston's petition was successful, and he was duly acknowledged as '21st Chief of the Whole Name and Arms of McBain'.

He once told a group of Scots businessmen that he became embarrassed among Americans at having constantly to explain why his title repeated itself in such a pompous way. He wrote to Lord Lyon (Sir Thomas Innes of Learney) asking permission to drop the 'of McBain'. Lord Lyon's reply was simple: by all means drop it, but then you will also drop the chiefship and revert back to being plain 'Mr McBain'.

The present Chief is Hughston's son, James McBain of McBain, 22nd of Kinchyle, who now lives in Finger Rock, Arizona. The clansman's crest badge is 'A Wildcat Holding a Targe' (shield), with the Clan Chattan motto 'Touch not the Cat Bot (without) a Glove'. There are two MacBean/McBain tartans.

A private in the Gordon Highlanders rose to become Major-General Sir Hector MacDonald.

MacDonald

Clan MacDonald is one of the oldest and most famous of all the Scottish clans. At one time it controlled, as overlords, a huge area of western Scotland and the Isles, where for generations the MacDonald Chiefs ruled like kings. The MacDonalds, therefore, posed a considerable potential threat to the Kings of Scotland, and often played a key part in anti-Stewart or anti-Government conspiracies and rebellions. This was largely because they claimed independence from the rule of the Scottish monarchy, by virtue of their origins as Lords of the Isles.

To be a member of the MacDonalds or of one of their vassal clans – and there were several of these – had many advantages. On the whole the chiefs of Clan MacDonald were bold, forceful leaders, often with a strong sense of justice and concern for the welfare of their folk. One distinguished Scottish genealogist and historian wrote that 'the civilization of the Hebrides [under the MacDonalds] never recovered from the loss of Home Rule'.

The clan's family name in Gaelic was, more accurately, *Domnallach*, meaning 'of the Donalds'. Only the chief was (The) Mac Dhomnuill. The surname MacDonald was not used before the 16th

Castle Tioram was once a stronghold of the MacDonalds of Clanranald.

MacDonald crest badge

century. The clan stems from Donald, grandson of Somerled, the half Norse/half Scot ruler of western Scotland and the Isles who was killed fighting the Scots in 1164. Somerled's son Ranald, by his second wife Ragnhild, daughter of Olaf, King of Man, died in 1207 and left three sons: Donald Roderick, and Comyn. The largest share of the huge Ranald empire, including South Kintyre and Islay, fell to Donald.

Donald's son Angus ruled his wide domains in the style of an independent king, with a court, laws, and an army. His son Angus Og supported King Robert the Bruce (1306–29) while retaining the MacDonald independence, which Bruce was not disposed to challenge. Angus Og's son John, Lord of the Isles (a title he assumed in the 1340s) married Amy MacRuari, and their son Archibald (or Ranald) became ancestor of the MacDonalds of Clanranald.

Probably in the 1360s, John married again, his second bride being Margaret, daughter of Robert the Steward, later King Robert II (1371–90). When he died in 1387, their son Donald inherited the Lordship of the Isles and became the next chief of the clan. By virtue of his marriage to the aunt of the young Countess of Ross, Donald also laid claim to the Earldom of Ross.

Regarding himself as an independent prince and so free to make whatever treaties he liked with whomever he liked, Donald came to several agreements with England in the 1390s, and in 1408 he renewed this alliance with King Henry IV of England. When the Countess of Ross renounced her titles and retired to a nunnery in 1410, Donald saw his chance to renew his claim to the Ross Earldom. But another claim was lodged by the son of the Regent, the Duke of Albany (brother of the late King Robert III, who had died in 1406), and war broke out between the rival claimants. Donald marched his army across Scotland and fought the Battle of Harlaw near Aberdeen (1411), a gory stalemate after which he withdrew to his lands in the west. He never forgave the English, who had promised to support him.

In the 1430s, however, Donald's son Alexander MacDonald was recognized as Earl of Ross as well as Lord of the Isles. Under his son John MacDonald, Earl of Ross and 10th Lord of the Isles, the MacDonald power reached its zenith, with John maintaining the princely state of his forebears, even holding Parliaments at the clan seat of Ardtornish. But before long the entire MacDonald empire came under threat from the Scottish crown, in the formidable person of King James IV (1488–1513).

The conflict began in 1491 when John's nephew, Alexander MacDonald or Lochalsh, raided Inverness, seized its castle, and ravaged the neighbouring lands of Clan MacKenzie. A battle followed in which the MacDonalds were worsted by the MacKenzies. King James then discovered that Lord John had been intriguing with King Henry VII of England, and decided to put an end to the MacDonald power once and for all. In 1494 the King stripped John MacDonald of all his titles, with the Crown now assuming the Lordship of the Isles. John MacDonald died four years later, it is said a broken man in a common lodging-house in Dundee.

John MacDonald's son and grandson tried in vain to resurrect the MacDonald empire, and when Donald Dubh MacDonald died in 1545 the clan broke up. It remained divided into some nine more or less independent minor branches, which the Scottish Crown was ready to recognize as separate clans, many of which had already begun to come to terms with the House of Stewart. In the 1680s, Sir James MacDonald of Sleat, Chief of Clan Huistean, was recognized as Lord of MacDonald, and his heir Alexander MacDonald of MacDonald was later accepted as Chief when the Sleat lands were raised to the Barony of MacDonald. The Chiefs were raised to the Peerage as Lords Macdonald in 1776.

In the Great Civil War and the First Jacobite War of 1689–90, the MacDonalds fought loyally for the House of Stewart, and paid for this loyalty in 1692 by suffering the infamous Massacre of Glencoe. This came about when, after recovering from its defeat at Killiecrankie by the Jacobite army of John Graham, 'Bonnie Dundee' (1689), William III's Government determined to make an example of the MacDonalds in its drive to bring the Highlands to heel. The chosen victims were the MacDonalds of Glengarry and Glencoe. They were required to swear an oath of allegiance to William on pain of having their homes burned and themselves put to the sword – but under conditions which made it impossible for the oath to be sworn by the required date. Government orders were, therefore, sent to Captain Robert Campbell, one of the Glen Lyon Campbells, to 'fall upon the rebels . . . and put all to the sword under seventy'. On 13 February, 1692 the Campbells moved into Glencoe and accepted the hospitality of the unsuspecting MacDonalds, with Robert Campbell dining in apparent friendship with the MacDonald Chief. But before daybreak on the next day the Campbells rose silently from their beds and fell upon the sleeping MacDonalds, slaughtering 38 people including two women and a child of six. Neither King William nor the Campbells were ever forgiven for this frightful deed, which apart from its sheer savagery violated every ancient bond of mutual consideration between host and guest.

Among the nine branches of the MacDonalds were the MacDonalds of Clanranald, the first to rally to Bonnie Prince Charlie in 1745, with their junior branch, the MacDonalds of Glengarry. There were also the MacDonnells of Keppoch who descended from Alasdair MacDonald.

The present High Chief is Godfrey Macdonald, Baron Macdonald of MacDonald.

MacDougall

The Dougall after whom the MacDougalls take their name was one of three sons of Somerled, the half Norse/half Scots King of the Isles of the 12th century. When Somerled was killed in battle (1164) with the royal army of Malcolm IV (1153–65), his extensive territories passed to his sons, and Dougall received among his share the valuable province of Lorn. Dougall's son Duncan MacDougall inherited Lorn, and he appeared in a record of 1244 as Lord of Argyll. His son Ewen MacDougall, Lord of Lorn, wisely refused to support the campaign of King Haakon of Norway against Alexander III (1249–86), which ended in a decisive Scottish victory at Largs.

Ewen's son Alexander of Lorn, 4th Chief of the MacDougalls, became Sheriff of Argyll in 1292, presumably appointed by John Baliol, King of Scotland. In the early years of the 14th century, he also sided with the Red Comyn (whose aunt he had married) in Comyn's quarrel with Robert the Bruce. Ewen's other son Ian Bacach MacDougall offered support to the English in their attempt to overthrow Bruce in the years before the Battle of Bannockburn (1314). On one occasion the MacDougalls nearly captured Bruce in a skirmish, but he got away after throwing off his cloak, which was buckled by a brooch and which he left lying on the ground. This came to be called the 'Brooch of Lorn', and it is still in the possession of the MacDougalls today.

The MacDougalls paid dearly for their opposition to Bruce; after Bannockburn the victorious King deprived them of all their lands. Some were restored later in the century, but the MacDougall power was never the same again. When John MacDougall, 6th Chief of Lorn, died in 1388 without male issue, the remaining lands passed via John's daughter to the Stewarts, who became Lords of Lorn. But the clan itself continued in the MacDougall line through Ian MacDougall, a cousin of the last Lord of Lorn.

In 1457, Ian's great-grandson John, 10th Lord of Dunollie, was granted extensive lands around Dunollie Castle, which his descendants held for nearly 300 years. The MacDougalls supported the Old Pretender, Prince James Edward, in the Jacobite rising of 1715, and forfeited their possessions as a result. Having learned their lesson, they stayed out of the rising of 1745–46, after which some of their land was restored. Including the ruins of Dunollie Castle, it remains MacDougall land today. Madam Coline MacDougall of MacDougall and Dunollie, 30th hereditary chief, died on 5 May, 1990, aged 85.

Left: MacDonald of Clanranald crest badge
Right: MacDougall crest badge

MacDowall

Like the entirely distinct MacDougalls of Lorne in Argyll, the MacDowalls of Galloway, in the far south-west of Scotland, have a surname revealing descent from a 'namefather' called Dougal.

Galloway boasts Scotland's earliest historic link with Christianity. More than 150 years before Columba's mission from Ireland to Iona, and a full 200 years before Augustine arrived in Kent from Rome, a church was founded at Whithorn on the Solway Firth by the Scoto-Celtic missionary Ninian in AD 397. The wealth of Gaelic place-names and surnames in Galloway, and their structural elements, indicate direct influence from Ireland from the 6th century onwards, with the addition of renegade Irish associates of pagan Norsemen. Irish chronicles of the mid-9th century refer to them as the *Gal-gaidil*, whence the name 'Galloway'.

Whether the original Dougal was one of the ancient Lords of Galloway is difficult to establish, but the suggestion cannot be dismissed. The name *mac Dhughaill* preserved its early sounds of 'Dowell/Doo-ul', and the variant 'Cole/Cool', through Fergus 'McDhuile' (1296); Duncan 'MacDuel' (1307); Gilbert 'Macduyl' (1416); Uhtred 'Mcduwell' (1515); John 'McCoull' (1609); and John 'McQuhoull' (1621). MacDowells who settled in Ireland after the notorious 'Plantation of Ulster' in the early 17th century often became 'Madole'.

The 'Duwall' family which flourished as Swedish mercenaries in the 17th century are more likely to have been MacDowalls from Galloway than MacDougalls from Lorne. One prominent merchant, Patrick McDowall, settled in America before 1758. Samuel McDowell, a lawyer from Newton-Stewart in Wigtonshire, migrated to Camden, South Carolina in 1824 before moving to Chicago to ply his trade.

The MacDowall heartland is around Stranraer, in the extreme south-west, where their neighbours are the Agnews, Kennedys, McCullochs, and Hays. The principal family has its seat at Garthland, and the present Chief is Fergus MacDowall of Garthland.

The clansman's crest badge is 'A Hand Holding a Dagger' with the motto *Fortis in arduis* ('Strong in Adversity'). There is no specific tartan for Clan MacDowall, but either of the two Galloway patterns would be quite appropriate.

MacDuff

Clan MacDuff is sometimes described as Scotland's premier clan. Certainly it is a very old one, and until the 15th century its chiefs took second place only to the kings of Scotland at gatherings, led the van of the royal armies, had the right to enthrone the kings on the Stone of Scone (before that was stolen by Edward I of England and taken to London in 1296), and thereafter to crown the kings.

The chiefs of the Clan Macduff were from the late 11th century earls of Fife, and they also had extensive lands in the Highlands, Stirlingshire, and in the Lothians. The first two known chiefs were Constantine MacDuff, Earl of Fife from 1107, and his brother Gillemicheal, Earl of Fife in about 1127. Their father had been the eldest son of Aedh, Abbot of Dunkeld, who was the eldest son of Malcolm III (1057–93) and his wife Margaret, grand-daughter of the English King Edmund 'Ironside' (died 1016). Aedh was therefore the elder brother of King Edgar (1097–1107), Alexander I (1107–1124), and David I (1124–53). Aedh had not been able to succeed because he was a churchman.

In 1306, Robert the Bruce had himself crowned King at Scone. He was anxious to observe the ancient coronation traditions of the Scottish monarchy, but the then Chief of the MacDuffs, Duncan, 10th Earl of Fife, was a minor and a ward of Edward I of England. Bruce therefore arranged for Fife's sister, Isabel, Countess of Buchan, to place the golden circlet on his head, in the presence of the leading bishops and lords. Edward's response was to send an army into Scotland to arrest Bruce. The latter gave battle but was defeated and escaped, branded as an outlaw. Isabel Buchan was not so fortunate; nor were two of Bruce's brothers. She was displayed in a latticework cage hung from the walls of Berwick Castle; the brothers were hanged.

Duncan, the 12th and last MacDuff Earl of Fife, died in 1353. The earldom passed to Robert Stewart, brother of the future King Robert II (1371–90). He later became Duke of Albany and Regent of Scotland during the first 14 years of James I (1406–37), who spent 18 years in captivity in England (1406–24). Albany died in 1420 and was succeeded by his son Murdoch, who also became Earl of Fife. When James I finally came home to his

MacDuff crest badge

Duff House, a William Adam masterpiece built in 1735, in the heart of the once extensive lands of the Clan MacDuff in the north-east.

kingdom, he had Murdoch put to death along with other lords, largely for acts of misgovernment, corruption, theft, and murder during the previous years.

The eclipse of the main branch of Clan Macduff was not the end of the family, which survived in several branches as the Duffs. Some Duffs fought with the Jacobites during the risings of 1715 and 1745–46. In 1759 the earldom of Fife was revived when William Duff, of Braco, was created Earl of

Fife – but in the peerage of Ireland, not of Britain. He had offered his services to the Hanoverian Duke of Cumberland before the Battle of Culloden in 1746. His great-great-grandson Alexander, the 6th Earl, was advanced to Duke of Fife, when in 1889, he married Princess Louise, the eldest daughter of the Prince of Wales (afterwards Edward VII). Their daughter became Duchess of Fife, and she married the son of Arthur, Duke of Connaught, Queen Victoria's youngest son.

MacEwan

The 'namefather' of the MacEwans was *Eoghainn*, an early Celtic name meaning 'sprung from a yew tree'; but medieval manuscripts point to strong connections through the female line back to Anrothan O'Neill, of the Irish royal dynasty. The clan itself was known in Gaelic as *Clann Eoghain na h-Oitrich* ('MacEwans of the Otter'). In their heyday they were of considerable importance, especially in Cowal, where Castle MacEwan once controlled part of the coastline of Loch Fyne.

In the 12th century, the MacEwans controlled the entire region in concert with the Lamonts and the MacLachlans. But with the death of Swene, the 9th and last of the MacEwan 'Otter' chiefs in the mid-15th century, the clan lands were annexed by the Campbells of Argyll, to whom Swene had once unwisely granted a charter to a portion of those lands. By the time the Roll of Clans was published in 1587, Archibald Campbell was being described as the 'Laird of Otter'. The MacEwans had become a 'broken clan', with some MacEwans seeking the protection of the MacLachlans and others throwing in their lot with the Campbells of Argyll. One family is said to have become hereditary bards to a Campbell chieftain and received land with the position. Donald Dow M'Coull McQuhewin, although only part MacEwan, fell foul of the notorious Campbell Laird of Glenorchy, who 'heddit' (beheaded) him.

Other families moved *en masse* and formed MacEwan groupings in Dunbartonshire and Galloway, where the name is more common than in the clan's old heartland. In Galloway there were 'McEwyns' as early as the 14th century – probably long-distant kin. In 1698, Elspeth MacEwan won the dubious family distinction of being the last witch to be burned at the stake in Kirkcudbright. A branch which settled in Ayrshire, where there was a McEwinstoun as early as 1622, produced the 1st MacEwan Baronet, of Marchmont and Bardrochat, in 1953.

The MacEwan chiefship is vacant today. The clansman's crest badge is 'An Oak Stump With New Leaves Growing From It' with the motto *Reviresco* ('I Grow Again'). There is a specific 'MacEwan' tartan.

MacFarlane

The name MacFarlane comes from *mac Pharlain*, or 'son of Parlan', which is said to be a version of the Old Irish name Partholon, the equivalent of Bartholomew. The clan founder was Parlan, whose great-grandfather had been Gilchrist of Arrochar, a younger son of the then Earl of Lennox, who lived in the last quarter of the 12th century and the first quarter of the 13th. Parlan was contemporary with King David II (1329–71).

When Duncan, last of the old line of the earls of Lennox, died early in the 15th century, the Chief of Clan MacFarlane claimed the earldom but it was

Left: The winding road up Glen Croe in MacEwan country.

MacEwan crest badge   MacFarlane crest badge

given instead to the Stewarts of Darnley, descendants of Duncan of Lennox. The 10th Chief of Clan MacFarlane, Sir Andrew, married a daughter of the new Earl of Lennox, and their son Sir Iain fell at the Battle of Flodden in 1513. Sir Iain's grandson, the 13th Chief, was killed in the battle of Pinkie Cleugh when the English defeated the Scots. The next MacFarlane chief mustered some 300 clansmen to fight against Mary, Queen of Scots, in her last struggle before abdicating: the Battle of Langside in 1568. There is a suggestion that the MacFarlanes were trying to get their own back for not obtaining the Lennox earldom, for Mary's second husband, Lord Darnley, was the Lennox heir.

In the early 17th century, during the campaigns of James VI and I against some of the more unruly clans (such as the MacGregors), the MacFarlanes were proscribed and their lands forfeited. Many emigrated to America, some went to Ireland, and others moved to different parts of Scotland, where they changed their names.

In 1853, James MacFarlane, a pedlar, walked from Glasgow to London to have a volume of his lyrics published.

The chiefship is vacant.

MacFie

This surname can also be correctly spelled 'MacPhee', not to mention 'Duffie', 'MacDuffie', and a score or so variations on those four. ('Duffie' is often mistakenly assumed to be an Irish surname, as people have a tendency to confuse it with the quite separate Irish name 'Duffy'.) The oldest form of the surname, recorded around 1240, is *macdufthi* – close to the sound of the Gaelic *MacDubhsithe*, which could be translated as 'Son of the Secret Peacemaker' or even 'Son of the Fairy People'. It is one of the oldest surname constructions in the western world.

The homeland of the clan was the island of Colonsay, and the Hereditary Keeper of the Records of the Lords of the Isles was always a MacDuffie of Colonsay. The clan was closely linked with the fortunes of the Lordship, and its chief was beheaded after the last attempt to restore that lost kingdom of the Western Isles to the MacDonalds in 1615. Colonsay passed to the MacDonalds and thence via the Campbells to the McNeills, who sold the island in 1904.

As a 'broken clan', the MacFies/MacPhees/MacDuffies scattered around the world. For a while, in the United States, there were rival clans for each name. Lord Lyon appointed a Dr MacPhee as Clan Commander in the 1970s, upon whose

death the commander designate was believed to be Sylvia MacPhee of Toronto.

The clansman's crest badge is a 'Lyon Rampant' with the motto *Pro rege* ('For the King'); there are three acknowledged tartans for the name.

Left: MacFie crest badge
Right: MacGillivray crest badge

MacGillivray

The progenitor of this small clan was Gillivray – *gille bhruth* in Gaelic, 'servant of judgement' – who pledged allegiance for himself and his descendants to Farquhar Mackintosh, killed in 1274. The MacGillivrays are, therefore, one of the oldest branches of the powerful Clan Chattan confederation which was led by the Mackintoshes, but their original roots were in Argyll. The MacGillivrays settled at a place called Dunmaglas, which became the territorial designation of their chiefs. The first Laird of that name was Duncan MacGillivray, around 1500.

The MacGillivrays were deeply involved in the Jacobite risings of 1715 and 1745–46, and their Chief, Alexander, died fighting beside the 'Well of the Dead' at Culloden in 1746. The last chief in the direct line died in 1852, since when the chiefship has been vacant. In 1989, Lord Lyon appointed Colonel George Brown MacGillivray as Commander of the Clan for an interim period of five years, after which the clan must either re-elect him or nominate an alternative commander. The commander's function is that of a steward: to hold the clan together until such time as a rightful claimant to the chiefship is acknowledged by Lord Lyon.

The MacGillivray clansman's crest badge is a Clan Chattan variant: a 'Rampant Wild Cat' with the motto 'Touch Not This Cat'. (*Dunmaghlas*, from the name of the castle, is also used.) There are three acknowledged tartans of the name.

Among the most interesting members of this clan was Alexander MacGillivray, who became a North American Indian chief in 1777.

MacGregor

Clan Gregor, as it should properly be called, carries the proud Gaelic motto 'S'rioghal mo dhream', meaning 'Royal is my blood'. Predating the clan's claim to royal descent by centuries, the motto serves to reinforce the enduring sense of outrage felt by most MacGregors at the centuries of repression suffered by their forebears. But this story is also one of an unparalleled talent for survival.

The old claim that the 'Gregor' who was the clan's namefather was either the brother or the son of Kenneth MacAlpin, first paramount King of Scotland, is unproven. In fact, Gregor (he of 'the golden bridles') was probably the 2nd Chief of the clan; he succeeded his father, 'One-eyed' Iain, as late as 1390.

The ancestral homeland of the MacGregors was the three glens of the Rivers Strae, Orchy, and Lochy, which are now in the heartland of the

Campbells. And therein lie the seeds of the clan's tragedy, for it was the ruthless expansion of the all-powerful Campbells which led to the MacGregors becoming landless and outlawed. In this process the most unscrupulous branch of the Campbells, by 1519 calling themselves by the old MacGregor territorial title 'of Glenorchy', promoted as Chief of Clan Gregor a younger chieftain who had been forced to marry a Campbell heiress whom he had ravished.

The true chiefly heirs to the *Grigorach* were forced to continue the struggle as guerrillas in the mountains of Argyll and Perthshire, earning the evocative nickname of 'Children of the Mist'. Their chief was captured in 1552 and personally 'beheddit' by Black Duncan Campbell of Glenorchy, brother of the ravished heiress who was by then the wife of the puppet MacGregor chief.

But the hard times of the Children of the Mist had barely begun. Half a century later, the MacGregor policy of exacting dramatic revenge for any persecution led to a 400-strong force of Colquhouns (allies of the Campbells) being despatched to exterminate 'the haill tribe, root and branch'. To this end they carried the authority of King James VI himself. But the guerrillas of MacGregor and their allies ambushed and routed the Colquhouns in Glen Fruin, to the west of Loch Lomond, slaughtering over a hundred in the process.

The response was draconian. A Special Order in Council was issued by the King, outlawing the whole Clan Gregor and even forbidding anyone, on pain of death, to bear the dreaded name of MacGregor. The Chief, Alexander MacGregor of Glenstrae, was hanged with many of his followers in Edinburgh, and thereafter the clan was harried until 1774, when the Act of Proscription against the clan, its people, and its name was repealed.

As a result, many people of MacGregor stock today bear one of the many names adopted during the two centuries during which the true clan name was proscribed. The best-known figure in the clan's chequered history is probably 'Rob Roy', but for much of his life he called himself Robert Campbell, taking his mother's surname. The 'Roy' echoes the sound of the Gaelic *ruadh*, used to describe someone with red hair or a florid complexion. A legendary swordsman, Rob Roy perfected the ancient Scots art of 'blackmail' – the original protection racket – and despite an action-packed life managed to die in his bed at the age of 70.

Many other MacGregors were not so fortunate. Of the present chief's immediate ancestors, 22 were hanged, five died fighting, four were beheaded, three were assassinated (two by arrows in the back), and one – desperate to get away from the violence of life in 17th-century Scotland – migrated to America, only to be scalped by Indians.

Above: Loch Katrine, immortalized in the novels of Sir Walter Scott, is deep in MacGregor country.

MacGregor crest badge

It almost goes without saying that of those MacGregors who made a name for themselves on the world stage, most did so by fighting. An example of their other skills is provided by the story of the MacGregor who was – literally – the forefather of well over a thousand of the clan in Mexico City. He arrived there in 1799, married a local girl, and produced 22 sons by her.

The fighting MacGregors are best represented by General Gregor MacGregor, Simon Bolivar's right-hand-man in South America's liberation from Spain; General Sir Colin Campbell, born into Clan Gregor as Colin McLiver and famous for commanding the 'Thin Red Line' in the Crimea and the Relief of Lucknow in the Indian Mutiny; and Sir Samuel Carlevitch Greig, Admiral of All the Russias, born in Fife and seconded as a young Royal Navy officer to Catherine the Great's Russia, becoming the 'Father of the Russian Navy'. (For a brief period in the 1780s he had under his command in St Petersburg the 'Father of the American Navy', Admiral John Paul Jones.)

Macintyre

Clan Macintyre, whose name comes from the Gaelic *Mac-an-tsaor*, 'son of the wright', originally came from the Hebrides. After settling in Glen Noe in Lorn in the 14th century, the Macintyres became hereditary foresters to the Stewarts, Lords of Lorn, and also provided pipers for the Clanranald Macdonalds.

The earliest identifiable Chief of the Macintyres was Duncan, who died towards the end of the 1690s. A descendant, Donald Macintyre, emigrated with his immediate family to the United States in the 1780s, immediately after the American War of Independence. But the Macintyres who remained in Glen Noe eventually lost the estate, which left the clan almost landless.

There is a tradition that the Macintyres held Glen Noe from the Campbells, to whom it had passed from the Stewarts, for an annual tribute to be paid – in summertime – of a snowball and a white calf. The snowball was no great problem, even in summer, as Glen Noe backs on to the mountains of Ben Cruachan, almost 1,130 m (3,700 ft) high and often capped in snow. The white calf was also easy, as the clan bred white cattle. Apparently this arrangement lasted until the late 18th century, when the Macintyre chief agreed to commute the payment to cash. This in turn became rent, and was soon stepped up so high that the Macintyres were unable to pay, and were forced to sell Glen Noe. Given the Campbells' track record of voracious land acquisition, the only wonder is that it took

them so long.

Probably the clan's greatest descendant was Duncan Ban Macintyre (1724–1812), a poet of love-songs and satires – the last and greatest exponent of the Gaelic tradition of nature poetry.

MacKay

The Gaelic name for 'MacKay' is *Mac Aiodh*, which means 'son of Aiodh' (or Aedh). The clan's original lands were in Moray, which, in the 12th century, included Inverness and Ross. Malcolm MacKay, Chief in the time of David I (1124–53) was known to the Norsemen as Jarl (Earl) of Moray, and is said to have married a sister of the great Somerled, the half-Norse/half-Scot Lord of the Western Isles. As such, Malcolm was an opponent of the Scottish King.

Malcolm's eldest son Donald was captured by David I's grandson and successor, Malcolm IV, but they were reconciled and Donald MacKay was made Earl of Ross. This earldom died with him. A descendant, Kenneth MacKay, attempted to recover

it by force but was put to death.

Meanwhile, the MacKays had moved into Sutherland and settled in Strathnaver, a district which in later centuries came to be known as MacKay country. In about 1415 one of the clan chiefs, Angus Dubh MacKay of Strathnaver, married a sister of Donald MacDonald of the Isles; his bride was also granddaughter of King Robert II (1371–90). In 1427 it is recorded that the MacKays were able to muster a force of 4,000 men for battle, indicating considerable power for north-eastern Scotland where the chief rival of the MacKays was Clan Sutherland. Indeed, much of MacKay history from the 15th century to the 18th was taken up with a struggle to prevent Strathnaver from being swallowed up by the Sutherlands.

In 1626, Sir Donald MacKay, Clan Chief in the reign of Charles I (1625–49), was given permission by the King to raise an army of 3,000 men to fight in Germany during the Thirty Years War (1618–48). The specific intention was to come to the aid of Frederick, Elector Palatine, Charles I's brother-in-law. The force raised by MacKay included about 1,000 of his own clan and dependants. After service with Frederick, MacKay's men joined up with the army of Gustavus Adolphus, King of Sweden and champion of the Protestant cause. MacKay won such renown that the Swedish King described him as 'my right hand in battle'. Charles I created MacKay 1st Lord Reay in 1628, but the raising of the MacKay regiment for the German wars had been immensely costly, and parts of the Strathnaver lands had to be sold.

The MacKays remained loyal to Charles I in the Great Civil War (1642–51) but refused to support the cause of the exiled King James II and his Jacobite heirs. In the Scottish campaign of 1688–89 Hugh MacKay, a cousin of the clan chief, commanded the Government forces which were defeated by Graham of Claverhouse at Killiecrankie. In the Jacobite risings of 1715 and 1745–46, the MacKays quietly supported the Hanoverian side.

Left: Among the most beautiful of Scottish scenery is Sandwood Bay, with the little Sandwood Loch just inland from it. This is the roadless wilderness of the MacKay homelands, topped by Cape Wrath.

MacKay crest badge

MacKenzie

The MacKenzies were not so old a clan as some in Scotland, but for a time they controlled huge areas of land in the north, at one time owning most of Ross and Cromarty. They began as one of a number of clans in Ross, holding land between the Aird and Kintail.

The MacKenzies traced their ancestry back to one Gilleon of the Aird, but the fist MacKenzie of importance was Alexander, 7th Chief of Kintail, who received a summons to the court of James I (1406–37) in 1427. He lived another 60 years. His grandson John MacKenzie, at the head of his clan, accompanied King James IV to the Battle of Flodden in 1513, and unlike his sovereign and most of the Scottish nobility, he surviveid the battle. (The Kintail lands had been made a Barony in 1508.) John MacKenzie also fought the English at Pinkie Cleugh, in 1547, and afterwards supported Mary, Queen of Scots. His grandson Colin MacKenzie also supported the Queen, but when she was compelled to abdicate in 1547, he made his peace with the Regent, James, Earl of Moray.

By the time that Colin's son Kenneth was created 1st Lord MacKenzie of Kintail in 1609, the clan had skilfully built up its power in northern Scotland. The MacKenzies owned the castle of Eilean Donan on Loch Duich, plus large areas of Strathconon, and had won Lochalsh from the MacDonnells. Two branches sprang from the new peer: the MacKenzies of Pluscarden and the MacKenzies of Lochslinn. The clan could claim to own lands stretching from coast to coast in Ross, from Black Isle to Gairloch, and a few years later they took the Isle of Lewis from the MacLeods.

Lord MacKenzie's son Colin was created Earl of Seaforth in 1623, and he was succeeded by his half-brother George who was later Secretary of State for Scotland. Kenneth MacKenzie, 3rd Earl Seaforth, was an active Cavalier and was deprived of his estates by Cromwell. His son Kenneth, the 4th Earl, was one of the first members of Scotland's own order of chivalry, the Order of the Thistle, and died in 1701. William, the 5th Earl, supported Prince James Edward, the Old Pretender, in 1715 and was attainted when the rising collapsed. His grandson raised one of the most famous of the Highland regiments, the Seaforth Highlanders, in 1778 and took it to India. The MacKenzie River in New Zealand is named after the explorer Sir Alexander MacKenzie. Among its several branches today, Clan MacKenzie includes the Earldom of Cromartie and a number of baronetcies.

The clansman's motto is *Luceo non uro* ('I shine not burn').

Right: The extensive lands around Loch Maree had come under the superiority of the Clan MacKenzie by the 18th century, and include some of the finest mountain scenery in Europe.

MacKinlay

'Finlayson' in Gaelic becomes *mac Fhionnlaigh*, and because the Gaelic 'h' (for 'of') silences the initial letter, it is pronounced 'Mac Finlay' – sometimes with an intrusive 'd' after the 'n'. In early Gaelic it was rendered as *Fionnlaoich* – 'fair hero'. The suggestion that the name may have come from *Fionnlugh* – 'fair one of [the god] Lugh' can probably be dismissed; all early phonetic spellings suggest the *laoich* ('hero') suffix.

The MacKinlay surname appears in the Loch Lomond area, Glen Lyon, Balquhidder, and in Braemar, where the *Clann Fhionnlaigh* refers to the Farquharsons. That clan's 'namefather' was Farquhar Shaw of Rothiemurchus, but it takes its Gaelic clan name from Finlay *mor* who was killed at the Battle of Pinkie Cleugh in 1547, where he carried the Scots Royal Standard in that defeat by the English. Just as various Donaldsons can descend from quite different 'Donalds', so a number of 'Finlays' were the progenitors of quite separate small MacKinlay clans. Some were in areas where the aspirated 'h' form in Gaelic does not seem to have applied, and there are MacFinlay families in Caithness, Ross and Cromarty, and elsewhere.

In Ulster, the native name *mac an Leagha* is sometimes anglicized to 'Mackinley', but other MacKinlays arrived from Scotland after the Protestant 'Plantation' of the province in the reign of James VI and I (1603–25). William McKinley, 25th President of the United States (assassinated in 1901) was of 'Scotch-Irish' stock; his father David and mother, Rachel Stewart, were both Ulster-born.

There seems never to have been a MacKinlay chief – a 'MacKinlay of MacKinlay' – and, therefore, there are no unifying heraldic symbols such as a clansman's crest badge, slogan, or motto. There is, however, a 'MacKinlay' tartan.

MacKinnon

In the centuries when the Celtic Church functioned in Scotland without interference from Rome, priesthoods were often hereditary and monasteries were ruled by abbots who married and had children, passing on abbacies like temporal estates. For several centuries, many of the abbots of Iona were of the Clan MacKinnon. The name MacKinnon came from *mac Fhionnghain* – son of Fingon. Some early MacKinnons anglicized their name to 'Love', mistaking its Gaelic origin for *macionmhuinn* –

'son of the well beloved one'. The clan's original home was probably the Isle of Mull which overlooks Iona, but this was lost to the Clan MacLean in the 14th century, except for Mishnish and Dunara Castle.

Niall MacKinnon, son of the 14th-century Chief Gillebride MacKinnon, had a brother, who in 1358 succeeded as Abbot of Iona in the face of stern opposition from the Papacy. It seems to have taken about 40 years before his petition was accepted by the Pope. Lachlan MacKinnon, father of the last Abbot of Iona, John MacKinnon (who died in about 1500), had a Celtic cross erected at Iona, part of which can still be seen. The tomb of the last abbot has also survived.

MacKinnons supported the Jacobites in the risings of 1715 and 1745–46, and after the Government victory at Culloden in 1746, the then chief was taken as a prisoner to southern England and held for a time at Tilbury Fort in Essex. The fortunes of the MacKinnons had been in decline for a long time, and in 1791 the lands of Strathaird had to be sold to pay debts.

MacKinnon crest badge

Below: The original homeland of the Clan MacKinnon was in the north of the Isle of Mull, and many of the Abbots of neighbouring Iona were MacKinnons.

Mackintosh

This clan's name comes from *Mac an Toisach*, 'Son of the Chief'. The founder of Clan Mackintosh is said to have been a son of MacDuff, ancestor of the Earls of Fife, whose lands were in Moray. Clan Mackintosh was a member of the great clan confederation, Clan Chattan, of which the Mackintoshes remained the dominant clan for several generations. A charter of the 1330s from The MacDonald, Lord of the Isles, later confirmed by King David II (1329–71), mentions the Mackintosh Chief as the Chief of Clan Chattan.

Malcolm Mackintosh, Chief from about 1430 to 1464, also appears in a charter of 1442 as owner of various properties including Rait Castle in Nairn, referred to as Lord of Moy (Inverness). His son Duncan Mackintosh married Flora, daughter of John MacDonald, Lord of the Isles. In the 16th century, William Mackintosh, the 16th Chief, was accused by the Gordon Earl of Huntly, Sheriff of Inverness, of plotting against the latter's life. Tried in Aberdeen before a jury previously bribed by the Gordons, he was predictably convicted and executed in 1550.

Over the next century, the Mackintoshes were involved in a number of feuds with neighbouring and rival clans, such as the Camerons and the MacDonnells of Keppoch. Lachlan Mackintosh, Chief in the mid-17th century, was recognized as Chief of Clan Chattan in 1672 and died in 1704. His

Above: At the northern end of Loch Moy stood the ancestral seat of the Chiefs of the Clan Mackintosh – Moy Hall – which was built anew in 1957.

Mackintosh crest badge

son Lachlan fought for the Old Pretender, Prince James Edward, in the first Jacobite rising of 1715.

In the rising of 1745, Angus, the 23rd Chief of Clan Mackintosh, took the Government's part, but his wife, the brave and colourful 'Colonel' Anne Mackintosh, a Farquharson by birth, called out her husband's clan to fight for Bonnie Prince Charlie. She won a celebrated skirmish which passed into Jacobite legend as the 'Rout of Moy'. When a Government detachment of some 1,500 men arrived on the Moy estate in 1746, searching for the fugitive Prince, the gallant 'Colonel' managed to put the Government troops to flight with only a handful of men, by the use of some clever manoeuvering.

Lady Anne's martial prowess was not, however, held against Clan Mackintosh after the Government victory of 1746 and her son Aeneas Mackintosh, the 24th Chief, was made a Baronet in 1812. Today the seat of the Mackintosh of Mackintosh is still at Moy in Inverness-shire.

Above: Loch Fyne in mid Argyll with which Clan MacLachlan has been associated since the 13th century.

MacLachlan crest badge

MacLachlan

Lachlan Mor, the first member of the Clan MacLachlan who can be identified, was a powerful chief in the Lachlan Bay district of Loch Fyne in the 13th century. By tradition, the clan is said to have descended from the O'Neill kings of Ulster.

In 1292, Gileskil MacLachlan, Chief of the Clan, is listed as one of 12 chiefs and lords whose lands were formally declared part of the sheriffdom of Argyll by King John Baliol. Four years later, Ewen MacLachlan appears on the Ragman Roll as one of the chiefs who, probably under duress, swore fealty to Edward I of England. Gillescop MacLachlan, Ewen's son, was a supporter of Robert the Bruce and sat in that King's first Parliament.

Thereafter the Clan MacLachlan does not appear to have played any prominent role until 1656,

when Oliver Cromwell appointed Lachlan MacLachlan – probably the 14th Chief – a Justice of the Peace for Argyllshire. His son Archibald, the 15th Chief, was recognized as Lord of Strathlachlan in 1680, though the clan chiefs had in practice been lords of that territory for generations.

The MacLachlans were staunch Jacobites. They fought with Claverhouse ('Bonnie Dundee') at Killiecrankie in 1689, and the 16th Chief, Lachlan, was one of the signatories of the Address of Welcome presented to James Edward, the Old Pretender, when he landed in Scotland during the rising of 1715. The 17th Chief (also Lachlan) led the clan on Bonnie Prince Charlie's side at Culloden, but was killed in the action by a cannon ball. His home, Castle Lachlan on Loch Fyne, was bombarded by a Government warship.

There is a story that the 17th Chief's horse, accompanying the clan survivors on their retreat from Culloden field, broke loose when it reached Loch Fyne and swam across the water to the battered castle, thereby being the first to notify the family that some sort of disaster had taken place at Culloden.

The clansman's motto is *Fortis et fidis* ('Brave and trusty').

MacLaine of Lochbuie

This branch of the Clan MacLean, being a 'considerable family', now deserves to be considered as a clan in its own right, in the same way as do the Frasers of Lovat in relation to Clan Fraser.

The MacLaines and the MacLeans both descend

from *Gilleathain-na-Tuaigh* ('Gillean of the Battleaxe'). The Gaelic patronymic is thereby *mac gille Eoin* ('son of the follower, or devotee, of St John') – *Eoin* being an early form of 'Iain'. Like many short-cuts in language development, this Gaelic mouthful came to be pronounced as *mac 'ill Eathain* or 'Mac-lane' – never 'Ma-cleen' or even 'Ma-clane'.

The MacLaine branch, perhaps sensibly, decided to spell their surname in English more as it should sound, but argument persists as to whether it should be 'L' or 'l'. At the end of the day it becomes a matter of preference, and both chiefs use the small 'l'. Historic examples recorded in manuscripts between 1400 and 1700 include 'M'Claine', 'Maklayne', 'Makllane', 'M'Clane', 'Macklane', 'M'Clan', and 'Makclane', not to mention 'M'Klin', 'M'Leand', 'M'Gleane', 'Mc'illayn', 'M'Clean', and 'McGillichean'. The general convention, as with all Highland names is that proper nouns or personal names incorporated into Scottish surnames should retain the capital letter of that noun or name, even where it has been shortened (as in MacDuffie/MacFie).

The 5th Chief of *Clann Gillean* had two sons, Hector 'the Stubborn' and Lachlan 'the Astute'. Although Lachlan was the younger, he was, according to the accepted system of 'tanistry' (limiting the choice of chief's kin), nominated as successor by his father (who possibly felt that the clan had reached a point in its development where brains were more crucial than brawn). Upon which, Hector 'the Stubborn' also became, understandably, 'the affronted', and broke away from the clan to form his own branch of the 'children of Gillean' – known today as the MacLaines of Lochbuie after their castle stronghold. Later, the MacLeans of Dochgarroch broke away from the Lochbuie chiefship and joined the Clan Chattan confederation of smaller clans in Badenoch, becoming known as the 'MacLeans of the North'.

The inevitable rivalry between the two clan branches produced some colourful deeds of legend. Ewan 'Pin Head' MacLaine rebelled in the 16th century against his father, Iain 'the Toothless', who was forced to call upon his cousin, Hector *mor* MacLean of Duart for help. The young MacLaine was killed in the subsequent affray, but his headless ghost (or is it just that his tiny phantom skull is too difficult to see after dark?) rides abroad whenever and wherever a MacLaine dies. (The 'Headless Horseman' was last seen earlier this century.)

The story, however, was not over. After Hector *mor* MacLean had gleefully helped slaughter his rival's only son, he proceeded to incarcerate Iain the Toothless on the little island of *Cairn na Burgh*, away from womenfolk so that Iain could not produce a new heir. Happily for the future of the MacLaines, however, an ugly, hunchbacked servant woman had been overlooked; and the winning smile of Iain the Toothless led to the birth of a son (known almost inevitably as Murdoch 'the Stunted') who became the ancestor of all later MacLaines of Lochbuie.

In general, all branches of the MacLeans supported the exiled Stewarts during the 'Jacobite century' of 1688–1788, from the deposition of King James VII and II (1688) to the death of Bonnie Prince Charlie (1788). The Lochbuie chief who fought with 'Bonnie Dundee' in the Killiecrankie campaign of 1689, ambushed by five troops of Government horse while on the march with a small force of Highlanders, succeeded in routing the cavalry and killing their commander. The Lochbuie MacLaines, however, stayed at home during the Jacobite rising of 1745.

The Lochbuie lands were sold to pay debts in the 1920s, and the chiefs emigrated to South Africa. The present chief is Lorne Gillean Maclaine, 26th Chief of the Clan Gillean of Lochbuie and Feudal Baron of Moy. The clansman's crest badge is a 'Battleaxe', with the motto *Vincere vel mors* ('Conquest or Death'). There are three acknowledged MacLaine tartans.

MacLaren

Clan MacLaren takes its name from Labhran, a medieval Abbot described in contemporary manuscripts as *ab Achtus* or 'Abbot of Achtow', where there must have been an early religious establishment. What was believed to be the senior surviving branch of the clan, the MacLarens of Achleskine, was still farming at Achtow at the end of the last century. The farm lay in the shadow of *Creag-an-Tuirc*, 'The Boar's Rock', the rallying-place which gave its name to the MacLaren clan warcry and modern-day motto.

Until the 14th century, Clan MacLaren had enjoyed the benign protection of the Earls Palatine of Strathearn. The latter had been kings in Pictish times, giving them the presence to state that they ruled their lands and held their titles, not 'By the Grace' but 'By the Indulgence of God'. As proof of their descent from the same stock as the Earls, the MacLarens were permitted to bear on their Arms the Earldom's twin red chevrons on a gold field, 'differenced' by the addition of the black galley of Lorn. This established the MacLarens' even more important royal links with Loarn, son and successor of the founder of the Scots Kingdom of Dalriada in the early 6th century AD.

Unfortunately for the MacLarens, the mighty Clan Campbell stemmed from the very same Loarn.

143

When the Earldom of Stratherne was annexed by the Scottish crown in the 14th century, the MacLarens had no choice but to submit to the cousinly 'benevolence' of the Campbell chiefs which has weighed so heavily on other weaker clans down the centuries. Campbell patronage did not save the 18 MacLaren households massacred at Balquhidder in 1558. This slaughter was carried out by MacGregors from Glendochart in the north – who were themselves being harried by the Campbells. This was a classic ploy used by the Campbell Earls of Argyll: setting the smaller clans at each other's throats, then moving in to sweep up the pieces when the feuding survivors from each side were too enfeebled to resist.

With the MacLarens lying ravaged and broken after the MacGregor assault, the Campbell embrace tightened. The Earl of Argyll 'made over' the MacLarens to his kinsman in a curious document, which says 'We . . . grantis us to haif gevin . . . to our traist cousyng Colyne Campbell of Glenurquay [Glenorchy] and his airis male, the manrent, homage and the service quhilk our predecessouris and we had and has of the haill kyn and name of Clanlaurane and their posteritie . . .'

Enterprising MacLarens who sought better luck elsewhere did so mostly as soldiers of fortune in the armies of European monarchs. In 1498, Robin and Gibbie MacLaren joined the *Garde Ecossaise* or Scots Guard of the King of France. With them went Simon and Colin MacLaren, who joined the French King's mounted Archer Guard. Other MacLarens – out of the scores of other Scots who joined the service of Sweden – were ennobled for their services. 'Johan Laurin', a colonel in the Swedish Army and later Provost of East Gotland in Sweden, became Baron Lagergren of Sweden and died in 1673. Another 'John Laurin' became a Swedish baron in 1678; 'Magnus Laurin' became Court Lagerstrom in 1691. All were of unmistakable MacLaren stock, bearing the clan emblems of the twin red chevrons and the laurel crest on their Swedish heraldic achievements.

The 'children of Laurin' have flourished in other fields, too. Colin MacLaurin was a child prodigy in mathematics. Born in 1698, he was sent to Glasgow University at the age of 12, became Professor of Mathematics at Marischal College, Aberdeen, by the age of 19, and at the advanced age of 27 became Professor of Mathematics at Edinburgh University, dying in the chair at the age of 48. Charles MacLaren (1782–1866) was the first editor of *The Scotsman*. A family of legal MacLarens produced a judge and two Members of Parliament, one of whom became the 1st Baron Aberconway, while a 'tribe' of MacLaurins emigrated to North Carolina in 1798 and founded the town of Laurinburg.

Many 'MacLaurins' came from the Isle of Tiree in the Hebrides; the son of 'the Professor' was acknowledged by Lord Lyon in 1781 to be the head of that branch, which had been 'anciently proprietors in that island'. The family had probably been given refuge there after the dispersion of the clan in 1558, following the Balquhidder massacre. The Countess of Argyll at the time was by birth a MacLean, whose family owned Tiree.

The direct descendant of the original MacLarens of Achtow, Donald MacLaren was acknowledged by Lord Lyon in 1957 as 'Chief of the Whole Name and Arms of MacLaren'. The present chief is his son, Donald MacLaren of MacLaren and Achleskine. The clansman's crest badge is 'A Black Lyon, Crowned and Wreathed with Laurel', with the motto *Creag-an-Tuirc*. There are six acknowledged MacLaren tartans.

MacLaren crest badge   MacLean crest badge

MacLean

Clan MacLean stems from a 13-century Chief, Gillean, a descendant of the ancient kings of Dalriada. The clan has been associated for centuries with the mainland peninsula of Morvern in Argyll, the Isle of Mull.

Gillean's son, Gillemoir Macilyn, was one of the chiefs recorded on the Ragman Roll as having sworn fealty to King Edward I of England in 1296, but Gillemoir's grandson Gillecullum fought for Robert the Bruce at Bannockburn in 1314. Gillecullum's son Ian Dhu MacLean moved from Morvern to Mull, where his two sons, Lachlan and Hector, became the ancestors of two MacLean families: Lachlan in Duart and Hector in Lochbuie. (The Lochbuie MacLeans later altered the family name to 'MacLaine'.) Lachlan MacLean married a daughter of the MacDonald Lord of the Isles, and for many years the MacLeans supported the MacDonalds in their struggles against Scotland's Stewart kings. Sir Lachlan Maclean of Dewart, Bt. is the 28th Chief.

144

When the MacDonald Lords of the Isles were finally overthrown by James IV in the 1490s, the MacLeans made their peace with the Scottish Crown. In 1496, their Duart lands were made a barony. The breakup of the MacDonald supremacy resulted in a long feud between some of the MacDonalds and the MacLeans, who themselves now tried to build a power base in the west. In 1589 King James VI, angered by the continuing feud between the MacDonalds and the MacLeans, condemned the clan chiefs, pardoned them, then invited them to meet him for discussions. When they arrived James had them arrested and charged again with the same offences. In 1632 Lachlan MacLean of Morvern, heir to Hector MacLean of Duart, was made a baronet.

In the early 17th century, the MacLeans came under increasing pressure from the fast-growing power of the Campbells of Argyll, who used the tactic of buying up MacLean debts, then obtaining court judgements for possession of most of the MacLean territory. With such a score to settle it is not surprising that the MacLeans fought for the Royalist Montrose in the Great Civil War, briefly breaking the power of the Covenant of which the Campbells were the most powerful supporting clan.

The MacLeans supported Graham of Claverhouse against the Government army at Killiecrankie in 1689, and rallied to the Jacobite cause in the risings of 1715 and 1745–46. Sir Hector MacLean, Clan Chief in the 1740s, was in London when the first rumblings of the 'Forty-Five' were heard. He was detained and held as a political prisoner for about two years, but his clan nevertheless fought for Bonnie Prince Charlie at Culloden in 1746.

MacLennan

There is much confusion relating to this surname and its affiliations. Many authorities refer to the 'Clan *Logan* or MacLennan', but the 'Logan' is not satisfactorily explained. There is a quite separate clan which took its name from the lands of Logan in Ayrshire and whose last chief, the Logan of that Ilk, died heirless in 1802. There were also the Logans of Restalrig, whose last Laird died after being 'put to the horn' or outlawed when implicated in the plot to kill King James VI, in the 'Gowrie Conspiracy' of the 16th century.

The Lowland Logans are first mentioned in 1204, in the reign of William 'the Lyon'; the Highland MacLennans are associated by tradition with the Morayshire name of *loban* or *lobban*: a Gaelic term for an old style of cart or sledge for hauling peats. This vehicle was more properly called *carn-loban*,

with its stack or 'cairn' of peats held in position by side-pieces or 'lobban'. It needs some mangled Gaelic to conjure the name 'Logan' from that source, unless from an early mishearing or misreading of the north-east surname. William Lobane was a tenant in Drumderfit, Easter Ross, in 1560, and the MacLennans do claim a line of descent from that family. A story tells of a MacLennan around 1400, hiding under a 'lobban' to avoid capture and being given that name thereafter. This is exactly how many surnames have begun, but it still throws no light on the hard 'g' appearing in the name.

Another clan legend fits in better with a Gaelic word which looks like 'lobban' but would sound nearer 'Logan'. Apparently the Frasers fought with the small Drumderfit clan in the early 13th century and killed their Chief, Gilligorm, whose wife gave birth to a son some months later while under the 'protection' of her enemies. Tradition has it that the Frasers broke strategic bones in the infant's body to ensure that he would not grow up tall and strong to avenge his father. He is said to have been known as 'Crotair MacGilligorm', the 'hunchback son of Gilligorm'. But the Gaelic *lobhaireacan*, meaning 'stunted one', may have been the original name applied to the family because of a genetic deformity, which may have appeared in later generations and been rationalized by the Fraser horror story to arouse sympathy.

The story of Crotair MacGilligorm goes on to say that he later took Holy Orders and devoted himself to the old Celtic Church (which did not demand celibacy from its priests). His subsequent son and heir was dedicated to St Fillan – and this provides a straightforward Gaelic surname style, *mac gille Fhinnein*, which loses the 'F' when aspirated by 'h' as 'of Fillan'. The sound of the name thus becomes 'Mac l-eh-nan'. (The name of MacLellan/McClelland is often confused with MacLennan but is of quite separate origin, from Galloway.)

The MacLennans were once numerous in Kintail. 'Jonat' or Janet Lobane and others were accused at Inverness in 1614 of 'crewel vnmerceifull murther'. In heartening contrast, Roderick MacLennan and

MacLennan crest badge

his brother Donald are recorded as dying bravely in defence of their chief and his banner at the Battle of Auldearn, one of Montrose's famous victories in 1645.

In 1977, Ronald MacLennan was acknowledged by Lord Lyon as 'Chief of the Whole Name and Arms of MacLennan'; but subsequently William MacLennan of Sydney, Australia, came forward with proof of his direct descent in the male line from the senior MacLennan family, and his Arms were thereafter matriculated by the Lyon Court. 'Bill' MacLennan refused to contest the rights of 'Chief Ronnie', as he was popularly known, but both of them died in 1990. Ruaridh, the 13-year-old son of Ronald MacLennan, became the 35th Chief of the Clan – but the son and heir of William MacLennan retains the option to contest the succession. Until the smoke of internal strife in the Clan MacLennan disappears, Ruaridh – dubbed 'Wee Chiefie' by the popular press – carries on with his schooling, largely unaware that he is now part of his clan's living history.

MacLeod

There are two main branches of the MacLeods, the 'sons of Leod' of the Isle of Lewis, who was son of Olaf Lord of the Isle of Man and the Northern Isles. These two branches descended from Leod's two sons, Tormod and Torquil. Tormod was the ancestor of the MacLeods of MacLeod, of Glenelg, Harris, and Dunvegan. From Torquil came the MacLeods of Lewis and the MacLeods of Assynt.

Torquil was the 2nd Lord of Lewis, and his family held the island until thrown out by the MacKenzies at the beginning of the 17th century; they held Assynt much longer. Tormod MacLeod claimed the chiefship of the whole clan. One of his descendants supported Robert the Bruce. His son Malcolm MacLeod received a charter from David II (1329–70) giving him Glenelg lands. By then, the chiefs were calling themselves MacLeods of MacLeod. William, the 7th Chief, was killed in a feud

Dunvegan Castle has been a MacLeod coastal fortress on Skye for seven centuries, and *until 1748 could only be entered through its strongly guarded sea-gate.*

Left: MacLeod crest badge
Right: MacMillan crest badge

with the MacDonalds; he had already acquired Dunvegan. His son Alasdair Crotach, the 8th Chief, received a charter from James IV for Trotternish at the end of the 15th century.

After the death of the 8th Chief, there was a long-drawn-out dispute over the chiefship, but by the beginning of the 17th century Rory Mor MacLeod was recognized as 16th Chief. He was knighted in 1603 and died in 1926. The clan supported Charles I in the Civil War, and some of them fought for Charles II at the Battle of Worcester (1651). After the Restoration in 1660, the MacLeods felt a major grievance that Charles II had not been sufficiently grateful for their exertions on his behalf, and they never supported the Stewart kings again. The MacLeods took no part in Claverhouse's campaign of 1688–89, nor in the first Jacobite rising of 1715. In the second rising (1745–46), the MacLeods raised a battalion for the Government forces.

Torquil's line continued until the 16th century, but after the death of Malcolm, 9th Chief of the MacLeods of Lewis, there followed years of dispute over the chiefship. In the early 17th century, the direct MacLeod line became extinct and the MacKenzie Earls of Cromartie obtained the Chiefship of the Isle of Lewis. The Raasay estate remained in the MacLeod family until it was sold in the 1840s.

It is pleasant to quote some comments on the MacLeods by the clan historian, Dr I.F. Grant. *Throughout the history of the MacLeods there runs a thread of tenacity that worthily fulfils their motto, 'Hold Fast'. In nothing is this staunchness better shown than in the maintainance of the bonds uniting the chief and his clansmen. After the collapse of the second Jacobite rising and the general break-up of Highland society, . . . doctors were maintained . . . education was fostered, and heavy expenditure incurred in road-making. MacLeod's private post to Edinburgh was for long a boon to the community. Grain was imported in times of scarcity . . . the MacLeod estates were* never sullied by the blot of 'clearing' the people from their holdings.

MacMillan

The name MacMillan means 'son of the tonsured', and suggests that the beginnings of Clan MacMillan were as a family of priests. There were MacMillans beside Loch Arkaig in the 12th century; later, they moved to territory close to Loch Tay. The name Gilleonan MacMolan appears in a charter for 1263. The clan was clearly established by 1360, when Malcolm Mor MacMillan was granted a charter by the Lord of the Isles, confirming the ownership of land in Knapdale, including part of the western peninsula that ends at Knap Point. A couplet survives from old times as an interesting confirmation of the grant:

MacMillan's right to Knap shall be
As long as this rock withstands the sea.

Malcolm's grandson, Lachlan MacMillan of Knap, was slain in the great battle of clans at Harlaw in 1411, which was basically a showdown between the Stewarts and the MacDonalds of the Isles. The chiefs of the MacMillans of Knap continued to head the clan but branches settled elsewhere, such as at Lochaber in Argyll, and also in Galloway.

Langbank House in Renfrewshire, present seat of the chief of the Clan MacMillan.

Macnab

Clan Macnab, whose name means 'son of the abbot', sprang from the monastic house of Glendochart. In the 13th century, the abbots of Glendochart ranked equally with local earls. In the early years of the 14th century, Clan Macnab sided with the MacDougalls against Robert the Bruce – a miscalculation which, after Bruce's crushing victory over the English at Bannockburn in 1314, cost them many of their possessions. The Macnabs retained Bovain, probably because of their connection with the Church, and this lordship was confirmed in a charter of David II (1329–70) to the Clan Chief, Gilbert Macnab.

In the 15th century the Macnabs seem to have acquired new territories, but in the 1550s most Macnab lands had to be sold to pay off debts. When Parliament and the Scottish Covenanters fought Charles I in the Great Civil War, the Macnabs joined the Royalist forces led by Montrose on behalf of the King.

The chiefs of Macnab were more the stuff of legends than most. A contemporary of Francis Macnab, 16th chief of Clan *mac an abba*, said, 'All were insignificant beside the Macnab!' He ruled a small kingdom that had been unchanged for six centuries at a time when other chiefs had been crushed by progress. Strikingly tall and topped with three long eagle's feathers, he made an instant impression on London society on a visit in 1800. His presence at the notorious cock-pit in Fleet Street has entered into local lore. Having previously boasted that there were many cocks in Scotland that could beat the English champion fighting-cock 'The Pride of Lambeth', he brought a bird hidden in a huge sack. At the crucial moment he took off the sack to reveal a very angry cock golden eagle, which flew at 'The Pride of Lambeth' and tore its head off. Macnab won a 1000 guinea wager.

In 1612 the sons of the chief – known with a fine touch of sarcasm as Smooth John – carried out a daring night-time raid on the small Clan MacNeish. They carried a boat over the mountains and surprised the sleeping MacNeishes on their island stronghold in Loch Earn (except for one 'wee lad' from all future MacNeishes would descend). The sons triumphantly presented Smooth John with the head of the MacNeish chief when he rose for breakfast the next morning. More respectable Macnabs include the 19th-century Canadian Prime Minister, Sir Allan Macnab.

The present chief is James Macnab. The clansman's badge is the head of MacNeish with the motto *Timor omnis abestio* ('let fear be far from all').

MacNeil

The MacNeils were essentially an island clan although they also held territory on the mainland, which included Knapdale. The clan's oldest branch stemmed from Niall, a chief ruling the island of Barra in the Outer Hebrides in the mid-11th century. Almost inevitably this Niall, the founder of the clan, was later claimed by the MacNeils to have descended from the famous Irish King Niall of the Nine Hostages, in the early 5th century. Clan MacNeil's sense of antiquity is attested by the famous story of how Noah offered the MacNeil chief a place in the Ark, only to be loftily informed that 'The MacNeil has his own boat'.

The 6th Clan Chief, Neil Og MacNeil of Barra, supported Robert the Bruce, and was rewarded with a grant of lands in Kintyre. In the reign of King David II (1329–71), the MacNeils are recorded as holding Barra as vassals of the MacDonalds of the Isles. A charter confirming this, along with other properties, was granted to Gilleonan Ruari Murchaid MacNeil, 9th Chief of Barra, by Alexander, Lord of the Isles in 1427.

The MacNeils also held the island of Gigha, off the west coast of Knapdale, but by all accounts these MacNeils were little more than pirates. After the MacDonalds were broken by King James IV in the 1490s Gilleonan MacNeil, 11th Chief of Barra, was confirmed in his title to Barra by the King of Stirling in 1495. At about this time, the clan's seat was established at Kiessimul Castle on Barra, but from then on the MacNeils of Barra and of Gigha acted independently of each other, and other branches of the clan also took shape.

Neil MacNeil, the last of the Gigha chiefs, was killed in a skirmish in 1530. While the Barra MacNeils remained in the ascendant, the Gigha MacNeils declined as the Campbells strengthened their grip on Argyll. Gigha itself was sold in 1554 to a branch of the MacDonalds, but it was bought back in the 1590s by a MacNeil of Taynish, and it stayed in the family until the 19th century, when much of the MacNeil land was sold.

The MacNeils of Barra claimed the chiefship of all the MacNeils. Ruari Og MacNeil, 15th Chief of Barra, was described in the 1570s as 'a Scot that usually maketh his summer's course to steal what he can' – a pirate, in other words. For many years the King's Writ hardly reached Barra, and certainly carried little authority when it did. This same Ruari – 'Rory the Turbulent', as he was known in some quarters – was actually arrested for piracy, but he got off.

'Black Roderick' MacNeil, the 18th Chief of Barra, obtained a Crown charter from King James

VII & II making Barra a Barony. True to his salt, Roderick fought for the exiled King James at Killiecrankie in 1689 and for his son, the Old Pretender, in 1715. 'Black Roderick's' second son became the 19th Chief and Lord of Barra and fought for Bonnie Prince Charlie in the Rising of 1745–46. After spending two years in prison, he was released and died in 1763. His son and heir, Roderick, had been killed with General Wolfe at Quebec in 1759, winning Canada for the British Empire, and the chiefship passed in 1763 to the 19th Chief's grandson.

The direct MacNeil line came to an end with the death of General MacNeil in 1863, by which time Barra had already been sold. But a MacNeil descendant managed to re-purchase part of the island, including the ancient MacNeil seat of Kiessimul Castle.

MacNaughton

The MacNaughtons (or MacNaughtens) were the 'sons of Nechtan', one of whom lived in Lorn in the late 12th century. The first Clan Chief on record was Malcolm MacNechtan, whose son Gillechrist MacNechtan gave lands to Inchaffray Abbey in about 1246. In 1267, Gillechrist received a charter as hereditary castellan, or keeper, of the island castle of Fraoch Eilean in Loch Awe. He was one of the 12 barons and chiefs whose lands formed the sheriffdom of Argyll during the brief reign of King John Baliol (1292–96). By then the clan called themselves lords of MacNaughton, and they occupied territory between Loch Awe and Loch Fyne.

Early in the 14th century, the MacNaughtons under their Chief Donald joined the MacDougalls against Robert the Bruce. As a result they were deprived of many of their lands. Donald's son Duncan threw in his lot with David II, son of the

MacNaughton crest badge

Bruce, and his son Alexander MacNaughton was granted further territory.

Sir Alexander MacNaughton, Chief of the Clan in the early 16th century and a great-great-grandson of the Alexander MacNaughton above, was knighted by King James IV and fell beside him in the Battle of Flodden in 1513. The MacNaughtons remained faithful to the Stuart cause.

The present chief is Sir Patrick MacNaughten of MacNaughten.

Macneacail

This West Highland clan should not be confused with the Lowland 'Nicholsons', although many MacNeacaills/MacNicols have anglicized their name to this form over the years. The clan held the lands of Scorrybreac on Skye, and the senior chieftain in the 13th century, MacNicol of Portree, was one of the 14-man Council of the Lordship of the Isles. There seems to have been an unusually constant succession of father to son down the centuries, and it is said that over 100 chiefs of Scorrybreac have been buried in the traditional burial ground of Snizort.

The MacNicol chiefs lost their lands and migrated to Australia in the last century. When Lord Carnock was officially recognized in the 1980s as Chief of the Whole Name and Arms of Nicholson, Lord Lyon accepted a petition from Ian Nicholson of Scorrybreac, Chief of the West Highland Nicholsons, to change his name and re-matriculate his Arms as 'Iain MacNeacail of MacNeacail and Scorrybreac'. There are two MacNicol tartans.

Macpherson

Clan Macpherson emerged in the 12th century as part of the great confederation of clans, Clan Chattan, of which the Macphersons were to become a major branch. The clan stems from Ewen Ban, second son of Muiriach, Chief of Clan Chattan, who married a daughter of the Lord (Thane) of Cawdor in Moray. Ewen had three sons, Kenneth, Iain, and Gillies, and Kenneth's descendant Donald Mhor was the first to use the name Macpherson, in the 15th century. His descendant Andrew was described as the 8th Chief of the Macphersons.

Andrew's son Ewen, a supporter of Montrose in the Great Civil War, left a son, also Andrew, who did not marry. It may have been his brother Duncan Macpherson, the 10th Chief, who in 1672 tried

Left: Macpherson crest badge
Right: MacQuarrie crest badge

unsuccessfully to claim the chiefship of Clan Chattan. Duncan left no male heir and the chiefship passed to a cousin, Lachlan Macpherson, who died in 1746. His son Ewen had been a leader of the second Jacobite Rising. After the defeat at Culloden he had to hide in Badenoch territory for nine years, with a price of $1,000 on his head; eventually he got away to France. The present chief is the Hon. Sir William Macpherson of Cluny and Blairgowrie.

MacQuarrie

The MacQuarrie surname stems from the old Gaelic personal name *Guaire*. In the charter by John of the Isles, Earl of Ross in 1463, John 'M'Goyre of Wlua' was a witness. The Royal confirmation of this charter records him as 'M'Geir of Ulva' – the island off Mull which is the heartland of this small clan.

Followers of the MacDonald Lords of the Isles, the MacQuarries were forced to seek the protection of the MacLeans of Mull after the fall of the Lordship in 1493. MacQuarrie of Ulva was one of the clan chiefs who appeared before the Bishop of the Isles at Iona in 1609 to swear loyalty to King James VI and I.

The MacQuarries were a distinguished military family in the 18th century, and Major-General Lachlan MacQuarrie became Governor of New South Wales (the fledgeling colony of Australia) in 1809. (He replaced the ill-fated William Bligh, deposed from the Governorship – *see* MacArthur). He remained in this post until 1821, and is remembered as a liberal, reforming figure. He was cousin to the last of the Ulva chiefs, who died in 1819 aged 103. The chiefship today is vacant.

The clansman's crest badge is 'An Armoured Hand Brandishing A Dagger' with the motto *An-t-arm breac dearg* ('the red tartaned army'). Small though Clan MacQuarrie is, there are no less than seven acknowledged tartans for the name.

150

Finlay MacQuarrie, a deerstalker on the Isle of Colonsay, *photographed about 1845.*

Macrae

The Macrae surname is from the Gaelic *macrath*, 'son of grace' and is found in such various forms as Macrae, Macraith, and Mcrea. The clan originally lived in the Beauly district near Inverness, moving south-west into Kintail, in Ross, in the mid-14th century. The founder of the Kintail Macraes was Fionnla Dubh MacGillechriosd, who died in 1415. Duncan Macrae, 5th Chief of Kintail, was given lands around Inverinate on Loch Duich in the 1550s, and these were held by the Macraes for well over two centuries. There is still a Clan Macrae of Inverinate today, which claims chiefship of all the Macraes.

The Macraes were related to the Kintail branch of the great Clan MacKenzie. They were Chamberlains of Kintail for generations, and from about 1520 were also Constables of Eilean Donan Castle on Loch Duich. The Macraes are credited for having served the MacKenzies well, fighting for them with such vigour and courage that they were known as the MacKenzies' 'Shirts of Mail' – which may mean that they formed the bodyguard of the larger clan. At the Battle of Sheriffmuir in the first Jacobite Rising of 1715, it is said that the Macrae contingent fighting alongside the MacKenzies fell almost to a man.

The Reverend Farquhar Macrae (1580–1662) was Vicar of Kintail for 44 years. One of his sons, John Macrae, was ancestor of the Conchra branch of the clan.

The chiefship is vacant at present.

Macrae crest badge

Below: Eilean Donan Castle whose hereditary Constables were Macraes. The Royal Navy bombarded the Jacobite defenders in the 1715 rising.

MacSporran

Although the Macsporrans bear a name that many people suspect to be a music-hall joke, they are a genuine if small family – fewer than 400 are known around the world – who in medieval times were important vassals to the Lords of the Isles. The MacSporrans served as hereditary Pursebearers, treasurers in effect, to what was one of medieval Europe's most powerful offshore principalities until it was annexed by James IV of Scotland in 1493. Prince Charles is the present Lord of the Isles.

The Clan name – *Mac-an-Sporain* in Gaelic, 'Son of the Purse' – has undergone several changes over the centuries. A Paul na Sporan is reputed to have been Treasurer to Malcolm II, King of Scotland from 1005 to 1034. Certainly there are listed, among the tombs of the kings of Scotland and their notables on the island of Iona, 'the tombs of Gilbrid and Paul Sporran, antient tribes of the Mack Donalds'. In 1627, a Duncan M'Sparrane was one of the McNachtane (MacNaughton) chief's soldiers who took ship at Lochkilcherane for service in France, possibly with the famed *Garde Ecossaise* of Scottish soldiers who fought for the kings of France.

A Donald M'Sporran is recorded at Auchnagairoch in the Parish of Knapdaill in 1677, and the same spelling recurs with Gormla N'Sporran in the following year. The latter name displays the abbreviated female form of the patronymic, *Nic*, itself a contracted form of the Gaelic *Nighean mhic* – literally, 'daughter of the son of'. She was the wife of Donald M'Ilcher in Muastaill, Parish of Killean, in 1678. When clan names were proscribed after the Jacobite rising of 1745, the name of MacSporran is said to have been anglicized to 'Pursell'. The office of ship's 'purser' is the modern survival of the medieval office of 'pursebearer', which was not unique to Scotland.

In 1976, John MacSporran of Hilton, Dunfermline, was elected chief by a *derbfhine* (Council of Elders) from the Clan Society. The election was duly recognized by the Lord Lyon, but a few years later the Clan Society sought to 'de-select' John and elected lawyer Paul MacSporran in his stead. The question of the chiefship has still to be satisfactorily resolved. The best known of the name today is Seumas MacSporran, who is almost a clan in his own right. On the tiny, west coast island of Gigha, he is the one and only Harbour Master, Special Constable, Sub-Postmaster (and postman), rent collector, shopkeeper, taxi-driver, ambulance driver, volunteer fireman, insurance agent *and* petrol pump attendant.

MacThomas

Earlier this century a Lord Lyon, King of Arms, is said to have exclaimed, 'Clan MacThomas? All they have is a quarter of an acre and a telegraph pole in Glenshee!' He was referring to the last of the clan lands in Glenshee, a wooded knoll which is the traditional Gathering Place of Clan MacThomas. It stands on the west side of the A93 Blairgowrie–Braemar road, less than 6 km (4 miles) south of the Spittal of Glenshee.

Clan MacThomas seems to stem from a descendant of the Mackintoshes who led the great confederation of small clans which took the wild cat as its totem and became known as *Clann Chattan* (pronounced 'Hattan'). The validity of this claim can be seen in the old *red lyon* of the Mackintoshes, borne on MacThomas heraldic achievements. The *red lyon* itself in turn shows descent from the great Clan MacDuff of the 12th century, which controlled vast territories in central and eastern Scotland and whose younger sons were the seed of numerous smaller clans.

The Mackintosh ancestor of Clan MacThomas was Adam M'William of Garvamore in Badenoch, natural son of the 7th Chief of Clan Mackintosh. Some time thereafter there appears in the clan history a character who is the true namefather of the clan, leading his followers away from Badenoch into Glenisla and Glenshee. He was probably the legendary MacThomas or 'Big Tommy', rendered in Gaelic as *Mac Thomaidh* (pronounced 'Mak Combee'). In 1571 John McComy-Mhuir (*Mac Thomaidh Mor*) was confirmed in the lands of Finegand in Glenshee, of which his family had been ancient inhabitants.

In the mid-17th century the MacThomas chieftain supported Cromwell, and after the Restoration of Charles II in 1660 was described as having 'grate power with the late Vsurpers (*sic*) as their intelligencer and favourite' – in other words, a collaborator. In the Roll of Clans of 1587 there is listed 'Clan M'Thomas in Glenesche', while in 1594 they appear in the Roll of broken clans in the class of 'mony brokin men'. A generation later a poor widow, Kaithren M'Comey, was convicted of 'blooding the Lairdis ky (*cows*)', which suggests famine. Certainly the clan began to disperse across Inverness-shire and Perthshire around that time, so that the name MacComy was common in Breadalbane by the 1700s.

The Chief today is Andrew MacThomas of Finegand, 19th Chief of Clan MacThomas since the Lyon Court recognized his father as the rightful chief of the clan.

Maitland

One of the earliest mentions of this name in Scotland was that of Thomas de Matulant, in 1227. The early nickname of 'Maltalent', probably applied to a somewhat slow-witted Norman, implies a slur which the subsequent history of the Maitland family does not sustain. Sir Richard de Mauteland acquired the lands of Thurlestane by marriage to an heiress over 700 years ago, and the lands and castle of that name have been in the family ever since.

MacThomas crest badge

Below: Thirlestane Castle, a 12th-century fort which was rebuilt as a fortified residence by John Maitland about 1590.

The 1st Baron Maitland was Secretary of State and Lord Chancellor of Scotland in 1590. His son was created Earl and his grandson Duke of Lauderdale. This worthy fought both for and against Charles I, but later became the 'L' in the CABAL of ministers (the other four being Clifford, Ashley, Buckingham and Arlington) which served Charles II after his Restoration in 1660. Alternately repressive and conciliatory, the corruption of Lauderdale's regime finally brought about his downfall in 1679. His numerous titles became extinct when he died without male heirs, and the Earldom reverted to his brother. Since then, many other Maitlands have distinguished themselves in the Army and Navy, and as lawyers and statesmen.

The present Chief is the 17th Earl of Lauderdale, whose heir is styled 'Master of Lauderdale' in addition to his courtesy title of Viscount Maitland. (*His* son is styled 'Master of Maitland'.) The Earl is Hereditary Saltire Banner Bearer of Scotland. The clansman's crest badge is 'A Seated Lion, holding a Sword in the Right Paw and a Fleur-de-lys in the Left', with the motto *Consilio et Animis* ('By Counsel and by Thoughts'). A tartan was designed in the 1970s, the sale of which is strictly controlled by the chief.

153

Makgill

The Makgills of That Ilk descend from Malcolm, son of the Lord of Galloway who died in 1185, and their arms are recorded in one of the oldest heraldic manuscripts at the Court of the Lord Lyon. In Gaelic, *mac an ghoill* means 'descendant of the stranger' (or 'Lowlander'). Also spelled 'McGill' and 'MacGill', it is a common name in Galloway, but the family of the chief today, along with some others, prefer to retain the early form: 'Makgill'.

The Makgills of Rankeillour in Perthshire are one of the most senior branches of the clan. Sir James, of that branch, was deeply involved in the murder (1566) of David Rizzio, Secretary to Mary, Queen of Scots. Sir James Makgill of Makgill was created one of the earliest Baronets of Nova Scotia in 1627 and a Lord of Sesson (judge) in 1629, before becoming the Viscount of Oxfuird in 1651. The 2nd Viscount died in 1706, and the title lay dormant until the claim to the title of the present chief was successfully pleaded before the House of Lords in recent years. The heir to the Chiefship and Viscountcy is styled 'The Master of Oxfuird'.

The Makgill tartan only dates back to 1953. The clansman's crest badge is a Martlet, and the motto *In domino confido* ('In the Lord I Trust').

Malcolm

The Malcolms were originally the McCallums (although some historians argue that these were two different families). They are a small Argyllshire clan originally centred in Lorn, with territory in the Lochawe district.

The McCallums derived their name from *Mac Ghille Chaluim*, which means 'devotee of St Columba'. In 1414, Duncan Campbell made a grant of land by Loch Craignish to Ranald MacCallum of

Malcolm crest badge

Corbarron, who became hereditary castellan of Craignish Castle. In the 17th century, the last of the Corbarron MacCallums left his lands to another branch of the family headed by Sir Zachary Mac-Callum of Poltalloch, near Duntrune.

In the 1770s, Dugald MacCallum, 9th Chief of Poltalloch, changed the family name to Malcolm. The 15th Chief, John Malcolm, was created Lord Malcolm of Poltalloch in 1896, after many years as Member of Parliament for Argyll. At his death in 1904, he owned some 32,375 hectares (80,000 acres).

The original clansman's motto was *Deus refugium nostrum* ('God is our refuge').

Mar

A description of the Parish of Mar in Aberdeenshire in 1732 states: 'There are to this day, some people in this country of the surname of MAR, but of no account.' In fact, this small clan has the curious distinction of having always been classed 'The Tribe of Mar' and its chiefs, holders of one of the oldest Earldoms in Scotland. For Mar, with Buchan, was one of the great provinces of Pictish Scotland – Alba – to be controlled by a Mormaer, equivalent to the Welsh Princes. Mar was one of the seven great Earls or Princes of Alba, from all of whom the Royal Family can show lines of descent. For this reason an Earl of Mar is classed as a Prince, and is referred to by the Sovereign as 'Cousin'.

Donald, Mormaer of Mar, is reported to have been killed at the Battle of Clontarf, the great battle in Ireland at which High King Brian Boru died defeating the Vikings, in 1014. The Mormaer of Mar was present on the more peaceable occasion of the founding of Scone Abbey in 1114. Just a little over six centuries later, the Earl of Mar raised the Royal Standard in the name of Prince James Edward in the first Jacobite Rising of 1715.

The clansman's crest badge is a 'Pair of Wings' and the motto of Mar *Pan Plus*. The Mar tartan is not believed to be old and the present Chief, the Countess of Mar, has authorized an old pattern which is known to have been woven in the Mar lands of Glenbuchat in the first half of the 18th century, as an additional sett which she prefers to wear.

Marjoriebanks

Marjorie, daughter of King Robert the Bruce, was progenitrix of the Royal House of Stewart. When in 1316 she married Walter FitzAlan, High Steward of

Scotland, lands in the Barony of Ratho were bestowed on her *(terre de Ratho-Marjoriebankis).* The Johnstone family, which later acquired these lands, adopted the territorial designation as their surname. (It is pronounced 'March-banks'.) Joseph Marjoriebanks built the imposing Northfield House, near Prestonpans, in 1611.

The Chief of the Clan today is William Marjoriebanks of That Ilk; there is no known tartan for the name.

Matheson

'Matheson' is the anglicized version of *Mac-Mhathain,* a clan which was related to the Mac-Kenzies. The ealiest known clan chief was the 2nd Chief, Cormac MacMhathain, who in 1263 or 1264, was rewarded for assisting the Earl of Ross in the wars between the Scots and the Norsemen on the western coast and in the Islands. The greatest Scottish victory of these wars was at the Battle of Largs (1263), when Alexander III defeated the Norsemen under Haakon IV, King of Norway. Cormac's role in the struggle was mentioned in the saga of King Haakon: ' . . .the dispeace that the Earl

The bustling ferry port on the Kyle of Lochalsh, the lands bordering which were held by the Mathesons from 1476.

of Ross and Kiarnak Makamael's son [Cormac] and other Scots had made in the Hebrides . . . ' This does not prove Cormac's presence in Largs, but it does establish his involvement in the power-struggle for the Islands.

Clan Matheson held land in Ross, particularly in Lochalsh, and also in Sutherland. In 1427 the Matheson chief is noted for having the capability of raising 2,000 men from his clan and dependants when need arose. But in that year the Mathesons forfeited Lochalsh, and perhaps other territory, after a dispute with King James I (1406–37).

When John MacDonald of the Isles, last Earl of Ross, was overthrown by James III in the 1470s, the Mathesons remained loyal to the MacDonalds, only to pay for it with further confiscations.

James Matheson (of the Shinshess branch) founded the mighty Hong Kong company of Jardine Matheson in 1827, and was instrumental in getting the British government to insist that the Chinese authorities allow British merchants to import opium freely into China. After China was defeated in the ensuing Opium Wars, it ceded the 'barren island' of Hong Kong to the British. Matheson was knighted and made enough money to buy the Isle of Lewis in 1844.

The present chief is Sir Torquhil Matheson of Lochalsh, 6th Baronet and one of Her Majesty's Gentlemen-at-Arms. The clansman's crest badge has the motto *Fac et spera* ('Do and hope').

Alexander Matheson of Lochalsh was created a baronet in 1882. The baronetcy had to miss a generation on the death of the 3rd Baronet, whose three sons were all killed during World War I.

Maxwell

The Maxwell Clan territory lies mainly in the south-west of Scotland. The clan name comes from Maccus, a Norse chief who was an associate of David I (1124–53). His descendant Eumerus, or Aymer, had two sons. One of these, Herbert Maxwell, swore fealty to Edward I of England in 1296. His son Sir Eustace Maxwell held Caerlaverock Castle in Dumfriesshire for the English King, but before the Battle of Bannockburn in 1314 had changed sides to support King Robert the Bruce. One of his descendants, Sir Herbert Maxwell, was made Lord Maxwell in the 1440s and sat in the Scottish Parliament. Lord Maxwell died in 1452 and was succeeded by his son Sir Robert Maxwell, who died in 1488.

In common with many Scottish lords and clan chiefs, the 5th Lord Maxwell intrigued with both James V of Scotland (1513–42) and Henry VIII of England during the 1530s. By 1542 Maxwell was Warden of the Scottish Marches for James V, and in that year he organized an invasion of northern England. This was repulsed in the Battle of Solway Moss, and Maxwell was captured. The news of the defeat is said to have hastened the death of James V a few weeks later.

The 8th Lord Maxwell was one of the leading Scottish lords who remained Catholic after the Protestant conversion of Scotland in the 1560s. He was involved in a number of schemes to restore the Catholic Mary, Queen of Scots, to the throne. After Mary's trial and execution in England (1587) and the defeat of the Spanish Armada in the following year, Maxwell continued corresponding with Philip II of Spain with a view to helping the Catholic cause. Maxwell's letters were intercepted by spies of Walsingham, Elizabeth I's Secretary of State, but he seems to have been left unmolested. Maxwell was finally killed in 1593, in a clan feud between the Maxwells and the Johnstons near Lockerbie.

Maxwell's second son Robert, the 9th Lord Maxwell, was created 1st Earl of Nithsdale in 1620; he is remembered for having set up a community settlement at Langholm. His desendant, the 8th Earl (1676–1744), achieved one of the 'great escapes' of British history. A staunch Jacobite, he was captured in the Battle of Preston during the collapse of the 1715 rising, taken to London, tried, and sentenced to death for treason. On the night before his execution, aided by his brave wife, Nithsdale escaped from the Tower disguised as a woman. The Earl and his wife both escaped from England and settled in Rome; he died in 1744.

Maxwell crest badge

Below: Caerlaverock Castle in Dumfriesshire.

Melville

This surname was brought to Scotland by Norman knights from Malleville in Normandy; Galfridus 'de Malveill' is the first of the name recorded. In the last quarter of the 12th century he appears as a witness to the earliest-known charter of the Burgh of Aberdeen, and was the first recorded Justiciary of Scotland. Nine Melvilles or 'Malevilles' rendered homage to Edward I of England in 1296, by which time the Melville name had been given to lands in Fife as well as Midlothian. The famous scholar Andrew Melville (1542–1622), in turn Principal of both St Andrews and Glasgow universities, shows how the surname proliferated into over 50 variants. On one page in his diary he spells his own name 'Melville' and 'Melvin'.

Robert, 1st Baron Melville, was Ambassador to England in 1562. George, 1st Earl Melville, supported the rebellion of Charles II's illegitimate son, the Duke of Monmouth (1685) and was forced to flee to the Continent. In 1688 he returned in the train of William of Orange, who, when he came to the throne, heaped honours upon Melville. He married the granddaughter of the Covenanting general, the Earl of Leven (*see* Leslie); their son became 2nd Earl of Melville *and* 3rd Earl of Leven.

Menzies crest badge

The Chief of the Whole Name and Arms of Melville today is the 14th Earl of Leven and 13th of Melville. The clansman's crest badge is a 'Ratchet Hound's Head' with the motto *Denique coelum* ('Finally to Heaven'). For reasons which are not quite clear, the 'Melville' tartan is exactly the same as that used by the Oliphants.

Menzies

The name of Menzies probably derives from the Norman district of Mesnières, near Rouen. The first-known chief of that name known in Scotland was Sir Robert de Mesnières, who held lands in Tayside during the reigns of Alexander II (1214–49) and Alexander III (1249–86). He was Chamberlain of Scotland in 1240, and is known to have held territory around Weem near Aberfeldy and Durisdeer, further south in Nithsdale. A son (or maybe grandson) fought with Robert the Bruce at Bannockburn. In 1487 a descendant, Sir Robert Menzies, was confirmed as Clan Chief, and his son, also Robert, was created Lord Menzies by James IV in 1510.

A descendant of Lord Menzies, Sir Alexander Menzies, was made a Baronet by Charles II in 1665. His brother, James Menzies of Culdares, who had fought for the Covenant in the Civil War, quarrelled with the MacDonalds of Glencoe in the time of Charles II, and in one skirmish received nine arrow wounds in the legs – a reminder of how the bow and arrow, ideal for silent ambushes, remained in use in Highland warfare long after archery had disappeared from most other parts of Europe.

One of the Menzies of Culdares claims the distinction of having introduced the larch tree into Scotland from the Austrian Tyrol, sometime about 1738. Another famous Menzies descendant of more recent times was Sir Robert Menzies, Prime Minister of Australia 1939–41 and 1949–66, afterwards honoured in Britain with the title of Lord Warden of the Cinque Ports.

Moffat

The town of Moffat in Annandale, Dumfriesshire, is the origin of this Lowland clan name. The first appearance of the surname is a churchman named Nicholas de Mufet, who witnessed a charter by the Bishop of Glasgow around 1230. In 1268 he was himself elected Bishop of Glasgow, but died in 1270 without, for some reason, having been consecrated. Robert 'de Muffet' and Thomas 'de Moffet', both of Dumfriesshire, rendered homage to Edward I of England in 1296.

In 1587 the Act 'For the quieting and keping in obedience of the disorderit subjectis inhabitantis of the Bordouris, Hielandis an Ilis' specifically mentions the 'Moffetis of the West Marche' as being among the more unruly Border clans. (One of the spellings of the name around that time was 'Muffett'.)

The father-in-law of the famous African explorer, Dr David Livingstone, was the Reverend Robert Moffat of the London Missionary Society. Moffat founded the mission station at Kuruman in South Africa which Livingstone used as a base for his first African travels in the 1840s.

Today the Court of the Lord Lyon recognizes Francis Moffat of that Ilk as 'the direct line representer of the ancient Moffats of that Ilk, and thereby Chief of the Whole Name and Arms of Moffat'. There are two Moffat tartans.

Moncreiffe

According to Burke's *Peerage*, this is 'the oldest family in Perthshire to have retained their original lands in the male line'. The name derives from the feudal Barony which itself stems from the Gaelic place-name *Monadh Craoibhe*, 'hill of the sacred bough'. Moncreiffe Hill, to the south-east of Perth, was a stronghold of the Pictish kings: *Dun Monaidh*, conveniently sited in the triangle formed by the inauguration mound of the Kings at Scone, the Royal Abbey at Abernethy, and the Palace at Forteviot.

The early tenures held by the Moncreiffe chiefs, and the royal 'Red Lyon' borne on their heraldic arms, point to their descent from one of the younger branches of the Scottish-Pictish royal family – probably that of Maldred, brother of the King Duncan I slain by Macbeth in 1040. Maldred's lineage can be traced back to the great Irish king, Niall of the Nine Hostages, around AD 400.

The Moncreiffes were confirmed in their lands by a charter of 1248. Some 50 years later, William 'de Monncrefe' was forced to swear fealty to Edward I of England after being captured with other Scots barons on the return from a great raid into Northumberland.

The Moncreiffes have continued to be a famous military family to the present day. John Moncreiffe of that Ilk was killed at Flodden in 1513, along with his cousin, John of Easter Moncreiffe, while various lairds have been Archers of the Sovereign's Bodyguard. From Moncreiffes who joined the Scottish Archer Guard of the Kings of France (a regiment said to date back to the Crusades), three noble families evolved in France; the Marquis de Moncrif was guillotined during the French Revolution. In the last 100 years, the Moncreiffes have produced a bevy of big-game hunters and cattle ranchers in the American west.

When Sir David Moncreiffe, 10th Baronet of that Ilk and 23rd Laird of Moncreiffe, died in a fire which destroyed Moncreiffe House (1957), the Baronetcy passed to his cousin Iain. Sir David's sister, Miss Elisabeth, was denied the Baronetcy because this descended only to 'male heirs whatever'. However, she inherited the feudal Barony and became 24th Laird of Moncreiffe and Chief of the Clan.

Shortly afterwards, she made her cousin Iain 'liferenter' of the style 'of that Ilk', and thereby of the chiefship, but retained the style 'Moncreiffe of Moncreiffe' and the feudal Barony. To conform with tradition and the requirements of feudal legality, this transaction took place before the Bar of the Court of the Lord High Constable of Scotland – who happened to be Sir Iain's wife, Countess of Erroll in her own right (see Hay). The 'Court' took place in the stables at Moncreiffe House, which possessed a suitable rail which served as the 'Bar' before which the two parties could appear before the High Constable in session. When Sir Iain (Albany Herald at the Court of the Lord Lyon for almost a quarter of a century) died in 1985, the Moncreiffe chiefship reverted to Miss Elisabeth; the Baronetcy passed to his eldest son Merlin, who had already succeeded his late mother as Earl of Erroll and Chief of Clan Hay. The heir to Miss Elisabeth 'of Moncreiffe' is Peregrine Moncreiffe of Moncreiffe, Sir Iain's younger son.

The Moncreiffe clansman's crest badge is 'A Demi-Lyon Rampant Rising From the Golden Coronet of a Scottish Chief', with the motto *Sur esperance* ('Upon Hope'). As a result of a long association with Clan Murray, the Moncreiffes traditionally wore the Atholl tartan. But after he became Chief, Sir Iain, the 11th Baronet, arranged that Madam MacLachlan of MacLachlan assign to him a 'primitive' pattern of red and green squares which, though no longer favoured by Clan MacLachlan, Sir Iain felt was appropriate to the long history of the Moncreiffes 'before tartan became fashionable in its present form'.

Sir Iain Moncreiffe of that Ilk, Bt. (1919–85) Clan Chief and Albany Herald.

Montgomerie crest badge

Montgomerie

A Lowland clan, the Montgomeries stem from Robert de Mundegumri, grandson of Earl Roger de Montgomery, one of the Norman lords and supporters who accompanied William the Conqueror to England in 1066. Roger was granted lands in Shropshire, Herefordshire, and the border district with Wales. His grandson Robert was granted the territory of Eaglesham in Renfrewshire.

A descendant, the 7th chief, Sir John Montgomerie of Eaglesham, fought the English in the Battle of Otterburn in 1388 and captured the famous Harry Percy, 'Hotspur', son of the 1st Earl of Northumberland. John Montgomerie married the heiress to Sir Hugh de Eglinton, and the grandson of this union, Alexander, was created Lord Montgomerie in the 1440s. One of his sons, George, was the ancestor of the Montgomeries of Skelmorlie. The eldest son, Alexander, predeceased his father, with the result that his younger son Alexander became the 2nd Lord Montgomerie. His son Hugh, the 3rd Lord, was created 1st Earl of Eglinton in 1507. His great-grandson Hugh, the 3rd Earl, was a supporter of Mary, Queen of Scots.

The 6th Earl was a Covenanter at the outset of the Great Civil War, fought with the Scottish Army on the Parliamentary side at the Battle of Marston Moor in 1644, but later changed sides and supported the Prince of Wales, afterwards Charles II. Captured at the Battle of Berwick in 1651, he remained a prisoner until the Restoration.

Alexander, the 10th Earl of a Lord of the Bedchamber of King George III, was shot by an armed excise officer – a Campbell – who had wandered on to his land, and who opened fire when challenged by the Earl. Campbell was tried and convicted of murder, but hanged himself in his cell. The 10th Earl was succeeded by his brother,

Archibald Montgomerie, who had raised one of the first Highland regiments, the 78th Highlanders, and led it with distinction in the campaign that won Canada for Britain with the Battle of Quebec in 1759. The Regiment won special praise from General James Wolfe, the British commander who was killed at Quebec in the moment of victory. The portrait of Archibald Montgomerie by Sir Joshua

Eglinton Castle, ancestral seat of the Montgomerie chiefs and site of the 1839

'Eglinton Tournament', a romantic revival of the medieval practice of jousting.

Reynolds is held in the Royal Collection.

The present chief is the Earl of Eglinton and Winton.

Morrison

The Morrisons are often said to have been of Norse origin. They first appear as a clan in the Outer Hebrides, particularly on the Isle of Lewis. The family stemmed from Ceadhain MacMhuirrich, an offshoot of the Clan MacDonald which descendend from the great Somerled, the half-Norse/half-Scottish ruler of the Western Isles who died in 1164. The earliest Morrison clan chiefs were hereditary judges or *brieves* (another word for *brehon*, a Gaelic judge and lawmaker) of Lewis. The Morrisons held the brieveship until the 17th century.

Most of the history of Clan Morrison is obscure. A number of Morrison families moved from Lewis to Caithness and Sutherland in the 17th century, but it is interesting to note that Sir Thomas Innes of Learney quotes the 1861 Census as showing that there were just over 1,400 Morrisons in Lewis, which was about one-seventeenth of the island's total population.

Two Morrison descendants from the Hebrides have come to prominence in the present century: John Morrison, a leading Conservative back-bencher in the 1950s and 1960s, who became 1st Lord Margadale in 1964; and William Morrison, Speaker of the House of Commons and later Governor-General of Australia, created 1st Viscount Dunrossil in 1959.

Munro

The Gaelic name for Munro was *Rothach*, 'man from the Ro' (varied in time to 'Monrosse'); the clan first settled in the area of Foulis in East Ross. The first chief 'of Foulis' was Hugh, who died in 1126 and the next Munro Chief on record was George, who obtained a land grant from King Alexander II (1214–49). A descendant Chief was Robert Munro, who supported Robert the Bruce at Bannockburn in 1314. The 8th Chief, Robert, married a niece of Queen Euphemia, wife of King Robert II (1371–90) and half-sister of William, the last Celtic Earl of Ross. Robert Munro was killed fighting for the Rosses. The 12th Chief of Clan Munro was knighted by James IV.

The next Munro of interest was the 18th Chief, Robert of Foulis, who became a colonel in the army of Gustavus Adolphus, King of Sweden, the leading Protestant commander in the Thirty Years War (1618–48). Munro raised a company of his clan and their dependants to accompany him to Germany, at a time when there were 27 field officers and 11 captains in the Swedish army, bearing the surname

Munro. Chief Robert himself was mortally wounded at the Battle of Ulm in 1633, a year after the death of Gustavus Adolphus at Lutzen. He was succeeded as 19th Chief by his brother Hector, who was created a Baronet by King Charles I in 1634.

Sir John Munro, the 4th Baronet, fought on the side of William III in the Scottish campaign of 1689. The 6th Baronet, Sir Robert Munro, with his brother Duncan, fell at Falkirk, fighting for the Hanoverian King George II in the Jacobite rising of 1745–46.

James Monroe of Virginia (1758–1831) became 5th President of the United States of America in 1857, and served two terms. He was the originator of the famous Monroe Doctrine: a statement of American foreign policy (1823) opposing the extension of European control or influence in the Western Hemisphere, a doctrine to which all United States presidents have adhered ever since.

The present chief is Capt. Patrick Munro of Foulis.

Morrison crest badge   *Munro crest badge*

Murray

This was a very powerful clan that at one time had extensive landholdings in Scotland. Murray chiefs and leaders were often at the centre of great events and movements in Scottish history between the late 13th and late 16th centuries. The clan name originates from the northern province of Moravia, or Moray, which was once a kingdom in the days of Celtic domination over Scotland. The clan's founder is said to have been Freskin, variously described as an Anglo-Norman lord given land in the Lothians and in Moray (which at that time included parts of Inverness, Nairn, and Ross) by King David I (1124–53); or, alternatively, a Pictish–Scottish lord from the ancient race of Moray.

Freskin's grandson William de Moravia added to the Moray territory by obtaining parts of Lanark, including the lands of Bothwell; the Morays, as the clan was then known, were Lords of Bothwell from about 1200 to 1360. William's direct heir was Walter de Moravia, but there were other sons as well, one of whom founded the Tullibardine branch.

Walter de Moravia, Lord of Bothwell, acted as co-Regent of Scotland in the 1250s, when King Alexander III (1249–86) was still a minor. The 3rd Lord of Bothwell died in the Tower of London as a prisoner of King Edward I of England. His son (or brother) was Andrew de Moravia, the famous colleague of Sir William Wallace at the outset of the campaign to free Scotland from English rule at the end of the 13th century (*see* Wallace).

Andrew Moray, the 4th Lord of Bothwell, was Regent of Scotland during the first years of David II (1329–71). He died in about 1338 and was followed by his son, the 5th and last Lord of Bothwell who, having married his cousin (another Moray) died of the Black Death in 1360. For many years there was a dispute over which branch of the Morays should provide the chief, but by the 16th century the Murrays of Tullibardine in Strathearn were recognized as the chiefly line, and from 1541 they formally assumed the chiefship.

Murray crest badge

Below: The Duke of Atholl, chief of the Clan Murray, inspects his Atholl Highlanders, the last private army in Europe.

In 1606, Sir John Murray of Tullibardine was created Earl of Tullibardine. His father Sir William Murray, the 11th Chief, had been Comptroller of Scotland and had supported Mary, Queen of Scots during her last months as reigning monarch. At this time there were several Murray branches, including those of Abercairney, Cockpool, Cobairdy, Falahull, and Elibank. Since 1606, however, the supremacy of the Tullibardine Chief has never been seriously challenged.

The 2nd Earl of Tullibardine married the heiress to the Earls of Atholl, an Earldom which was advanced to the Marquessate of Atholl in 1676

and to a Dukedom in 1706. The 1st Duke of Atholl was a bitter opponent of the Act of Union with England of 1707, and he and his sons were active Jacobites in the Rising of 1715. One son, Lord George Murray, also took part in the Rising of 1745–46, and passed into Jacobite legend as the man who actually unfurled the Royal Standard of Bonnie Prince Charlie at Glenfinnan on 19 August, 1745.

The subsidiary title of the present Duke of Atholl is Marquess of Tullibardine.

Napier

The name of this small but influential clan is sometimes confused with the English surname 'Naper', which stems from the officer of a royal or noble household who was responsible for the 'napery' or linen. The Scottish Napiers take their surname from an indeterminate historical incident when a younger son of the Earl of Lennox changed, by his skill and bravery, the outcome of a battle which the King of Scots was on the point of losing. After the fight, the King declared to his nobles that all had fought valiantly but that one among them had 'nae peer', or no equal. He thereupon granted young Donald of Lennox the lands of Gosfield in Fife and commanded him to assume the surname of 'Na Per', later amended to 'Napier'.

John 'le Naper' obtained a charter for the lands of Kilmethew in Dunbartonshire from his kinsman, the Earl of Lennox, around 1290. This is undoubtedly the same John le Naper who rendered homage to Edward I of England in 1296. He was the forebear of the Napiers of Merchiston, whose 15th-century castle forms the core of Napier College in Edinburgh today.

John Napier of Merchiston (1550–1617) invented natural logarithms and spherical trigonometry; his calculating devices were known as 'Napier's Bones'. The family has always excelled in the fields of scholarship, science, and engineering, as demonstrated by the famous despatch of General Sir Charles Napier. When he captured the Indian province of Sind in 1843, he sent a punning despatch to London, the single Latin word *Peccavi* – 'I have sinned'.

Then there was engineer David Napier, who invented the 'steeple engine' in 1820. His more gifted cousin Robert Napier constructed his first marine engine in 1823, and began shipbuilding in 1841. He built the first four steamships of the Cunard Line, helping open up the Americas to a flow of better-educated immigrants who provided the entrepreneurial and management skills needed

to develop the continent. The Lieutenant appointed by the Clan Chief for the United States is a noted historian, Lieutenant-Colonel John Hawkins Napier III, USAF (retd).

The Chief today is The Rt. Hon. Major The Lord Napier and Ettrick, who is Private Secretary and Comptroller to Princess Margaret, Countess of Snowdon. The clansman's crest badge is 'An Arm Grasping a Crescent' with the mottoes *Sans tache* ('Without Stain') and 'Ready aye Ready'. The tartan is a typical pre-1800 design in blue and black on a white ground.

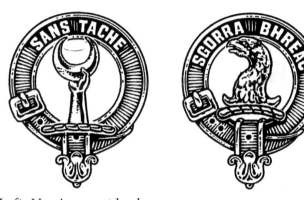

Left: Napier crest badge
Right: Nicolson of Scorrybreac crest badge

Nicolson

The Nicolsons, or Clan MacNicol as the family was known in its early years, originated in west Sutherland, beside Loch Assynt. The name appears in early documents in more than one form, such as 'MacNeacail' or 'M'Nicail'. Probably in the 14th century, a daughter of the last MacNicol of Assynt married Torquil MacLeod of Lewis, and the clan moved away from Assynt to the Isle of Skye. Here they settled at several places, the principal settlement being Scorrybreac, near Portree, where the clan chiefs lived for centuries.

In time the Skye MacNicols changed the family name to Nicolson (which means the same), while kindred MacNicols on the mainland tended to retain the older form. The Assynt lands, meanwhile, passed to the MacLeods, to earn infamy in 1650 as the place where Neil MacLeod betrayed the great Montrose to the Covenanters. The betrayer was condemned in verse by the fine Gaelic poet Ian Lom, here translated by Sheriff Nicholson: *Neil's son of woeful Assynt . . . Strippt tree of the false apples, Without esteem, or fame, or grace.*

Very little is known of the Nicolson history. One curiosity is the relationship of the Andrew Nicolson who fought on the losing side – in the army of Haakon of Norway – at the Battle of Largs in 1263. MacNicols are also said to have sat on the Council of the Lord of the Isles, and the clan played an important role in the history of Skye.

The last Chief of the Clan who lived at Scorrybreac was Norman Nicolson, who emigrated to New Zealand in the 19th century. The Nicolson line continues in Australia (see MacNeacail).

Ogilvy

Although the Ogilvies take their name from that of their baronial lands of Ogilvie near Glamis in Angus, the name itself may stem from a Celtic–British place-name describing the high ground of Glen Ogilvie – *Ocel Fa* – dating back at least 1,600 years. As 'Oggvlvin' (with 'u' and 'v' casually interchanged at that time), the lands were chartered to Gillebride, or Gilbert, by his father the Earl of Angus. King William the Lyon (1165–1214) later made him the feudal Baron of Ogilvie.

After more than 800 years the Ogilvies are still on those lands, but many Ogilvies could claim personal descent from the Pictish sub-kings of Angus, later styled earls, for another 500 or more years before that. Clan Ogilvie's main feud was with its powerful neighbours, the Crawfords. In one battle against the Crawfords in 1445, the Ogilvies were said to have been convinced that they were only beaten because their tartan contained too much of the fairy colour: green.

There are several variations on the surname, with one old east coast rhyme teasing the Ogilvies with 'Ugly you live and Ugly you'll die'. The main variants are 'Ogilvie', 'Ogilvy', and 'Ogilby', although many of the clansmen who served with the Scots Guard for the King of France after 1422 were recorded as 'Ohilby'.

As the 1640s opened, the Royalist sympathies of James Ogilvy, 1st Earl of Airlie, attracted the heavy hand of the Campbells under their Covenanting Chief, Argyll. In 1640, 5,000 Campbells of Argyll descended on the Ogilvies and destroyed Castle Airlie. Full revenge was exacted during the harrying of Clan Campbell by Montrose in the winter of 1644–45 (see Campbell). But after Montrose's defeat at Philiphaugh in 1645, Lord James Ogilvy found himself awaiting execution in the castle at St Andrews. After his sister arrived to bid him a tearful farewell, the guards were reluctant to bother the weeping lass as she went off into the night, and so failed to notice that the handkerchief into which she sobbed covered a growth of beard. After this escape, Ogilvy lived to become the 2nd Earl of

Ogilvy crest badge

One of the Ogilvy tartans is so complex that it is known as the weaver's nightmare, with 91 colour shuttle changes in one sett of the pattern.

Airlie and reach the ripe old age of 93. Happily, the brave sister who had taken his place in the death cell escaped punishment.

Today the Chief is David Ogilvy, 13th Earl of Airlie, who is also Lord Chamberlain to HM The Queen. His brother, the Hon Sir Angus Ogilvy, married Princess Alexandra of Kent in 1963. The clansman's crest badge is 'A Maiden Holding a Portcullis' with the motto *A fin* ('To the End'). There are three principal Ogilvy tartans, the oldest being dubbed the 'Weavers' Nightmare' because of its complex pattern.

Oliphant

After saving the life of King David I at the rout of Winchester in 1141, David 'Holifard' was rewarded with a grant of land in Roxburghshire. Of Norman origin, the family originally held lands in Northamptonshire.

Although the surname is often rendered 'Olyfat', 'Olifard', and even 'Oliver', there was a growing tendency to spell and pronounce the name in evocation of the semi-legendary beasts which Crusaders claimed to have seen on their travels: elephants. By the 1300s the surname was busily mutating through 'Olifaunt', 'Olyfant', Olyfawnt', 'Olyphaint', and 'Olephant', to 'Eliphant' in 1711 and 'Oliphant' by 1800.

The Oliphants received the lands of Gask and Aberdalgie from King Robert the Bruce. The lands at Ardblair, near Blairgowrie, passed by marriage with the Oliphants of Gask to the present-day owner, Laurence Kingston-Blair-Oliphant. Lady Caroline Nairne, who wrote some of the greatest Jacobite ballads, was born an Oliphant of Gask. Her forebear was the Edinburgh goldsmith who made for Prince Charles Edward the famous campaign canteen in silver which was found in his abandoned baggage train after Culloden.

The chiefship is vacant at present. The clansman's crest badge is a 'Unicorn's Head' with the motto *A tout pouvoir* ('To the Utmost'). The tartan is the same as the Melville.

Ramsay

The Ramsays are a Lowland clan of Anglo-Norman origin; their first-known Chief was Simon de Ramsay, granted land in the Lothians by David I (1124–53). The next Ramsay on record was William, who witnessed charters in 1198 and 1236. Another Ramsay, Sir Nessus, who may or may not have been a relative, witnessed a charter of Alexander II (1214–49) in 1217. William de Ramsay, son of the earlier William, was a member of the Council of Magnates of the Realm in 1255 and died in 1262. His grandson William Ramsay of Dalhousie was recorded in the Ragman Roll of 1296, became a supporter of Robert the Bruce, and lived to sign the Declaration of Arbroath in 1320.

His elder son, Sir Alexander Ramsay of Dalhousie, was Warden of the Middle Marches and Constable of Roxburgh Castle. In 1342 he was appointed Sheriff of Teviotdale by King David II. This appointment was bitterly resented by Sir William Douglas, the 'Knight of Liddesdale'; he had Ramsay kidnapped, imprisoned, and starved to death. The King made no attempt to punish Douglas for this outrage; indeed, he seems to have given Ramsay's offices to Douglas. But Douglas did not enjoy them for long. He turned traitor to Scotland and joined the English, whereupon the King confiscated Douglas's properties.

Despite Sir Alexander's untimely demise, the Ramsays of Dalhousie continued their line until Sir George Ramsay, Member of Parliament for Kincardine, was created 1st Lord Ramsay of Melrose in 1618. He had his title changed to Lord Ramsay of Dalhousie in the following year. His son William, the 2nd Lord, was advanced to the Earldom of Dalhousie by Charles I in 1633. Like so many others, Dalhousie repaid his monarch's favour by fighting against the King in the Great Civil War, leading an army for the Covenanters; but the Ramsays of Dalhousie kept their Earldom on the Restoration of King Charles II in 1660.

The 10th Earl of Dalhousie was a famous Governor-General of India. Appointed in 1847, when aged only 35 – the youngest ever to hold that important office – he introduced many constructive reforms. In 1849 his Earldom was advanced to a Marquessate, and he remained in office until 1856. When he died in 1860, leaving no male heir, the Marquessate died with him, but his cousin inherited the Earldom.

The present chief is the Earl of Dalhousie K.T. There is one acknowledged tartan.

Ramsay crest badge

Rattray

This small clan was one of a number which in recent times formed a bond of association with the powerful Murrays, whose Chief today is the Duke of Atholl. But in earlier centuries the Rattrays were constantly harassed by the Stewart Earls of Atholl, envious of the considerable Rattray landholdings in Perthshire. These lands had been inherited through the female line of the Stewart royal house, albeit through the wild, bastard son of King Robert II – the 'Wolf of Badenoch'.

After Sir John Rattray of that Ilk was slain at Flodden in 1513, the Atholl men drove his heir, Patrick, out of Rattray Castle and forced his niece Grizel to marry the 3rd Earl of Atholl. In 1533, Patrick Rattray was murdered by Atholl men in his own chapel at Craighall, the new tower house he had built close by what is now Blairgowrie, and which is still the seat of the Rattray family today.

The surname derives from the old Pictish *rath-tref*, 'dwelling fort', which had given its name to the Barony of Rattray. The first Laird on record is Alan de Rattray, around the year 1200. Sir Sylvester Rattray of that Ilk was Ambassador to England in 1463.

The clansman's crest badge is a 'Five-Pointed Star Impaling a Blazing Heart' with the motto *Super sidera votum* ('Wish Higher Than the Stars'). There are two Rattray tartans.

Rattray crest badge

Ardblair Castle, home of one of the senior chieftains of the Clan Oliphant, Laurence Blair-Oliphant.

165

Robertson

Clan Robertson descends from the ancient Celtic hereditary Abbots of Dunkeld. One of these, Abbot Crinan, married Bethoc, daughter of King Malcolm II (1005–34), and their eldest son was Duncan I (1034–40). Thus arose the Clan Donnachaidh or 'Children of Duncan' (the name 'Duncanson' was often used in later years.

One of Duncan's sons was Maelmare, Earl of Atholl, whose descendant Donnachaidh *Reamhar* ('Stout Duncan') led his clan at the Battle of Bannockburn. Another descendant, Robert *Riabhach* ('Grizzled Robert'), was created Baron of the lands of Struan in Tayside. He had rounded up the murderers of King James I (including Sir Robert Graham) and produced them at court, receiving the barony shortly afterwards as a reward. Grizzled Robert was probably the first to use the name 'Robertson' for the clan.

The Robertsons remained faithful to the Stuarts, right down to the Jacobite risings of the 18th century. In the Great Civil War, the Robertsons were called out to support the Covenanters (who fought on the Parliamentary side against King Charles I), but they were persuaded by Montrose to change sides and fight with him, representing the true government of Scotland.

With more supporters like Struan Robertson, the Stuarts would probably still be on the throne. Struan first brought forces to fight in Lord Dundee's army in the war against William III (1689–90). When the Stuart cause collapsed, Robertson was attainted and deprived of some estates. In the next generation he supported James Edward, the Old Pretender, in the 1715 Jacobite rising – and Bonnie Prince Charlie in 1745–46. Though by then Struan Robertson was much too old to fight, it was a remarkable 'triple'.

When the direct line of chiefs ended in 1936 with Miss Robertson of Struan, the claim to the senior line by George Duncan Robertson of Struan was contested on the grounds that he descended from the illegitimate progeny of the liaison between a Robertson of the chiefly line and a black slave girl who had been sold to him by his cousin, Macinroy of Lude. The Lyon Court found in favour of the Jamaican line on the grounds that de facto – unchurched – marriages were customary in Jamaica at that time (1747) and were, therefore, recognized as lawful under Scots Law, which had similar customs, such as 'handfast' marriages, in any event. Langton Robertson of Struan succeeded his father in 1949, and was succeeded by his son Gilbert.

The clansman's crest badge is a hand holding a crown, alluding to the capture of the murderer of King James I by Robertson clansmen. The clan slogan is *Garg'n nair dhussgear* ('Fierce when roused'). There are 18 tartans specific to the clan, plus three for the Mcinroys of Lude.

The western boundary of Robertson clan territory, was effectively the watershed between the Atlantic and the North Sea, at the edge of the Rannoch Moor.

Rollo

After a charter grant by the Earl Palatine of Strathearn, King David II confirmed the lands of Duncrub in Perthshire on John Rollo in 1382. The name is a diminutive of Rudolph and was more commonly varied to 'Rollock', 'Rook', or 'Rolly' in later centuries.

Robert Rollock was the first Principal of Edinburgh University in 1583, and his brother Hercules was Rector of Edinburgh High School in 1584. Peter Rollock was Bishop of Dunkeld in 1585. The 1st Lord Rollo was created in 1651, and the 4th Baron, a noted Jacobite, declared for the Old Pretender in

the rising of 1715. His son Andrew, the 5th Baron Rollo, served as a Brigadier-General in the Seven Years War against the French in North America.

The present Chief is The Lord Rollo in the Peerage of Scotland, and also Baron Dunning and Pitcairns in the Peerage of the United Kingdom. The clansman's crest badge is a 'Stag's Head', but the main Arms bear three boars' heads, adding the Rollos to the large group of medieval Border families who carry the totem of the boar on their Arms. The motto is *La Fortune passe partout* ('Luck Passes Everywhere') and there is a Rollo tartan.

Rose

The name Rose comes from the lordship of Ros, near Caen in Normandy, part of the lands of Odo, Bishop of Bayeux, half-brother of William Duke of Normandy. One of the Bishop's knights was the ancestor of Hugh de Ros, who was established in the Kilravock district of Nairn in Scotland by the 1280s. In the reign of King Alexander II (1214–49) a charter had been witnessed by Hugh Rose of Geddes, and it was his son Hugh who obtained the estate of Kilravock.

The Rose Clan does not figure in Scottish history for some time thereafter, but in the 1460s Hugh Rose, the 7th Chief, began to build Kilravock Castle. In 1474–75, Hugh was confirmed as Lord of Kilravock and other lands by King James III (1460–88). Kilravock Castle has remained a possession of the Rose chiefs ever since. Hugh Rose, 10th Lord of Kilravock, was captured by the English at the Battle of Pinkie Cleugh in 1547; he died 50 years later, aged over 90.

In 1706, Hugh, 15th Lord of Kilravock, voted against the proposed Union of Scotland with England ratified the following year, but he was chosen among others to represent Scotland in the first British Parliament. The clan supported the Hanoverian kings in both Jacobite risings, of 1715 and 1745–46.

Rose crest badge

Ross

This clan takes its name from the County of Ross. It began with an ecclesiastical family, a hereditary priesthood whose name was *Macc-in-t'sacairt*, or 'Son of the Priest'. The clan founder was probably Fearchar, son of the Abbot of Applecross in Wester Ross, who inherited the abbacy early in the 13th century. Despite his cloth, Fearchar helped King Alexander II (1214–49) resist several attempts to unseat him from the throne, and was knighted by the King in 1215. Fearchar was also made Earl of Ross (a name taken from the Gaelic *Ròs*, meaning 'headland').

Fearchar's grandson, the 3rd Chief, fought on the side of Robert the Bruce at Bannockburn in 1314. His grandson William, 5th Chief and 5th Earl of Ross, left no direct male heir when he died in 1372. His daughter Euphemia inherited her father's Earldom as Countess of Ross, with the chiefship of the clan passing to William's half-brother, Hugh Ross of Balganown. Euphemia's inheritance was repeatedly challenged, eventually successfully, by the MacDonalds of the Isles (*see* MacDonald).

Hugh Ross's descendants provided the clan's principal family until 1711, when David Ross of Balganown, 13th Chief of the Clan, died. The chiefship eventually passed to a family branch whose kinship with the Balganown was extremely remote.

One of the descendants of the younger son of Hugh Ross, 9th Chief of Balganown, was Colonel George Ross: an American officer in the Patriot Army which fought the British in the American War of Independence. His name appears as a signatory of the historic American Declaration of Independence of 1776.

Ruthven

The old baronial lands of Ruthven (correctly pronounced 'Rivven') in Angus were chartered to Sweyn Thorsson in the 12th century, but the territorial name was not adopted as a family surname until the time of Sir Walter Ruthven of Ruthven, around 1235. The Lordship of Ruthven was created for William Ruthven of that Ilk, Hereditary Sheriff of Perth, in the 15th century.

Sir William's grandson Patrick, 3rd Lord Ruthven, was a leader of the gang who murdered David Rizzio, Secretary of Mary, Queen of Scots, in 1566. His son William was created 1st Earl of Gowrie in 1581, an honour repaid by his kidnapping King James VI in the following year and holding him to

Ross crest badge

The family branch of Ballindean used their home as a surname until a special Act was passed in 1641, restoring their name to Ruthven of Ballindean 'as if the Act of 1600 had never been made against them'. The rehabilitation of the Ruthvens in Scotland had been preceded by generous payment for services rendered to the King of Sweden and the Protestant cause in the Thirty Years War. General Patrick Ruthven of Ballindean had been made Count of Kirchberg in the Swedish Peerage in 1632; he was created Earl of Forth in the Scottish Peerage in 1641. The 1651 Peerage, Ruthven of Freeland, is currently held in the female line. The Earldom of Gowrie was revived in 1945 for Brigadier Lord Gowrie of Canberra, VC, PC, Governor-General of the Commonwealth of Australia (1936–44).

The current Chief of the Whole Name and Arms of Ruthven is his son Patrick Ruthven PC, 2nd Earl of Gowrie. The clansman's crest badge is a 'Ram's Head', with the motto 'Deid Schaw' (Deeds show) There is a specific 'Ruthven' tartan.

ransom for ten months, for which he was beheaded at Stirling in 1582. John, the 3rd Earl, was killed in his own house by some of the King's entourage in the mysterious 'Gowrie House Affair' of August 1600. The Earldom of Gowrie was extinguished, and three months later Parliament enacted that 'the surname of Rithven sall now and in all time cumming be extinguischit and aboleissit for euir'. Bearers of the name who regarded themselves as innocent of treason were exhorted 'to take to themselves, their bairns and posterity' any other surname.

Ruthven Barracks were built in 1716 so that government troops could be on hand to suppress clan risings. They were destroyed by the Highlanders in 1746.

Scott

The earliest Scott on record was Uchtred, described simply as *filius Scoti* or 'son of a Scot', who witnessed a charter at Selkirk about 1130. He had two grandsons: Richard, ancestor of the Dukes of Buccleuch, and Michael, ancestor of the Scots of Balwearie.

Sir Richard Scott, a descendant of Richard, married the heiress to Murdochstone lands in Lanarkshire and swore fealty to King Edward I of England in 1296. His descendant Sir Walter received the Barony of Kirkuld from Robert II (1371–90) in 1389, and was killed at the Battle of Hambledon Hill against the English in 1402. His son Robert acquired parts of the Branxholm land in Roxburghshire, and Robert's son Walter helped suppress the Douglas revolt of 1455 against James II (*see* Douglas). For this he was rewarded with more lands, including the rest of the Branxholm property. His eldest son, who had acquired Buccleuch, sat in some of the Parliaments of James III (1460–88).

David's great-grandson, Sir Walter Scott of Buccleuch, had a life that was nothing if not adventurous. He was Warden of the Middle Marches, was knighted at Flodden Field before the disastrous battle of 1513, survived the slaughter, fought in the Battle of Pinkie Cleugh 34 years later, survived *that*, and was finally killed in a clan feud with the Kerrs on an Edinburgh street in 1552. (His son William also fought at Pinkie but, evidently lacking his father's survival gene, was killed.) Sir Walter Scott of Buccleuch was created 1st Lord Scott of Buccleuch in 1606. He had been Warden of the West Marches and later became a field commander under Prince Maurice of Orange-Nassau, son of William the Silent, ruler of the Dutch United Provinces.

Lord Scott's son, Walter, was created 1st Earl of Buccleuch in 1619. His son Francis, the 2nd Earl (1633–51), was succeeded by two young daughters: Mary, Countess of Buccleuch, who died in 1661 aged only 13; and her younger sister Anne, born in 1651. In 1663 Anne Scott was married to James, illegitimate son of King Charles II, who took the name of Scott before his marriage. On their wedding day, James and Anne were created Duke and Duchess of Buccleuch. Better known as the 'Protestant hero' Duke of Monmouth, James was a popular favourite and it was widely hoped that the King would declare Monmouth heir to the throne. But when Charles II died in 1685 he left the throne to his Catholic brother James, Duke of York, who became James VII and II – the last of the Stewart kings of Scotland. Monmouth's attempt to lead an armed revolt against the King was crushed at

Sedgemoor in the West Country in 1685, and Monmouth was executed in London. But his widow retained her title as Duchess of Buccleuch, and from her dukes descended to this day.

The Scotts of Balwearie founded by Sir Michael Scott *(see above)* received a Baronetcy in later centuries. A relative of Sir Michael was another Michael Scott, known as the 'Wizard', who died in 1232. A mathematician, physician, and scholar, he was one of the most learned Scotsmen of his time. But probably the most famous of all the Scotts was Sir Walter Scott (1771–1832), a descendant of the

Harden branch — the great Romantic historian, novelist, and patriot, whose writings did so much to give Scotland back her national pride after the humiliations of the failed Jacobite risings and the savage repressions that followed. Sir Walter Scott was made a Baronet in 1820.

The present chief is Walter Montague-Douglas-Scott, 8th Duke of Buccleuch and 10th Duke of Queensberry, K.T.

Scott crest badge

Above: Drumlanrig Castle in Nithsdale was built (1679–89) for the 3rd Earl of Queensberry, but he only stayed there for one night. It is now one of the seats of Chief of Clan Scott, the Duke of Buccleuch and Queensberry.

171

Scrymgeour

This resounding surname comes from the word for 'skirmisher' or 'skrymsher': an old Teutonic word for a swordsman or defender. Sir Alexander 'Skirmeschur' was granted the lands of Dudhope in Forfarshire, and was also created Constable of the City of Dundee, by William Wallace, Guardian of the Kingdom of Scotland, in recognition of services rendered as Hereditary Bannerman at the Battle of Stirling Bridge in 1297. In this crucial, almost legendary, battle for Scotland's independence, a small force of Scots under Wallace had held the strategic crossing on the River Forth against Edward I's vastly superior English army.

Sir Alexander was captured by the English seven years later, and hanged at York for having carried Robert the Bruce's banner at the Battle of Methven. His son Nicholas carried the Royal Banner at Bannockburn in 1314, and the Scrymgeours have been hereditary Royal Bannermen of Scotland ever since.

By a marriage in 1370 to a West Highland heiress, Agnes of Glassary, some 40,470 hectares (100,000 acres) of land in Argyll were acquired by the Scrymgeours, who were unjustly deprived of them by the predatory, all-powerful Duke of Lauderdale. This worthy, unhappily for Scotland, was Charles II's Secretary of State for Scotland for nearly 20 years following the Restoration in 1660 (*see* Maitland), and the 'L' in the notorious CABAL of ministers (the other four being Clifford, Arlington, Buckingham, and Ashley); he took advantage of the sudden death of John Scrymgeour, 1st Earl of Dundee. (Lauderdale was finally brought down by his own corruption in 1679.)

The 2nd Earl, however, compensated for this stroke of ill fortune by marrying the heiress to Wedderburn, acquiring her estates on the condition that he assumed the additional name and Arms of Wedderburn. Consequently, the chiefs of the clan who bear the hyphenated surname Scrymgeour-Wedderburn, though accepted on the Standing Council of Scottish Chiefs, are not formally recognized by Lord Lyon, King of Arms.

The present Chief of the clan is James Scrymgeour-Wedderburn, 11th Earl of Dundee, who was created Baron Glassary of Glassary in 1954 after the old lands in Argyll were re-acquired after nearly 300 years. His Gaelic designation – *Mac Mhic Iain* – refers to his Highland lairdship, and he bears the old 'Royal Lyon, Armed with a Scimitar' on his Arms. The clansman's crest badge is 'A Lyon's Paw, Brandishing a Scimitar or Cutlass', with the motto 'Dissipate'. There is a specific 'Scrymgeour' tartan.

Sempill

Robert de Sempill, Steward of the Barony of Renfrew, is the first of the name to appear in Scotland, around the year 1280. His son Robert acquired the lands of Elliotstoun in Renfrewshire around 1345, and his direct descendant was made a Lord of Parliament as Baron Sempill (1488) by King James IV, dying with his King at Flodden in 1513.

William Sempill served as a secret emissary of Spain to the Catholics of Scotland in 1588; he was arrested but later escaped, and founded the Scots College in Madrid. Hugh, 12th Lord Sempill, was Colonel of the Black Watch in Flanders in 1743, and was promoted to Brigadier-General to command the left flank of the Hanoverian Army at Culloden. By the marriage of his granddaughter to Sir Patrick Forbes of Craigievar, Bart., Craigievar Castle later became the seat of the Sempills, whose surname changed to Forbes-Sempill. The present chief – Ann Forbes-Sempill, The Lady Sempill in her own right and 20th Peer of the name – is therefore not recognized by the Lord Lyon, but is a member of the Standing Council of Scottish Chiefs.

The clansman's crest badge is a 'Stag's Head', with the motto 'Keep Tryst'. There is no specific Sempill tartan.

Shaw

The Lowland name 'Shaw' or 'Schaw', and the Highland name 'Shaw', represent two quite separate kindreds. The Lowland surname stems from the Old English word *scaga*, meaning a copse or grove of woodland. In place-names, the spelling evolved through *schaga* and *shaugh* to what was a familiar word for a small wood until recent times: 'shaw'. The first of the name in recorded history outside the Highlands was John 'de Schau', who witnessed a deed relating to the Abbey of Paisley in 1284. The core of the family has remained in the shires of Renfrew and Lanark since those times.

Symon 'de Schawe', Fergus 'de Shawe', and William 'de Schawe', of Lanark, all rendered homage to Edward I of England in 1296. Christian Shaw, of the Bargarran branch of the family, started the thread industry in Paisley around 1720 which was to make the town world famous. Other branches have also clustered in Kirkcudbrightshire and Ayrshire, and around the towns of Greenock and Stirling. The senior line of the Lowland Shaws seems to be the Shaws of Sauchie, whose motto 'I Mean Well' is a reassuring adjunct to their crest – a bearded savage brandishing a gnarled cudgel.

Shaw crest badge

Craigievar Castle (1626), a seat of the   *Clan Sempill till 1963.*

The playwright George Bernard Shaw, who received the Nobel Prize for Literature in 1925, descends from a Scot called William Shaw, who was a captain in Michelburn's Regiment in the army of William III, fought at the Battle of the Boyne in 1690, and settled in County Tipperary thereafter. Less renowned in the gentle arts was 'Big Jack' Shaw, a pugilist of prodigious strength who served with the Life Guards in the Waterloo campaign of 1815. He fell in the battle after killing ten French *cuirassiers* in a hand-to-hand encounter.

The life and death of 'Big Jack' Shaw suggested that he probably descended from the Highland clan, whose fighting prowess was legendary. Farquhar Shaw died leading his warriors against 40 from a rival clan in the famous 'Battle of the Clans' on the North Inch of Perth in 1396. This was actually less of a battle than a trial by combat, fought out in the presence of King Robert III (1390–1406) to decide some point of honour or precedence, the details of which are now obscure.

Like the Farquharsons and the MacThomases, the Shaws descend from early chiefs of Clan Mackintosh (*mac an toiseach* or 'Son of the Chief', or leader.) The original Gaelic name became anglicized to 'Shaw' as the nearest approximation that Anglo-Saxon ears and tongues could muster. It stems from a very ancient Indo-European word which was probably the root of *toiseach* and a number of names for 'ruler' or 'leader' throughout the western world – 'shah', 'sheikh', 'tsar', 'caesar', and 'kaiser'.

The Old Celtic word with the 'sha' sound would have been written as *sheach* or *sheagh*, and the longest surname derives from that: *Macghillesheughnaich* (recorded phonetically in Islay, in 1506, as 'M'Gilleshaanich'). The genitive form of the word provides the construction of *Clann Ay* ('Children of Shaw').

Along with Clan Mackintosh, Clan Ay or Shaw traces its origins to the renowned Clan MacDuff of the early Middle Ages which, although centred in Fife, held vast lands in the north-east and the Highlands. The sept names of the Shaws – Ayson, Aison, Easson, MacAy, MacHay, Scaith, Seith, Shaith, Shay, Scheach, Sheath, and Schiach – are a reminder that this surname is one of the oldest in the English-speaking world.

The original Shaw heartland was Rothiemurchus, and the great Farquhar Shaw is buried in the eerie little churchyard there, at the centre of what is today one of the last remnants of the once-great Caledonian pine forest. These lands were lost to the Gordons in the 14th century, passing to the Grants in the 16th century. The Chief of the Shaws located himself at Tordarroch in neighbouring Strathdearn, only to see that revert to the Mackintoshes around 1760. The Shaw family has now bought back the Tordarroch lands, which form the territorial description of the representer of all the Highland Shaws: John Shaw of Tordarroch, 22nd Chief of Clan Shaw (*Clann Ay*). The clansman's crest badge is 'A Hand Holding a Dagger', with the motto *Fide et Fortitudine* ('With Faith and Courage'). Clan tartans include the Shaw; the 'Red Shaw of Tordarroch', and the 'Hunting Shaw of Tordarroch'.

Sinclair

The St Clairs, or Sinclairs, came from the Cotentin peninsula in Normandy. One Henri de St Clair had lands in Lothian in the mid-12th century; one of his descendants, Sir William Sinclair, was Sheriff of Edinburgh in the 1280s and received the Barony of Rosslyn in Lothian. He opposed King Edward I's attempt to impose direct rule over Scotland after the deposition of King John Baliol in 1296, but was captured and imprisoned. His son, Sir Henry Sinclair, supported Robert the Bruce and was one of the Scottish lords and chiefs who signed the Declaration of Arbroath, in 1320.

By the time Sir Henry died (about 1334–35), his son Sir William of Rosslyn had been killed in Spain with Sir James Douglas ('The Good') while taking the embalmed heart of Robert the Bruce for burial in the Holy Land. The chiefship passed to a grandson, Sir William Sinclair, who married the heiress to the Earl of Orkney. The son of this marriage, Henry Sinclair, was in 1379 created Jarl (Earl) of the Orkneys by King Haakon VI of Norway, ranking above all other Norwegian nobles. Henry was something of an explorer, who is thought to have reached Greenland (first discovered around 985 by the Norwegian Erik the Red). When he was killed in about 1404 he was followed by his son Henry, 2nd Earl of Orkney, who was for a time Guardian of the young James Stewart, later James I (1406–1437).

Henry's son William was created Earl of Caithness in 1455, but had to surrender his earldom of Orkney to the Scottish Crown. His heir William, 2nd Earl of Caithness, was killed with James IV at Flodden Field in 1513. His grandson George Sinclair, 4th Earl of Caithness, imprisoned his eldest son the Master of Caithness for seven years in Girnigoe Castle (1571–78), eventually starving him to death. During this imprisonment the younger son, William, amused himself by tormenting his elder brother in his cell until one day the Master rounded on his brother and killed him.

The result of this lurid family incident was that the 4th Earl was succeeded by his grandson George as 5th Earl in 1582, who in turn was succeeded by a great-grandson, the 6th Earl, who virtually sold his title to Sir John Campbell of Glenorchy to pay debts. This Campbell became Earl of Caithness, but when the Sinclair earl died, the title reverted to a Sinclair cousin (the second son of George, the 5th Earl) and Campbell was compensated with the Earldom of Breadalbane. The present chief is Malcolm Sinclair, 20th Earl of Sinclair and chief of the Whole Name and Arms of Sinclair.

Sinclair crest badge

Spens

A 'Spense' was a medieval officer, a custodian of provisions in a noble or Royal household, one who thereby 'dispenses'. This has yielded the name 'Spencer' in England, but the more frequent Scots variant is 'Spens'.

In the early 13th century, there are references to Roger *Dispensator* and Thomas *Dispensator*, with 'Spens' and 'de Spensa' appearing in the same period. A ship belonging to John 'de Spense' and other Scottish merchants was wrecked near Newcastle in 1365. By 1428 we hear of John Spens, 'custodier' of Stocket Forest; and Thomas Spens, Bishop of Aberdeen in the latter half of the same century, was an influential figure. In 1529, there was an entry in the Royal Accounts of Livery for 'John Spens at the cupboard'. And a portrait by Sir Henry Raeburn of Dr Nathaniel Spens shows the sitter wearing the 'Government Tartan' uniform of the Sovereign's Bodyguard for Scotland, The Royal Company of Archers.

The connection of the Spens family with the MacDuff Earls of Fife is disputed, but there seems to have been a long association in that county – by association, with the Clan MacDuff. Sir John Spens of Wormiston in Fife was Recruiter-General for King Gustavus Vasa of Sweden in the 1520s. Sir John encouraged many younger sons of Scottish families to join the Swedish Royal service, and his own dynasty was established in the Swedish House of Nobles.

In 1959, Sir Patrick Spens, PC, QC, of the Chiefly House of Spens of Lathallan, was created Baron Spens of Blairsanquhar in the Peerage of the United Kingdom. This Crown appointment was made under the law of succession to chiefships, implying a grant to Lord Spens as Chief of the Whole Name and Arms of Spens. The existing chief was thereby deposed without cause.

The clansman's crest badge is a 'Stag's Head', with the motto *Si Deus quis contra* ('If God is With Me, Who Can Oppose Me?') Although the 'Spens' tartan appears in the 1816 collection of the Highland Society of London, it is unknown today.

Stewart

The Royal House of Stewart had its beginnings in the reign of David I (1124–53), when the King appointed his friend Walter FitzAlan as High Steward of Scotland. Walter was a son of Alan Fitzflaald, nephew of Alan 'the Red', a Breton noble who came to England with William the Conqueror in 1066. In the reign of David I's grandson, Malcolm IV (1153–65), Walter's Stewardship was made an hereditary title. For the next two centuries, the chiefs of the family were known as 'The Steward', which in time became the surname 'Stewart'.

Walter, the 6th Steward, commanded a wing of Robert the Bruce's army at Bannockburn in 1314. After this crushing Scottish victory Walter married Marjorie Bruce, the King's daughter, and their son became King Robert II (1371–90). The Stewart Royal dynasty ended in the male line with James V

(1513–42), when the latter died a few weeks after the catastrophic defeat at Solway Moss in 1542, but the succession continued through James's daughter Mary, Queen of Scots. It was indeed strengthened when Mary married her second husband: Henry Stewart, Lord Darnley, a direct descendant of the 4th High Steward. Their son, James VI & I, was, therefore, heir to the House of Stewart through both the male and the female lines.

The Stewarts were more than just a royal dynasty. Not only did they provide all Scotland's monarchs from 1371 to 1603, and those of the United Crowns of Scotland and England from 1603 to 1714; they also held at one time or another in Britain 13 dukedoms and 17 earldoms. Besides three Cardinals and two British prime ministers, they provided one Duke in Italy, three in France and 10 in Spain. Stewarts also served as Regents during the reigns of Robert III (1390–1406) and James I (1406–37). James Stewart, Earl of Moray, was Regent from 1567 to 1570 during the infancy of James VI.

The several Stewart branches in the Highlands included those of Appin, Ardsheil, Atholl, and Lorn. Not all of them were automatic supporters of the Royal House at all times, though the Appin Stewarts were a notable exception, from the Great Civil War in the 1640s to the second Jacobite rising a century later. But the Stewarts were implacable foes of Clan Campbell, its apparently insatiable hunger for the lands of others, and its ambitions to dominate all rival neighbour-clans in the Highlands, even to the extent of acting as an agent for a remote Government in London. Here again the Appin Stewarts were well to the fore. The long enmity between Stewart and Campbell is brilliantly

Stewart crest badge   *Stewart of Appin crest badge*

After the 'Black Watch', the 'Royal Stuart' sett is the world's most popular tartan, although it should, in fact, be worn only by the Royal Family and Pipers of the Royal Regiments. The highly professional Tokyo Pipe Band wear the 'Stuarto tartano-check' in full Highland dress with great aplomb.

captured by Robert Louis Stevenson's *Kidnapped*, based on the alleged 'Appin Murder' of a Campbell by Alan Breck Stewart six years after Culloden.

The chief of the Name and Arms of Stewart is not, in fact, H.M. The Queen, but Sir Randolph Stewart, 13th Earl of Galloway. The crest is a nesting pelican, and there are more than 58 tartans.

Stirling

The medieval town from which this family takes its name was called 'Strivelin' for centuries after Walter 'de Striveling' witnessed a charter of King David I in the year 1152. A celebrated Scottish family, the Stirlings of Keir, whose great house sits on the ridge to the north of the town, spelled their surname in no less than 64 different ways in manuscripts dated between the years 1160 and 1677.

The Stirling family is said locally to have been at Keir 'since God was a boy', yet seems to have avoided receiving any honours for the best part of a millenium until Colonel David Stirling was knighted as a personal gift of HM The Queen just months before his death. He had founded the renowned Special Air Service, the SAS, in the Western Desert in World War II.

The Lairds of Cadder began with Thoraldus, who was created *Vicecomes* (petty Earl, or Viscount) *de Strivelyn* in 1147. The Stirlings of Keir acquired the Cadder estates by a marriage to the heiress, and the descendants of her brother acquired the lands of Cragbernard and then Glorat, which was elevated into a Baronetcy of Nova Scotia in 1666. That title died out with Sir George Murray-Home-Stirling, 9th Baronet, in 1949, after his eldest son had been lost at sea in 1938, and his youngest – a captain in the Black Watch – died of wounds received in the battle for Tobruk in 1941. The present chief is Fraser Stirling of Cadder.

The clansman's crest badge is a 'Swan', with the motto 'Gang Forward'. There is no specific 'Clan Stirling' tartan. A pattern which is often called by that name was in fact created for the Stirling and Bannockburn Caledonian Society.

Sutherland

The name of Sutherland comes from *Sudrland*, the Norse name for the north-east coast of Scotland below Orkney and Shetland, which the Vikings occupied from time to time. The first mention of a Sutherland lordship is found in the early 12th century. Hugh de Moray, grandson of a Flemish nobleman, became Lord of Sutherland in about 1210. His younger brother, William de Moray, was the ancestor of the Dukes of Atholl, the Earls of Dunmore, the Earls of Mansfield, and the Lords of Elibank. Hugh's son William – the first of the family to choose the name Sutherland – was created 1st Earl of Sutherland in about 1235.

William, 3rd Earl of Sutherland, was one of the signatories of the Declaration of Arbroath in 1320; Kenneth, the 4th Earl, was killed at the Battle of Halidon Hill in 1333, when the English longbowmen defeated the Scots. William, the 5th Earl, married Robert the Bruce's daughter Margaret; their son would have been declared heir to the throne but died of the Black Death instead, in 1361. After Margaret's death in 1358 William married again. It was through his son Robert (of this second marriage) that he became ancestor of all the Earls and (later) Dukes of Sutherland. Robert, the 6th Earl, married a daughter of Alexander Stewart (known as the 'Wolf of Badenoch' for his violent nature), younger brother of King Robert III (1390–1406). It is said that the family seat of Dunrobin in Sutherland is named after this Robert Sutherland.

The 8th and 9th Earls of Sutherland were a unique 'double': both were named John and both went mad, with the 9th Earl dying unmarried in 1514. He was therefore succeeded by his sister Elisabeth, who became Countess of Sutherland. She married Adam Gordon, a son of the Earl of Huntly, and was succeeded as 11th Earl of Sutherland by their son, John Gordon, widely known as 'Good Earl John'. (He was poisoned in 1567.) His descendant John, the 16th Earl and a Knight of the Thistle, resumed the ancient family name of Sutherland and was recognized as clan chief. His great grand-daughter became the second countess in her own right in the earldom. In 1785, she married George Granville, Viscount Trentham. He was created Duke of Sutherland in 1833, having already 'cleared' thousands of his wife's clansfolk from what he regarded as their primitive homes and rehoused them in 'modern' townships on the coast, destroying centuries of family traditions and kinship patterns.

When the 5th duke died childless in 1963, the dukedom devolved upon his kinsman in the male line, but the ancient earldom – the premier in Scotland – fell to his niece. She became the third in a line of countesses in their own right, all of whom have been called Elisabeth Sutherland. The latest is still chief of the clan. There are seven tartans associated with the name.

Opposite: Dunrobin, the seat of the Clan Sutherland, was named after Robert, the 6th Earl. It was built about 1275, but was extensively remodelled 1845–51.

Swinton

A Henry de Swyntoun rendered homage to Edward I of England in 1296, but the lands of 'Swyntoun' were chartered a century earlier to Edolf, probably an Anglian nobleman of Northumbria. The land-name is a typical construction from north-east England, signifying a 'village' or 'homestead' where pigs were kept. (In the village of Swinton, there existed for some centuries a family called 'Swine' who finally sought permission from the Lord of the Manor to change their name to 'Swinton'.)

Hugh of Swinton acquired the 'thanedom' of Arbuthnott as heir to Walter Olifard (whose heiress he probably married) when that knight failed to return from a Crusade. Hugh's son Duncan adopted the name of his thanedom, and began the Arbuthnott line, which still holds those lands in Kincardineshire to this day. John, Lord of 'Swyngton', was granted a safe conduct in England in 1377. He is clearly the same as John 'de Swyntoun', who received a charter from the great Abbey of Dunfermline as 'Lord of Little Swinton, of the lands of the whole Lordship of Great Swyntoun'. John Swyntoune of that Ilk was the first Laird so named, in 1530. Alexander Swinton was captured at the Battle of Worcester in 1651, but became a Lord of Session (Judge of the Court of Sessions) after the Restoration of Charles II in 1660.

Predictably, in typical 'canting' or punning form, swine appear in the Arms of the Swintons of that Ilk. The clansman's crest badge is 'A Boar Chained to a Branch of Oak With Acorns'; the motto is J'espère ('I hope'). There is no Swinton tartan.

Urquhart

A small but ancient clan, the Urquharts take their name from the district on the south side of the Cromarty Firth. The clan also held lands on the north side of Loch Ness and in the Black Isle.

The clan's beginnings are not known, but in the first years of the 14th century, William of Urquhart was Sheriff of Cromarty, an office that was to become hereditary. The Urquharts increased their influence by judicious marriages, with Sir William marrying a daughter of Hugh, Earl of Ross. Sir William's son Adam was given land by his grandfather Ross, and his grandson Alexander Urquhart received further grants from King David II in 1358. Later, the Urquhart chiefs became Constables of Urquhart Castle on Loch Ness — familiar to millions as the most prominent lochside landmark in photographs purporting to show the famous Monster.

In the early 16th century, one of the Clan Chiefs, Sir Thomas Urquhart of Cromarty, married Helen, daughter of Lord Abernethy, and is said to have had 25 sons by her. (Such terrifying fecundity is a not uncommon attribute claimed, presumably as a compliment, for Scottish clan wives.) Seven of these sons fell in battle with the English at Pinkie Cleugh in 1547. The eldest Urquhart son, Alexander, had been granted a charter by King James V granting property in Ross and Inverness.

Alexander's great-nephew was Sir Thomas Urquhart (1611–60). Born in Cromarty, he was an adventurer and a scholar who was knighted by King Charles in 1641, and succeeded as clan chief. He was also a celebrated author, producing the first and probably the most rumbustious translation of the works of François Rabelais, most notably the satirical novels Gargantua and Pantagruel. Sir Thomas died in 1660, it is said from choking with delight on hearing the news that King Charles II had been restored to the throne.

The direct line of the Urquharts passed to the American branch.

Urquhart crest badge

Right: An internal view of Castle Urquhart, showing the 13th-century royal fortress which was blown up in 1691.

Below: Castle Urquhart, the 'fort on the knoll'.

Wallace

The name of Wallace has a variety of suggested origins. It could have come from 'Walais' or 'Galais', a common name in 13th-century England, or from *Le Walays* ('The Welshman'). One of the likeliest derivations is from *Walensis*, meaning a Briton from the Strathclyde region of Scotland, where the inhabitants were once of the same British stock as the Welsh.

There is a record of a Richard Walensis of Riccarton, near Kilmarnock in Ayrshire, in the 1160s. His grandson Adam Walays, the 3rd of Riccarton, had two sons: Adam Walleis (the 4th of Riccarton) and Malcolm of Elderslie in Renfrewshire, who was the father of Scotland's immortal hero, William Wallace.

Wallace was born *c* 1274, and was drawn into the campaign for Scottish independence, after the death of King Alexander III in 1286, by a personal injury. His wife was murdered by English soldiers on the rampage from their base in Lanark, and his household was assaulted. Wallace responded by killing the English garrison commander and then, finding great sympathy for his act among friends and neighbours, decided to mobilize it into an anti-English liberation movement. He gathered a tough and determined band of warriors, who lived and trained in hiding and who would suddenly pounce upon an English-held castle or town and capture it by surprise. It was a form of guerrilla warfare, and for a time the English had no answer to it.

Meanwhile, in the north, a similar campaign was being organized and waged by Sir Andrew de Moravia (Moray). Calling themselves the 'Commanders of the Army of the Kingdom of Scotland', Wallace and Moray joined forces. In 1297, the two men and their joint army took on an English army near Stirling and utterly routed it.

Ignoring the writ of Edward I of England after his deposition of the puppet King John Baliol (1296),

the two men started to govern Scotland. But Moray died and Wallace was left on his own. Declaring himself 'Guardian of Scotland', he championed the cause of Baliol – which did not please the ambitious Bruce family or their supporters. Edward now responded to the challenge to his 'rule' in Scotland by leading an army into the rebel Kingdom, and at Falkirk (1298) Wallace was defeated. But despite the price on his head after fleeing into hiding, he fought on, emerging now and again with small bands of patriots to raid a castle or town.

Wallace crest badge

Right: The Castle on Dumbarton Rock stands on the site of the ancient fort of the Britons of the kingdom of Strathclyde, whose capital this was.

180

The end came for Wallace in 1305, when he was betrayed to the English, taken to London, and tried for treason – a charge of utter cynicism when one considers that he had never accepted the over-lordship of Edward, and was a patriot fighting in and for his own country. Nor had Wallace claimed royal power for himself, as Bruce was to do in the following year. His trial was an act of judicial murder, made more hideous by the fate devised for Wallace: hanging, drawing, and quartering

But what the English could not do was to erase the fame of Wallace – of, more practically, the lessons he had taught on how the Scots could, given the correct use of resources and terrain, fight and beat the English. Luckily for Robert the Bruce, who put those lessons into telling effect, Wallace left no male heirs to challenge the authority of Scotland's new and self-proclaimed King. But the Wallace family continued, and several branches of it still exist today.

The present chief is Lt. Col. M.R. Wallace of that Ilk.

Wedderburn

The 'Wautier de Wederburne' who rendered homage to Edward I of England in 1296 is the first of this surname on record in Scotland, and he took his name from the lands of Wedderburn in Berwickshire. With the decline of the family in the south of Scotland, the lands of Wedderburn passed to the powerful Homes, who dominated Berwickshire.

By the year 1400, four distinct yet closely related Wedderburn families could be found in Dundee, with another influential family, the Wedderburns of Kingennie, in Forfar. The lineal descendant of that line obtained a Crown charter in 1708 to elevate lands at Easter Powrie into a Barony, to be called 'Wedderburn'. When David Wedderburn of Wedderburn died there in 1761, the estates passed to the line now incorporated in the Scrymgeour-Wedderburn family, who are Earls of Dundee (*see* Scrymgeour).

James Wedderburn, Professor of Divinity at St Andrews in 1617, had risen to become Bishop of Dunblane by 1636. Other Wedderburns were prominent in the law, especially Alexander Wedderburn (1733–1805). He made his name as an advocate for Clive of India, as Member of Parliament for Inverary, and as Solicitor General for Scotland. He was created Lord Loughborough in 1780 and Earl of Rosslyn in 1801. The present chief is Alexander Wedderburn of Wedderburn, Master of Dundee.

The clansman's crest badge is an 'Eagle's Head', with the motto *Illaeso lumine solem* ('Unscathed by the Light of the Sun'). There is no specific 'Wedderburn' tartan.

Wemyss

The place-name from which the surname of Wemyss derives is a phonetic rendering of the Gaelic *uaimh*, 'cave', of which there are two beneath 'MacDuff's Castle' at Easter Wemyss. At the end of the 13th century, Michael de Methkil was also known as Michael 'de Wemeth'. Despite paying homage to Edward I of England in 1296, he seems to have made a bad impression on that monarch, to whom Michael was an unwilling host for a night in 1304. Two years later the 'Hammer of the Scots' wrote to Aymer de Valence, his Royal Guardian for Scotland, complaining that he had 'found neither good speech nor good service in him' [Laird Michael], and ordering that his lands and gardens be 'burned, stripped, and destroyed . . . or worse if possible'.

John Wemyss of that Ilk was one of the Conservators of the three-year truce with England in 1484. The Muster Rolls of the King of France's Scots Guard in the 16th century show the Wemyss name as 'Oysmes', while James 'Wemysse' was General of 'Artelerie' in Scotland in 1666. David Wemyss, Lord Elcho, raised a troop of horse guards for Bonnie Prince Charlie which fought at Culloden. When Elcho died in exile, his younger brother assumed the family name of their maternal grandfather, Colonel Francis Charteris (who was somewhat startlingly dubbed the 'Rapemaster-General of Great Britain'), and succeeded as 7th Earl of Wemyss.

A younger brother inherited the extensive lands which used to be called 'Wemyss-shire', the ancient Barony, and the succession to the chiefship of the clan. His descendant today, Captain David Wemyss of that Ilk, is Chief of the Whole Name and Arms of Wemyss. The clansman's crest badge is a 'Swan', with the motto *Je pense* ('I think'), and there is a specific 'Wemyss' tartan.

James, 5th Earl of Wemyss, in his tartan uniform as Captain-General of the Royal Company of Archers, 1715.

Chronology of Events

SCOTLAND	THE WORLD OUTSIDE
AD80 Romans under Julius Agricola invade Scotland inflicting major defeat on Caledonians.	Romans suppress Jewish revolt in Judaea. Buddhism gains ground in China. Christians persecuted in Rome.
c.500 Massive migration of Scot tribe from Ulster to Argyll.	End of West Roman Empire. Beginning of Middle Ages. Saxons establish Kingdom of Wessex.
c.800 Vikings attack Scotland.	Empire of Charlemagne. Vikings attack Ireland.
843 Kenneth MacAlpin merges Pictish and Scots Kingdoms.	846 Arabs sack Rome. England resists Vikings.
1493 Norse-Celtic Lordship of the Western Isles overthrown by King of Scots.	Spain and Portugal aportion the unclaimed parts of the globe between themselves.
1560 Reformation isolates the mainly Catholic Highlands.	Widespread discord between Protestants and Catholics.
1587 Act for quieting the clans of Borders, Highlands and the Isles. Mary Queen of Scots executed at Fotheringay.	First African slaves sold to New World colonists.
1688 Birth of son and heir to James VII and II who attempts to impose religious toleration and is deposed in Revolution. His 'Jacobite' supporters fail to re-instate him. King and the 'Old' Pretender flee to exile in Rome.	French seize trading posts in North America, and invade what is now Germany. William of Orange accepts offer of British throne.
1692 Government conspires to massacre MacDonalds of Glencoe; 39 killed.	'Massacre' in Massachusetts after hysterical witchcraft trial; 19 killed.
1701 Scottish colony in Panama (Darien) abandoned. James II dies. French hail Old Pretender as 'King of England'.	English Woollens Act prevents internal trade in American wool goods. Act of Settlement provides for Protestant succession in England.

1707 England and Scotland lose their parliamentary independence to a Parliament of Great Britain at Westminster.	Britain at war with France, which attacks colonies in America.
1708 Landing of Old Pretender's army thwarted by British Navy.	Marlborough successful against French in Europe.
1714 Succession of Hanoverian – George I – to throne of Great Britain.	King Felipe V bans Catalan language in Spain.
1715 Jacobite rising. 'Disarming Act' passed.	Japan comes under rule of the Shogun. Indian rising in S. Carolina.
1725 Native levies raised to police the Highlands. Roads built to make trouble spots accessible to troops.	Spain at war with Britain. Peter the Great of Russia dies.
1739 Native levies formed into regular Line Regiment (43rd – later Black Watch).	War of Polish Succession.
1745 Last Jacobite rising. Prince Charles Edward ('Young Pretender') lands in Scotland, achieving early victories and marching on London.	British defeated at Fontenoy by French. British take Louisburg, Canada.

Scottish Names

Names have been applied to individuals in groups or communities since the dawn of human communication, probably before organized language developed. Early tribal personal names were of the style 'cat-like', 'strong-spear' or 'world mighty', (still surviving today as Catannach, Gerard and Donald). Christianity introduced the concept of the baptismal or given name (of a saint), and 'Christian' names like 'Malcolm' and 'Gillanders' (devotees/servant of St Columba and of St Andrew) are survivors of the early Scottish form which have evolved into surnames. France and Ireland, perhaps because of the narrow range of saints' names used as first names, began a system of additional or 'sur' names as early as the 10th century, but in Scotland, such names did not appear for a further 200 years, until after the first Normans settled there and took the names of their new lands and baronies as their last names.

For ordinary people in Scotland, surnames developed differently in the (mainly) Presbyterian Lowlands and the Catholic – Gaelic speaking – Highlands. In more populous areas such as towns, additional names were necessary much earlier, because of the hundreds of Johns, Davids and Marys who needed to be identified as individuals. This was achieved by adding a surname, derived from one of the following:

patronymic (father's name or petname): Davidson, Dawson, Davie, Dawes

toponymic (name of place of origin): Fleming, Dunbar, Clyde, Lochhead, Wood

occupational name: Stewart, Taylor, Hunter, Slater, Clarkson, Smithson

nickname or *to-name*: Cruikshank, Aydrunken, Little, Lang, Smart, Armstrong, Redheid

Surnames of origin and occupation – common in towns, where there were many incomers and numerous trades – gradually became fixed. Somewhat later, patronymics became fixed, too. For example, after centuries of a pattern such as David Johnson's son being called Robert Davy or Davidson, whose son in turn was called Patrick Robertson, Robson or Robbie, whose son in turn might be either George Paton or Paterson, George's descendants began to call themselves 'Paterson', regardless of the fact that their actual father was not 'Patrick'.

In the Highlands, and to some extent in that unique Gaelic enclave which survived in Galloway, there were areas where most families were known *outwith* their territory by the name of the chief whose *clann* – or children – they were. Some were families who had merely come under the protection of the chief and later adopted the name.

However, until the 16th century, in the Clan Donald, for instance, only the chief would be known as 'MacDonald' *within* the clan territory. An ordinary member of the clan, where there would be thousands of Donalds, Iains and Alasdairs, would be distinguished by a physical characteristic or proximity to a topographical feature, in conjunction with the name of his father and his father's father. So that Iain Ruadh mac Alasdair mhic Aonghais mhic Dhomhnuill (John of the florid features, son of Alasdair, (grand) son of Angus (great grand) son of Donald), which would *sound* as 'Ian Roy mac Alister vic Engus vic Awnell', would be clearly distinguished from his equally florid cousin, 'Ian Roy *mac Dougal* vic Alister vic Awnell'. To reinforce the importance of their ancestry, children were often required to recite their own lineage for 50 generations or more. Today, many people have no idea of their grandmother's maiden name, a situation compounded by our system of only preserving the name of the principal male name in our ancestry. Your name today may be Campbell, but if your Campbell ancestor of 10 generations ago had gone to live among his MacDonald wife's people, *all* the 1,022 individuals in that genetic matrix might well be MacDonalds, except for the ten males in the direct line who passed on the surname Campbell.

Highland names are also complicated by the way in which the *mac* style came to be fixed at some point in the 16th century. A man's surname became *mac* followed, not by the first name of his actual father, but that of a forebear, often, but not always, the namefather of the whole clan. *Mac* now means 'descendant' rather than 'son', with the 'of' still expressed in the Gaelic form of a possessive noun, by generally aspirating (adding an 'h' sound to) the first letter of the proper name which follows. Mac-Donald becomes *MacDhomnuill* producing a sound like M'Cawnull. As a result, it was often written as McConnell in the past, when MacDonalds might also describe themselves as 'Donalds' (Domhnullach or 'Donnelly') or 'of the Donalds' (Dhomhnullach or 'Connelly'). As an extra complication, until the last century, a daughter of, say, Angus MacDonald, bore the surname not 'son of Donald', but 'daughter of the son of Donald'. This was rendered in Gaelic as *Nighean mhic* (shortened to *Nic Dhomhnuill*), with the sound of Ni'Cawnull.

The emphasis is generally on the first syllable of Gaelic names, except the names beginning with *mac*. MacDonald should *not* be said MACK Donald, but with a short, soft *Mc* and the emphasis on the DONALD.

The guide to the spelling of names is to give a capital letter only to proper names – MacGregor, MacFarlane etc. Others appear in the form Macpherson, Mackintosh, Mactaggart, Macintyre etc.

There were only 18 letters in the Gaelic alphabet:
d/g/i is for the 'j' sound
c for 'k'
cua/cea/cei for 'q'
f/bh/mh for 'v'
ui for 'w'
s for 'x'
oi/ui/ua/ia/io for 'y'
s for 'z'
a/e/i/o/u for 'h', which is dropped at the beginning of words; elsewhere it is merely an inserted instruction to aspirate.

The 'Z' that appears in the names 'Menzies' and 'MacKenzie' are mistranscriptions of the old Scots (not Gaelic) scriptic 'y', which looked like the English 'z'.

For convenience, old baptismal registers and so on listed all the *Macs* in the abbreviated form *M* or *Mc*. Irish *Mac* names employed exactly the same procedure. Clan chiefs in the Lowlands tend to use the term John or Juliet Blackvillage 'of that Ilk', as a form of old shorthand for 'Blackvillage of Blackvillage'. Highland clan chiefs tend to emphasize their tribal authority over all those of the name, by being 'Duncan/Jane Macabre of Macabre', although they may also add their territorial designation, as 'Macabre of Macabre and the Craigs'. Neither chief should ever be addressed in letters as 'Mr' 'Ms' or 'Mrs', but as 'Dear Blackvillage' or 'Dear Macabre'. This is sometimes prefixed by Madam if a female chief so prefers.

Glossary of Useful Terms

n = noun; v = verb; adj = adjective; adv = adverb

Archers, the popular name for the Royal Company of Archers (founded in 1676), the Sovereign's Bodyguard for Scotland

auld lang syne times past or long since

baillie n. magistrate of a burgh; (cf. alderman of a borough)

bairn n. child, infant

band n. a written agreement or promise

bannock n. thick flat cake made of oatmeal, baked on a girdle/griddle

beg/beag adj./adv. Gaelic for small, little, short, etc (pronounced *bake* with a 'Q' sound)

Belltane n. the Celtic May Day festival

black house n. low, thatched house of natural stone or turf (Gaelic, *taigh dubh*) as opposed to the 'new' houses of dressed stone with slate roofs

black mail n. 'mail' is old Scots for a contribution or levy; 'black mail' was an illicit levy extracted in return for 'protecting' cattle or lands

Black Watch, the Gaelic *am freicadan dubh*; the nickname applied to the Independent Companies which were raised in the Highlands in the late 1600s as undercover (see 'dubh') units or special forces, to keep watch on the activities of the Jacobite clans. Embodied as 43rd Regiment (later 42nd) in May 1740

Black watch tartan old highland sett, named from the Regiment which adopted it and not for its colouring. The dark shades we know today are post-1856

bothy n. hut or shelter, for travellers or farm servants

brae n./adj. the slope of a hill

Brae Laird n. proprietor of estate or land in the foothills (braes) of the Highlands

breacan n./adj. Gaelic for 'chequered' or 'multi-coloured', the nearest word to describe tartan; *breacan-an-fheilidh* is the Highland term for the belted plaid

broadsword n. double-edged sword, generally with a 'basket' hilt

broch n. massive, drystone circular tower from Iron Age and earlier

burgh n. borough established as: [1] Royal; [2] Barony; [3] Police

cadet n. of the same family as the clan chief, but descended from the younger sons or daughters of an earlier chief

cairn n. commemorative or marker heap of stones; prehistoric burial mound

carse n. fertile, alluvial land, generally adjacent to a river

chief n. Gaelic *ceann-cinnidh* or head of the kindred effectual leader of all those who bear his surname or who accept his authority

chiefdom n. a ranked society where every member has a position in the heirarchy

chieftain n. Gaelic *ceann-tighe* or 'head of a house'. The sub-chief of a branch – often territorial – of the clan

cist/kist n. wooden, metal or stone chest; prehistoric stone coffin

clachan n. hamlet of (originally) stone houses (Gaelic *clach* 'stone')

clan n. Gaelic *clann* 'children, offspring'. Effectively, a group of families who claim descent from common ancestor, real or mythical, without actually knowing the genealogical links to that ancestor (see *lineage*)

claymore n. (Gaelic *claidheamh-mor* 'great cleaver or sword'. Originally the great two-handed sword. Used by army as term for a basket-hilted broadsword

Clearances n. the systematic eviction, or encouragement to emigrate, of tenants on the great estates after 1750, to clear lands for 'improvement'

crannog n. artificial island created in a loch or marshland, for security

crest n. the heraldic device surmounting a Coat of Arms, originally worn on the crest of a knight's battle helmet. A clan chief's crest, surrounded by a 'strap and buckle', showing allegiance, may be worn as a badge

croft n. piece of leased arable land; not the house built thereon

dirk n./v. long Highland dagger worn at waist; to stab with same

drystane v. method of building in natural, undressed stone without mortar

dubh adj./adv. (pronounced 'doo') widely mis-interpreted Gaelic word, which is translated as 'black' but can mean secret, illicit, concealed etc. (as in the English 'black market', does not refer to colour)

dyke n./v. a wall; to construct a wall

fermtoun a hamlet, village or town that grew up around a medieval farm

feu n./v. a tenure of land; to create such a tenure

feuar n. one who receives a feu in his/her name

Fifteen, the n. the '15 or Jacobite Rising of 1715

fillibeg n. the kilt (Gaelic *feileadh beag* 'little fold or wrap') a length (3–10 m) of single width cloth, sewn with fixed pleats (also 'philabeg')

forestall v. to buy up the whole stock of a commodity before it comes to market

Forty-five, the n. the '45 or Jacobite Rising of 1745

gait n. a way or thoroughfare (see *yett*)

gang v. go, walk or proceed

gey adj./adv very, extreme, excessive or 'over the top' (the 'Gey Gordons')

ghillie n. (Gaelic *gille* 'lad') a youth, bachelor young man, an attendant. Used today for a paid attendant/porter at golf, fishing etc.

gilfine n. quorum of nine 'elders' in a clan, who can form an *ad hoc* council

girdle n./adj. (or 'griddle') circular, iron baking plate hung over fire or stove

glen n. a narrow, 'V' shaped Highland valley

haggis n. savoury pudding of oatmeal and offal, 'steamed' in a sheep's stomach

heritor n. a landholder in a parish

Hogmanay m. New Year's Eve

horning n. to be declared outside the law. 'Put to the Horn' or outlawed

Ilk n. in the term, 'of that Ilk', meaning 'of the same place', where a proprietor's surname is the same as his property ('John Newton of Newton')

ken n./v. knowledge; to know

kirktoun n. village or town that has grown up around an ecclesiastical site

laird n. landed proprietor (similar to 'squire' in post-medieval England)

lineage n. the close family group within a clan, who can actually trace their genealogical links to the common ancestor from whom they claim descent

Lord Lyon As King of Arms, an Officer of the Crown, presiding over his own Court and deciding all matters relating to heraldry and succession in Scotland

Manrent n. by a written Bond, a man 'rented' his service, assistance and allegiance to someone more powerful, in exchange for a Bond of Maintenance (protection)

march n. boundary

mercat cross n. central feature of burgh, where proclamations were read and criminals punished

muckle adj./n./adv. (or 'mickle') big, great; a large amount; much, greatly, very

oxter n./adj. armpit, or thereof; 'oxter knife' is one hidden under the arm

pickle n./adj. small quantity; little ('mony a pickle (not *mickle*) maks a muckle

plaid n. pronounced 'plad' not 'played' (Gaelic *plaide*, 'blanket'). 'Plaid patterns', derive from the mostly, white-based patterns on the family blankets which early emigrants took among their personal effects

procurator n. old Scots for 'advocate'. The Public Prosecutor is 'Procurator Fiscal'

quaich n. Gaelic *cuach*; traditional shallow drinking bowl

reiver n. lowland term for robber or thief

sasine n. the legal instrument giving lawful possession of property

Sassenach n. Gaelic *sasannach*, literally 'Saxon', and actually referring to all non-Highlanders and not just 'the English'

sept n. family group within a clan, bearing a different name or a variant of the main name. In some cases, descendants of strangers who sought chief's protection

skene dhu Gaelic *sgian dubh* not a 'black' handled knife, but one which was concealed (see *dubh*) from period when carrying weapons was forbidden. Only worn conspicuously in hose top since early 19th century.

Standing Council independent body of more than 100 Scottish chiefs

tacksman n. (tack, a lease) holder of lease from chief, often a close kinsman, who rents land to other clansmen in return for military service when required

wean n. child, infant

yett n. gate

Index

engaged in the new leisure pursuit of caravanning. In June 1907 he and ten other enthusiasts established the Caravan Club of Great Britain and Ireland. Membership of the club grew steadily and its affiliates were able to compare new concepts for mobile dwellings at annual meetings, which quickly developed into forums for the exchange of ideas. Early caravan enthusiasts tended to fall into two camps: those who did not want to sacrifice the luxuries of home while on the move and those who were willing to forgo comfort in favour of increased mobility. The former used caravans as capsules that preserved their sense of propriety while on the move. Stables was positioned firmly in this camp and distanced himself from traditional travellers such as showmen and tinkers.

The popularity of caravan holidays grew rapidly in the early decades of the twentieth century. The new demand for lightweight touring boxes led to many experiments by amateur builders that shaped the leisure caravan and the mobile home as they stand today. Just like traditional nomadic dwellings, such as the Mongolian yurt, the North American teepee and the Bedouin black tent, the first leisure caravans were designed, built and developed by the people who used them. The massive industry that has grown up around caravans and mobile homes started out in the back yards of enthusiastic self-builders. Arthur Sherman, a Minnesota bacteriologist, was just one of those pioneering self-builders. In 1929 Sherman designed and began production of an inexpensive, plywood caravan named the Covered Wagon. He was inspired to do so after struggling to erect a tent in the rain on an earlier family vacation. Sherman started making the trailers in his garage but, by 1936, he was one of the biggest manufacturers of travel trailers in America.

Better vehicles and a network of reliable highways enabled the trend for motoring holidays to boom. Those making long journeys across America would regularly stock up on canned provisions, resulting in them being dubbed 'tin can tourists'. The affectionate moniker took on a new meaning in 1936 when Wally Byam unveiled the Clipper, the first in a long line of classic American trailers. The Clipper was revolutionary in design and featured the characteristic rivet-fastened aluminium body and bullet-shaped nose that Airstream is now famous for. Inside were four bunks, a tubular metal dinette and a separate fitted kitchen. Other selling points included advanced systems for heating, electric and ventilation. Airstream struggled to meet all the orders it received.

Seasonal and itinerant workers in America began adopting recreational trailers as temporary homes during the Great Depression of the 1930s. Then, during the Second World War, the need to build instant communities around munitions factories, shipyards, and other manufacturing works led to the rapid development of trailer parks. Such parks continued to grow as soldiers wanting to set up home returned from overseas and large, all-weather travel trailers with electricity and heating—such as the 1946 Spartan—were used as models for year round occupation. These early trailer homes were streamlined and dynamic; they looked like they were intended to move; and at speed. However, by the late 1960s, manufacturers of trailer homes were making them bigger: introducing double and then triple wides (two or three separate trailers fastened together to create a single, larger home). Mobile homes no longer looked mobile and began to resemble traditional site-built homes. 'Modular' or 'manufactured' is the preferred term for mobile homes today and this is quite appropriate because the only move made by the majority of them is from the factory to the intended resting site.

It wasn't until the 1960s that mobility and mobile dwellings became a major source of interest for architects. Young, avant-garde architecture groups including Archigram in Britain, Utopie in France, Ant Farm in America, Haus-Rucker-Co and Coop Himmelb(l)au in Austria and the Metabolists in Japan, envisioned the city of the future as a dynamic entity of constant change. Mobile dwelling units, inspired by the space age and the rapid onset of the throwaway consumer culture, were central to these visions.

The architects devised inflatable capsules, plastic pods and plug-in apartments capable of continuous transformation to new situations. These groups did not want to erect huge stone monuments that would be around for hundreds of years. They called instead for an architecture more in keeping with the time: an architecture that was transient, flexible and even disposable. They envisaged the city of the future as a giant trailer park.

Other forward-looking architects from that period created some of the most dynamic looking mobile dwellings, while the conventional trailer settled down to a life of immobility. Futuristic plastic pods were marketed as space age ski cabins and hi-tech holiday retreats. Jean Maneval's Six-Shell Bubble House, 1968, signalled the arrival of a new breed of portable home. As its name suggests, the dwelling consisted of six separate self-supporting shells that were fastened and sealed together by flexible joints. However, the Six Shell Bubble House was in commercial production from 1968 to 1970 and only 30 were ever made. Most of those were used as accommodation units at an experimental holiday resort in the village of Gripp in the Pyrenean Mountains. Finnish architect Matti Suuronen designed an equally short-lived plastic house. His Futuro House, 1968, was first developed as a ski cabin that could be delivered to remote mountain locations, either in one piece by helicopter or transported by truck and assembled on site. Futuro House was shaped like a flying saucer and went into production in 1968. The house received an enormous amount of publicity on its launch but failed to live up to its billing as the home of tomorrow.

Elements of the American counter culture hit the road in the 1960s as an attempt to establish a way of life free from what they saw as the excessive consumerism of mainstream society. Many took up residence in converted vehicles such as delivery vans and old school buses. A spirit of improvisation reigned in these homes. Some were psychedelic eyesores covered in swirls of Day-Glo paint and random slogans, whereas others were clad in wood and adopted the folk-like appearance of a prairie home on a roller skate. Some of the most unusual examples were created by welding the shell of a camper van onto the top of a bus to form a DIY double-decker. Redundant vehicles were given a whole new lease of life and were often fitted with other found objects such as discarded furniture and old stoves. The development of these mobile homes followed a similar pattern to the evolution of the first leisure caravans. They were not commercially available products. The campers who built the first caravans experimented with different materials and designs and shared their innovations with others. Bus dwellers did the same.

Bus dwelling also proved popular in Britain where the travelling community continued to grow through the late 1970s and into the 1980s. The improvised mobile homes were again created from buses, vans and other vehicles that could be obtained cheaply and satisfied motor transport regulations. They varied in layout and style but many seemed to celebrate the new found freedom offered by life away from the recession-hit inner cities. A circuit of free festivals provided the foundation of the traveller economy. The growing popularity of these events led to many confrontations with the authorities. One of the biggest clashes erupted near Stonehenge in June 1985 after the police ambushed a massive convoy of travellers. It represented a new and violent era of intolerance by the British government toward the travelling community. New Acts of Parliament were introduced to curb the freedom of the travelling community and life on the road became increasingly difficult. The change of mood was reflected in the vehicles the travellers used as homes. They became more discreet with little or no exterior decoration so as to appear indistinguishable from a normal van or passenger coach. This stealth look was also adopted by the mobile sound systems that appeared on the free festival circuit in the late 1980s. DJ collectives such as DiY, Desert Storm and Spiral Tribe took to the road to play at impromptu rave parties across Britain. Some of the vehicles used by the travelling sound systems were adorned with camouflage patterns and military insignia that symbolised the escalation in tension between them and the authorities.

Battles with the law, in this case the building codes of Iowa, also helped shape Jay Shafer's tiny mobile home, Tumbleweed, 2000. Shafer previously lived in an Airstream trailer and used his experience to design and build this compact wooden dwelling based on the hardy, weather-beaten homes found in Cape Cod. It was originally conceived as a site built home, but Shafer found he could not build it in the location he wanted as it was deemed too small. "Minimum size standards", he contends, "have been established to keep small dwellings from popping up and lowering the property value and prestige of larger homes in America's urban and suburban communities".[3] In order to steer his way around the regulations Shafer mounted his home on wheels; transforming it into a travel trailer. However, Shafer's altercations with the law didn't end there. He wasn't able to buy a city lot on which to park his mobile home legitimately and instead had to buy another house so that he could live in the garden.

Living in converted vehicles is still a popular option for those wanting to break away from the grid. Andy Thomson, an architect from Vancouver, Canada, has lived in various reconfigured vehicles with his wife and daughter since 2001. Vanzilla, a reconditioned GMC delivery van, was one of his first mobile home projects. The truck was fitted with an array of energy saving devices and even generated its own electricity through an on board solar power system. The architect is part of a substantial network of eco-RV enthusiasts who advocate self-sufficiency and a low-impact lifestyle. His second mobile home was VeZaMx, a renovated GMC/Corsair RV. Many cities have bylaws that prohibit illegal camping and, when parked, Thomson's motor home was far less conspicuous than his previous delivery van. Vancouver is home to an extensive population of RV enthusiasts who take to the roads in droves during the vacation season. Most of these vehicles are used purely for recreational purposes, however, their presence provides ample cover for those motor homes that are lived in full-time. Thomson estimates that, in Vancouver alone, there are up to five hundred people residing in motor homes. Many of these people share his passion for low-energy, low-cost living outside the mainstream property market. In 2004 Thomson designed a purpose-built autonomous dwelling, named miniHOME, which embodies his aim of making off-the-grid housing more accessible.

Travelling communities tend to be viewed with suspicion by mainstream society. It's easy for the media to make a group of travellers—such as those that descended on Stonehenge in the 1980s—appear threatening or criminal even; but a new breed of traveller might help change such perceptions. Australian photographer, Rob Gray, is part of a growing international community of retired people who spend most of their time on the road. A conventional RV was nowhere near sufficient for his adventurous retirement plans so in 2001 he designed and built Wothahelizat, an enormous mobile home constructed on the chassis of an old fire truck. The robust foundation gives the vehicle extraordinary off road capabilities, which means it can be driven across terrain that might destroy a regular RV. Wothahelizat also has enough storage capacity to endure lengthy stays in Australia's remote outback without having to stock up on supplies every two or three days. "If you are going to spend time and effort getting to a remote spot", says Gray, "it doesn't make sense to stay for only a day or two".[4] To overcome this he has built a monster truck that can carry ample supplies to live comfortably in the bush for up to a month.

Shafer, Thomson and Gray embody the spirit of innovation that spawned the very first caravans and trailer homes. Just like the first people to take up caravan life as a leisure pursuit, the three men represent the two major trends of caravan life: Shafer and Thomson paring down their belongings to the bare minimum in order to make as little impact on the earth as possible, and Gray, travelling with all the comforts of home—and then some.

Endnotes

Informal Architectures: Space and Contemporary Culture
Anthony Kiendl

1 Baudelaire, Charles, *The Painter of Modern Life and Other Essays*, Jonathan Mayne ed., London: Phaidon, 1964, p. 9.
2 DeLillo, Don, *Underworld*, New York: Scribner, 1997, p. 184.
3 Benjamin, Walter, "Theses on the Philosophy of History", *Illuminations*, Hannah Arendt ed., New York: Schocken Books, p. 258.
4 Greenberg, Clement, *Clement Greenberg: The Collected Essays and Criticism, Volume I: Perceptions and Judgements 1939-1944*, John O'Brian ed., Chicago: University of Chicago Press, 1986, p. 20.
5 Greenberg, *Clement Greenberg: The Collected Essays and Criticism, Volume I: Perceptions and Judgements 1939-1944*.
6 Rancière, Jacques, *The Politics of Aesthetics*, Gabriel Rockhill trans., London: Continuum, 2004, p. 26.
7 Rancière, Jacques, *The Future of the Image*, Gregory Elliot trans., London: Verso, 2007, p. 91.
8 Perec, Georges, *Species of Spaces and Other Pieces*, John Sturrock ed., London: Penguin Books, 1999, p. 39.
9 Correspondence with the artist, 2005.
10 Willats, Stephen, "City of Concrete", *Bewitched, Bothered and Bewildered: Spatial Emotion in Contemporary Art and Architecture*, Heike Munder and Adam Budak eds., Zurich and Gdansk: Migros Museum Für Gegenwartskunst and Laznia Centre for Contemporary Art Gdansk, 2003, p. 66.
11 Boym, Svetlana, *The Future of Nostalgia*, New York: Basic Books, 2001, p. 84.
12 Habermas, Jürgen, *The Theory of Communicative Action*, Boston: Beacon Press, 1984.
13 Krauss, Rosalind E, *The Originality of the Avant-garde and Other Modernist Myths*, Cambridge: MIT Press, 1985, p. 282.
14 Vidler, Anthony, *Warped Space*, Cambridge: MIT Press, 1985, p. ix.
15 Iain, Borden, "Another Pavement, Another Beach: Skateboarding and the Performative Critique of Architecture", *The Unknown City: Contesting Architecture and Social Space: A Strangely Familiar Project*, Iain Borden and Joe Kerr et al eds., Cambridge, MA.: MIT Press, 2001, p. 195.
16 Hunn, David, *Skateboarding II*, London: Duckworth, 1977, p. 6.
17 Vidler, *Warped Space*, p. 102.
18 Pomorska, Krystyna, "Foreword", *Rabelais and His World*, Bloomington: Indiana University Press, 1984, p. viii.
19 Pomorska, "Foreword", p. 49.
20 Krauss, *The Originality of the Avant-garde and Other Modernist Myths*, p. 279.

21 Willats, "City of Concrete", p. 66.
22 Bataille, Georges, *The Accursed Share: An Essay on General Economy*, Robert Hurley trans., New York: Zone Books, 1993, p. 21.
23 Denis Hollier, *Against Architecture: The Writings of Georges Bataille*, Betsy Wing trans., Cambridge: MIT Press, 1989.
24 Bataille, *The Accursed Share: An Essay on General Economy*.
25 Bois and Kraus, *Formless: A User's Guide*, p. 186.
26 Sartre, Jean-Paul, *Being and Nothingness*, Hazel E Barnes trans., New York: Simon and Schuster, 1956, pp. 777-778.
27 Lazier, Benjamin, "Abject Academy", *Filth; Dirt, Disgust and Modern Life*, William A Cohen and Ryan Johnson eds., Minneapolis: University of Minnesota Press, 2005.
28 Bärtås, Magnus, and Fredrik Ekman, "The Soil Eaters", *Cabinet*, No. 3, New York: Immaterial Incorporated, 2001, pp. 42-43.
29 Bärtås and Ekman, "The Soil Eaters", p. 779.
30 Kelley, Mike, *Minor Histories: Statements, Conversations, Proposals*, John C Welchman ed., Cambridge: MIT Press, 2004, p. 401.
31 Kelley, *Minor Histories: Statements, Conversations, Proposals*, p. 402.
32 Lazier, "Abject Academy", p. 294.
33 Brisley, Stuart, *Beyond Reason: Ordure*. London: Book Works, 2003, p. 1.
34 Yve-Alain and Kraus, *Formless: A User's Guide*, p. 189.
35 Denis Hollier, *Against Architecture: The Writings of Georges Bataille*, p. 55.

Popular Science
Patrick Keiller

1 This text was first printed in the British Council exhibition catalogue: *Landscape*, Ann Gallagher, Introduction and ed., London: British Council, 2000, pp. 61-67, and in *The Independent*, 6 March 2000.
2 Reprinted in *Comedy*, Wylie Sypher ed., John Hopkins University Press, Baltimore and London, 1980.
3 Published in *Language in Literature*, Krystyna Pomorska and Stephen Rudy eds., Cambridge: 1987; first published in *Volne Smery* 30, 1933-1934
4 See Bregant, Michel, "Poems in Light and Darkness: The Films and Non-Films of the Czech Avant-Garde", *Umeni* Vol. XLIII, 1995, pp. 1-2.
5 de Certeau, Michel, *The Practice of Everyday Life*, Steven Rendall trans., University of California Press, Berkeley, 1984, pp. xi, xxiii-iv. The quotation is from *Cosmos, Witold Gombrowicz*, Eric Mosbacher trans., MacGibbon & Kee, London, 1967, p. 126.

The Centre for Land Use Interpretation
1 See www.clui.org

Emptiness and Imagination
Marie-Paule Macdonald

1 *Essays in Idleness, the Tsurezuregusa of Kenkô*, Donald Keene trans., New York: Columbia University Press 1967.
2 *Essays in Idleness, the Tsurezuregusa of Kenkô*, p. 192.
3 Bataille, Georges, "A Documents Dossier", *October*, No. 60, Spring 1992, p. 27.
4 www.archinect.com/schoolblog/blog.php?id=C0_109_39
5 Bataille, Georges, "A Documents Dossier", p. 25.
6 Bataille, "A Documents Dossier".
7 Žižek, Slavoj, *The Sublime Object of Ideology*, London: Verso, 1989, pp. 45-46.
8 Žižek, Slavoj, "Appendix" in *The Puppet and the Dwarf*, Cambridge, MA.: MIT Press, 2003, pp. 145-146.
9 Barthes, Roland, *Empire of Signs*, New York: Hill and Wang, 1982, p. 24.
10 Barthes, *Empire of Signs*, p. 32.
11 Summerson, John, "The Case for a Theory of Modern Architecture", *Architecture Culture 1943-1968*, Joan Ockman ed., New York: Rizzoli, 1993, pp. 226-236.
12 Fretton, Tony, "Camden Arts Centre", *Icon*: www.icon-magazine.co.uk/issues/011/camden.htm
13 Vacchini, Livio, "Interview", *Casabella*, No. 724, July/August 2004, p. 35.
14 Macdonald, Marie-Paule, *Rockspaces*, Toronto: Art Metropole, 2000.
15 Movible 1: A simple 7.3 x 2.4 x 4.9 metre plywood box with a series of movable parts: window, door, stair, etc. A full-scale model as a prototype was constructed and displayed in the summer of 2000 on the lawn of Dalhousie University's School of Architecture. Developed out of a proposal by Marie-Paule Macdonald, it was constructed as one of the Freelab projects by students Richard Boro, David Cameron, Roger Green, Christopher Holmes, Robert Huber, Bernard Mhaladi, Sakgomo Maniping, Lee Miller, Arnold M Nasha, Peter Osborne, Wayne Pai, David Vera, Brian Warford and David Yuen.

Bungalow Blitz: On Art, Architecture and Curating
Aoife Mac Namara

1 Smithson, Robert, "Cultural Confinement", *Conceptual Art: A Critical Anthology*, Alexander Alberro and Blake Stimson eds., Cambridge, MA: MIT Press, 2000, pp. 280-283.
2 Johnson, Philip, "In Berlin: Comment on Building Expositions", *Philip Johnson: Writings*, Oxford: Oxford University Press, 1979, p. 49.
3 Mies van der Rohe 1905-1938 exhibition at the Whitechapel Gallery, London, December 2002 to March

2003. The exhibition was curated by Terence Riley and Barry Bergdoll and organised by The Museum of Modern Art, New York and Andrea Tarsia at the Whitechapel Gallery. Exhibition design by Fern Green.

4 Thomas Ruff, *l.m.v.d.r.* (Ludwig Mies van der Rohe) series of eight chromogenic prints, 1999-2000.

5 Aoife Mac Namara (curator) Bungalow Blitz: Another History of Irish Architecture, an exhibition including work in video, painting, installation, photography and spoken word by Paul Antick, Jim Grant, Meadhbh Grant, Andrew Kearney, Aoife Mac Namara and Michael Sherrin. Oral history research by Joanne Lacey, London: MoDA, September 2001 to February 2002.

6 See Beryl Graham's "Materials for Art-Practice-Led-Researchers": www.sunderland.ac.uk/~as0bgr/learnmat.html

7 See Altschuler, Bruce, *The Avant-Garde in Exhibitions: New Art in the Twentieth Century*, Berkerly: University of California Press, 1994.

8 See *Exhibition History at MoMA* for an account of the changing conventions of architectural display at MoMA.

9 See *Architecture Without Shadow*, Gloria Moure ed., Barcelona: Ediciones Polígrafa, 2000.

10 See Schulze, Franz, "Mies van der Rohe: The Unabridged Version", *Art in America*, October 2001, pp. 118-127.

11 Thomas Ruff is one of many highly regarded German photographers (including Thomas Struth, Axel Hütte, Candida Höfer and Andreas Gursky) to have studied under Bernd and Hilla Becher at the Kunstakademie Düsseldorf in the 1970s and 80s. See Herzog, Jacques, and Pierre de Meuron, *Architectures of Herzog and de Meuron, Portraits by Thomas Ruff*, New York: Peter Blum, 1995.

12 Higgs, Matthew, "Uta Barth in Conversation with Matthew Higgs", *Uta Barth*, Lee Higgs and Gilbert-Rolfe, eds., London: Phaidon, 2004, p. 12.

13 See Mac Namara, Aoife, "Bungalow Time: An Interview with Andrew Kearney" for a further discussion of the artist's use of foreground.

14 Sudjic, Deyan, "Clash of the Titians", *The Observer*, 27 May 2001.

15 The German photographer Candida Höfer (a graduate of the same art school as Ruff) has produced a series of images of the interiors of Mies van der Rohe's buildings. See Glenn, Constance, "Candida Höfer: Absence in Context", *Candida Höfer*, Hiller and Glenn eds., New York: Aperture, 2004, pp. 14-21.

16 The phrase "illustrative exhibition practice" is used here to distinguish between exhibitions designed as showcases to clarify, explain or provide examples of already existing works of art, architecture and design and those whose purpose is more speculative and prospective: exhibitions that are provisional inquiries rather than unambiguous assertions.

17 Mies van der Rohe retrospective exhibition, New York: MoMA, 1947. Johnson, Philip, *Mies van der Rohe*, New York: MoMA, 1947.

18 See "List of Exhibitions at the Museum of Modern Art" and Barr, Alfred, "Present Status and Future Direction of the Museum of Modern Art: Confidential Report for Trustees Only", *Alfred H Barr, Jr Papers*, New York: MoMA Archives, August 1933, p. 122.

19 The second edition of the catalogue was produced in 1953. In 1978 a further edition was published, this time with an epilogue in the form of a conversation between Philip Johnson, Ludwig Glaeser and Arthur Drexler.

20 The images used in the film were panning shots of photographs taken of the installation by Charles Eames and Hubert Matter, collection of the Lily Auchincloss

Study Centre for Architecture and Design, MoMA.

21 Riley, Terence, "Making History: Mies van der Rohe and the Museum of Modern Art", *Mies in Berlin*, Riley and Bergoll eds., New York: MoMA, 2002, pp. 10-24.

22 Huxtable, Ada Louise, "Memo to Miss Newmeyer from Mrs Huxtable Re: Mies van der Rohe exhibition", 25 July 1947. Archives of the Department of Architecture and Design: MoMA, quoted in Riley, Terence, "Making History: Mies van der Rohe and the Museum of Modern Art", p. 12.

23 Riley, "Making History: Mies van der Rohe and the Museum of Modern Art".

24 According to Riley, the seven principal photomurals were installed as part of this installation; two unbuilt projects from the 1920s–Friedrichstrasse Skyscraper, 1921; Glass Skyscraper, 1922; Mountain House Studies, 1934–and four realised works–Monument to the November Revolution, 1926; German Pavilion, Barcelona, 1928-1929; Concrete Office Building Project, 1925; Tugendhat House, 1934.

25 Huxtable, Ada Louise, label copy for Mies van der Rohe exhibition, 1947, quoted in Riley, "Making History: Mies van der Rohe and the Museum of Modern Art", p. 11.

26 Riley, "Making History: Mies van der Rohe and the Museum of Modern Art", p. 13.

27 While the exhibition at MoDA was developed in response to the architecture of the galleries and display spaces of the museum, the exhibitions at Limerick and Letterkenny were less developed in this way. These exhibitions were formed of already existing exhibition prints, paintings and text panels, and while the context of each varied according to the available space, no new work was commissioned for either venue.

28 Here I am specifically referring to Constructivist, Dadaist, Surrealist, Situationist and later conceptual interventions in the more traditional divisions between object and exhibition.

29 The term 'space' and the related phrase 'spatial culture', are used following de Certeau, to mean that which "exists when one takes into consideration vectors of direction, velocities and time variables. Thus space is composed of intersections of mobile elements… space occurs as the effect produced by the operations that orient it, situate it, temporalise it, and make it function in a polyvalent unity of conflictual programmes or contractual proximities." de Certeau, Michel, *The Practice of Everyday Life*, Berkeley: The University of California Press, 1984, p. 117.

30 The term 'practice-based research' is enjoying considerable currency now that national and international research councils, and not simply dedicated arts councils, have begun to fund research in creative and performing art.

31 For a more detailed analysis of Mies' relationship with Mondrian and other painters of the European avant-garde, see Cohen, Jean-Louise, *Mies van der Rohe*, London: E & FN Spon, 1996, pp. 36-37.

32 While Mies' floor plan for the 1947 exhibition includes a provision for a mural called "Illinois Institute of Technology", the mural does not appear in Herbert Matter or Charles Eames' photographs of the exhibition.

33 van der Rohe, Mies, "Exhibition Plan, Museum of Modern Art, 1947", The Lily Auchincloss Study Center for Architecture and Design, MoMA, New York. Reproduced in Riley, "Making History: Mies van der Rohe and the Museum of Modern Art", p. 12.

34 Johnson, Philip, *Mies van der Rohe*, p. 34.

35 Riley, "Making History: Mies van der Rohe and the Museum of Modern Art", p. 13 and Johnson, Philip, *Mies van der Rohe*, pp. 34, 98-101.

36 Dadaist and Surrealist artists, architects and designers claimed that photo collage, montages, and assemblages–techniques derived from modern technology and developed in opposition to the media of painting and sculpture–could transform the work of art into a piece of reality. See Sheppard, Richard, *Dada, Dada, Dada: Studies of a Movement*, St-Giles: Alpha Academic, 1979, and Lewis, Helena, *Dada Turns Red: The Politics of Surrealism*, Edinburgh: Edinburgh University Press, 1988.

37 See Benson, Timothy O, *Raoul Hausmann and Berlin Dada*, Ann Arbour: University of Michigan Press, 1987.

38 Exhibitions and installation design were integral to Mies' architectural work since the 1920s. See *Mies van der Rohe: European Works*, Sandra Honey ed., London: Academy Editions, 1986.

39 The distinction between Mies' avant-gardist aesthetics and his politics is important, for as Richard Pommer has noted: "Not only was Mies monumentally indifferent to the formal politics of parties and governments: even more significant of his ideological position was his attitude toward social reform as manifested in his commissions and project." See Pommer, Richard, "Mies van der Rohe and the Political Ideology of the Modern Movement in Architecture", *Mies Van der Rohe: Critical Essays*, Franz Schulze ed., New York: MoMA, 1989, pp. 96-148.

40 See Eisenstein, Sergei, "Montage and Architecture", *Eisenstein: Vol. 2–Towards a Theory of Montage*, Michael Glenny and Richard Taylor eds., London: BFI, 1991, pp. 59-60.

41 In *The Power of Display: A History of Exhibition Installations at the Museum of Modern Art*, Mary Ann Staniszewski argues that exhibitions were central to the presentation and dissemination of the innovations of the international avant-gardes of the 1920s and 30s. See Staniszewski, Mary Ann, *The Power of Display: A History of Exhibition Installations at the Museum of Modern Art*, Cambridge, MA: The MIT Press, 1998, p 27.

42 Staniszewski, *The Power of Display: A History of Exhibition Installations at the Museum of Modern Art*.

43 In *The Language of New Media*, Lev Manovich speaks of this as an aesthetic of juxtaposition and dissonance, which he claims was the dominant aesthetic throughout the twentieth century. Manovich, Lev, *The Language of New Media*, Cambridge, MA.: MIT Press, 2002, p. 144.

44 Here I am making a distinction between Mies' work as an exhibition designer of trade, union or national exhibitions and his work as the designer of an architectural retrospective.

45 Eisenstein, "Montage and Architecture", *Eisenstein: Vol 2–Towards a Theory of Montage*, pp. 59-60.

46 de Certeau, *The Practice of Everyday Life*, p. 118.

47 de Certeau, *The Practice of Everyday Life*.

48 Eisenstein, "Montage and Architecture", *Eisenstein: Vol. 2–Towards a Theory of Montage*, p. 81.

49 de Certeau, *The Practice of Everyday Life*, pp. 117-119.

50 Benson, *Raoul Hausmann and Berlin Dada*, p. 32.

51 According to Graham, these photographs were conceived originally as part of a conceptual layout piece to be published in "a mass circulation magazine along the lines of *Esquire*", which was a focus of the New Journalism in the 1960s.

52 Dan Graham in Birgit Pelzer "Double Intersections: The Optics of Dan Graham", *Dan Graham*, New York: Phaidon, 2001, p. 38.

53 Riley, Terence, "Architecture as Subject", *Architecture without Shadow*, Gloria Moure ed., Barcelona: Ediciones Poligrafa, 2000.

54 This research material included notes made during visits to the Mies van der Rohe 1905-1938 at the

Whitechapel, magazine layouts and photographs that constituted Dan Graham's *Homes For America* and Row Houses projects, my collection of Bungalow Bliss letters, articles and editorials from the *The Irish Times* and copies of Irish legislative debates.

55 The photographs were taken between 1999 and 2004 over the course of five different research visits to Ireland.

56 The design of the book was conceived by Combine Design in Calgary, and developed from encounters with the exhibition at the Walter Phillips Gallery, archival material such as the newly commissioned work by Antick and Kearney, images from *Bungalow Bliss* and cuttings from the 1970s DIY magazine *Golden Homes*–a series popular with many of the bungalow builders in the 1970s.

57 While Mies' 1947 exhibition and Dan Graham's 1966 magazine work served as concrete points of departure for the development of both exhibition and book, our respective art, curatorial and installation practices were informed by a much broader context, particularly the history of the exhibition in the context of the European avant-gardes and conceptual artists including Tatlin, Haacke, Piper, Latham, Beuys, Rosler, Smithson, Snow, Matte-Clark, Durham and others.

58 While hung in quite different ways and in conjunction with different objects and images, the Limerick, Letterkenny and MoDA exhibitions all included the same three series of photographs.

59 For varied examples of these perspectives see Myers, Kevin, and Frank McDonald in Mac Namara, Aoife, "The House that Jack Built", *Bungalow Blitz: Another History of Irish Architecture*, Banff: The Walter Phillips Gallery, 2006

60 The walls of the sculpture were designed to be randomly extended over the course of the exhibition. This strategy led to some of the walls reaching around 3.7 metres in height, while others remained at 0.9-1.2 metres.

61 While the overstuffed couch or sofa has been a recurring motif throughout Grant's work on Bungalow Blitz, appearing as it did–albeit hung from a stairwell– in the first version of the exhibition at MoDA, he did not include any of the paintings and drawings he had exhibited at earlier stages of the project.

62 In the first three exhibitions in the series, Antick included photographs of couples, single-generation families and larger cross-generational family groups.

63 Moure, *Architecture without Shadow*, p. 17.

64 A crucial difference between Antick and Barney's photographs is that, while Antick focuses on ordinary interiors of everyday houses, Barney's images "transport us inside large rooms adorned with exquisite and expensive paintings and furnishings, and onto porches and yards that speak of carefree leisure and always balmy weather". See Grundberg, Andy, "Tina Barney: An Afterword", *Tina Barney Theatre of Manners*, Zurich: Scalo, 1997, p. 250.

65 Photographs of Mies van der Rohe's designs for *The Dwelling of our Time* (Die Wohnung unserer Ziet) at the German Building Exhibition in Berlin in 1931 were also an important reference point for the development of the exhibitions at the Lighthouse and Walter Phillips Galleries.

Termination of View
Bernie Miller

1 From Alan Tregebov's part of our unpublished presentation "Termination of View" at the Architecture School, University of Manitoba, 16 September 2003.

2 From the proposal booklet for Veer, a memorial to Emma Goldman. This was a finalists' entry in the Public Art Competition for the Bloor/Spadina Parkette, Toronto, Canada.

3 From the proposal booklet for Veer.

4 Borch-Jacobsen, Mikkel, "Analytic Speech", *The Ends of Rhetoric: History, Theory, Practice*, David Wellbery and John Bender eds., Stanford: Stanford University Press 1990, p. 128.

5 Borch-Jacobsen, "Analytic Speech", *The Ends of Rhetoric*, p. 128.

6 *The Death of Discourse*, Ronald KL Collins and David M Skover eds., Westview Press, p. 121.

7 *The Death of Discourse*, pp. 83-121.

"Post-Peasant Architecture: The House Bunică Built, A Case Study"
Donald Goodes

1 Bunică is the Romanian word for 'grandmother' and Mosu (pronounced 'moshu') is the Romanian word for 'grandfather'.

2 Kearney, Michael, *Reconceptualising the Peasantry: Anthropology in Global Perspective*, Bolder, Colorado: Westview Press, 1996.

3 Roediger, David R, *Working Towards Whiteness: How America's Immigrants Became White, the Strange Journey from Ellis Island to the Suburbs*, Basic Books, 2005.

itourist? Notes on the Affective Economies of Holocaust Tourism
Paul Antick

1 Baer, Ulrich, *Spectral Evidence: The Photography of Trauma*, Cambridge MA.: London MIT Press, 2002, p. 54.

2 There are numerous texts that deal with the Holocaust and the role of the Polish death camps. For a definitive text see Hilberg, Raul, *The Destruction of the European Jews*, New York: London Holmes & Meier, 1985.

3 Pollock, Griselda, "Holocaust Tourism: Being There, Looking Back and the Ethics of Spatial Memory", *Visual Culture and Tourism*, David Crouch and Nina Lubbren eds., Oxford: New York Berg, 2003.

4 This is not to say that the actual experiences of both tourists and Jewish pilgrims are wholly incommensurate with Pollock's description of them. However, I suggest that were Pollock to jettison the binary model she adheres to here–the pilgrim is everything that the tourist is not and vice versa–in favour of a dialectical approach that would produce a more suggestively nuanced account then two productive shifts in the analysis might emerge.

5 Young, James E, "Memory Against itself in Germany Today: Jochen Gerz's Countermonuments", *At Memory's Edge: After Images of the Holocaust in Contemporary Art and Architecture*, New Haven: London, Yale University Press, 2000.

6 Young, James E, "Memory Against itself in Germany Today: Jochen Gerz's Countermonuments", p. 124.

7 Pollock, "Holocaust Tourism: Being There, Looking Back and the Ethics of Spatial Memory", p. 176.

8 Pollock, "Holocaust Tourism: Being There, Looking Back and the Ethics of Spatial Memory", p. 177.

9 Pollock, "Holocaust Tourism: Being There, Looking Back and the Ethics of Spatial Memory".

10 Pollock, "Holocaust Tourism: Being There, Looking Back and the Ethics of Spatial Memory".

11 Pollock, "Holocaust Tourism: Being There, Looking Back and the Ethics of Spatial Memory", p. 178. Pollock borrows the expression 'Auschwitzland' from Tim Cole (see *Images of the Holocaust: The Myth of Shoa Business*, London, Gerald Duckworth & Co, 1999).

12 Baer, *Spectral Evidence: The Photography of Trauma*, p. 69.

13 Pollock, "Holocaust Tourism: Being There, Looking Back and the Ethics of Spatial Memory", p. 177.

14 For Gold, speaking in 1970, the most effective way to overcome the 'assimilation crisis' is by "searing into the memory of a generation born after the Second World War a sense of being Jewish". This could best be brought about by "instilling in youth a deep-rooted awareness of what the Holocaust means to contemporary Jewry". Quoted in Charlton, Linda, "Jews Fear Anti-Zionism of New Left", *The New York Times*, 14 August 1970.

15 There are many excellent examples of this in the American media in particular. Larry David's curmudgeonly Jewish sit-com writer in the HBO show, *Curb Your Enthusiasm*, declares that, "I hate myself, but not because I'm Jewish". He subsequently arranges for an orchestra to perform a medley of Wagner tunes on his Wagner-hating, Jewish neighbour's front lawn.

16 Novick, Peter, *The Holocaust in American Life*, New York: Boston, Mariner Books, 2000, p. 3.

17 Novick also refers to anxieties regarding the Jewish community's identification with a set of 'universalist' American values, the Cold War and its impact on the representation of the Nazi genocide. Here he quotes Charles Silberman: "Without anti-semitism Jews will lose their group solidarity." Novick, *The Holocaust in American Life*, p. 185.

18 Novick quotes Rabbi Joachim Prinz who argued that young Jews' "unwillingness to consider Jewish identification and solidarity", their "indifference in matters Jewish", was "largely attributable to the European catastrophe". Novick, *The Holocaust in American Life*, pp. 157-161.

19 For an incisive account of the Weimar period see, Burleigh, Michael, *The Third Reich: A New History*, Basingstoke, Oxford: Pan Books, 2000, pp. 27-149.

20 For an incisive account of the Weimar period see, Burleigh, Michael, *The Third Reich: A New History*.

21 Kugelmass, Jack, "Why We Go to Poland: Holocaust Tourism as Secular Ritual", *The Art of Memory: Holocaust Memorials in History*, James E Young ed., New York: The Jewish Museum, 1994, p. 178.

22 Zemel, Carol, "Emblems of Atrocity: Holocaust Liberation Photographs", *Image and Remembrance: Representation and the Holocaust*, Shelley Hornstein and Florence Jacobowitz in eds., Bloomington: Indiana University Press, 2003 p. 165.

23 Zemel, "Emblems of Atrocity: Holocaust Liberation Photographs", p. 211.

24 For an account of the critical approaches that characterise 'essentialist' and 'constructionist' positions on the representation of the Holocaust see Mintz, Alan, *Popular Culture and the Shaping of Holocaust Memory in America*, Seattle: London, University of Washington Press, 2001.

25 Quoted in Abercrombie, Nicholas, Stephen Hill and Bryan S Turner, "Determinacy and Indeterminacy in the Theory of Ideology", *Mapping Ideology*, Slavoj Žižek ed., London; New York: Verso, 1994, p. 154.

26 According to Louis Althusser "the interpellation of individuals as subjects presupposes the 'existence' of a Unique and central Other Subject, in whose name the religious ideology interpolates all individuals as subjects". The individual subject is thus "subjected to him by his very interpellation... a subject through the Subject and subjected to the Subject". See Althusser, Louis, "Ideology and Ideological State Apparatuses",

Visual Culture: The Reader, Jessica Evans and Stuart Hall eds., London: Sage Publications, 1995, p. 322.

27 Quoted in Eagleton, Terry, "Ideology and its Vicissitudes in Western Marxism", *Mapping Ideology*, p. 217.

28 Eagleton, "Ideology and its Vicissitudes in Western Marxism".

29 Not only does Griselda Pollock present the reader with a homogenous account of the tourist but, by implication, she does precisely the same thing with regards the Jew identity in general.

30 Hitler, Adolf, *Mein Kampf*, Helmut Ripperger trans., New York: Reynal & Hitchcock, 1939, pp. 416–417.

Evacuations: De-colonising Architecture
Eyal Weizman

1 The information on which this chapter is based has been gathered mostly first-hand in the process of my involvement with planners from the Palestinian ministry in preparation for the evacuation and in debates and plans regarding possible re-use of the settlements in case they were left in tact by Israeli forces. Some of the conversation and the quotes are taken from other meetings, including a round table discussion at Shaml, the Palestinian Diaspora and Refugee Centre, on 6 November 2004.

2 Zandbreg, Esther, "A Pile of Garbage with a View to Gaza's Beach", *Ha'aterz*, 1 September 2005.

3 Zandbreg, "A Pile of Garbage with a View to Gaza's Beach".

4 Gutman, Natan, and Shlomo Shamir, "Rice: There is no Place for the Wholesale Destruction of Settlers' Homes in the Gaza Strip during Evacuation", *Ha'aretz*, 7 April 2005.

5 Yoaz, Yuval, and Aluf Ben, "Sharon: Ideally I would have left the Homes standing", *Ha'aretz*, 3 May 2005.

6 "Arab Billionaire Offers to Buy Evacuated Gaza Settlements", *Ha'aretz*, 10 February 2005.

7 Quoted in Myre, Greg, "Homes of Israeli Settlers Pose a New Set of Anxieties", *The New York Times*, 23 January 2005.

8 Myre "Homes of Israeli Settlers Pose a New Set of Anxieties".

9 Vidler, Anthony, *The Architectural Uncanny*, Cambridge, MA.: MIT press, pp. 3–62

10 Myre, "Homes of Israeli Settlers Pose a New Set of Anxieties".

11 A draft text attached to the planning document I was showed read: "The colony blocks and the sand dune areas in the north and south shall not be used for urban development and must be cleared of all colony elements… these are the finest landscapes; areas of rare and exceptional landscape and nature values."

12 Abbas signed a government decree that the land reverts to the Palestinian government, but the decision met resistance.

13 Ben, Aluf, "Pullout still poses Rubble Trouble", *Ha'aretz*, 13 July 2005.

14 The Foundation for Middle East Peace, "Settlement Database and Suitability Assessment" or "Regional Plan of the Southern Governorates 2005-2015".

15 This in itself could explain why there are 12,000 people registered as residents in refugee camps such, but only 8,000 actually living there.

16 See this discussion in the specific context of the reconstruction of the Jenin refugee camp in Weizman, Eyal, "Walking through Walls", 2006.

17 Marxist revolutionaries of the nineteenth century were the first to employ this strategy. They believed that the pace of change could be accelerated by acts of indiscriminate violence designed to provoke the ruling power to throw off the mask of legality and reveal itself to the peasants and workers in all its brutality. See: Ignatieff, Michael, *The Lesser Evil*, Princeton: Princeton University Press, 2004, pp. 61, 67-68, 102.

18 Norma Masriyeh Hazboun, *Israeli Resettlement Schemes for Palestinian Refugees in the West Bank and Gaza Strip since 1967*, Shaml, the Palestinian Diaspora and Refugee Centre. http://www.shaml.org/publications/monos/mono4.htm#Introduction

19 Knesset Minutes, 4-6 December 1967.

20 See "The Architecture of Ariel Sharon", *Third Text*, No. 3, 2006.

21 Weitz, Joseph, *My Diary and Letters to the Children*, Ramat Gan: Masadah Press, 1973, p. 292.

22 "Levy Eshkol, The Third Israeli Prime Minister, Jerusalem: State Archive, the Series for the Commemoration of Israel's Presidents and Prime Ministers", Yemima Rosenthal ed., Jerusalem, 2002, p. 582.

23 See "The Architecture of Ariel Sharon", *Third Text*, No. 3, 2006.

24 Sharon, Ariel, *Warrior*, Simon & Schuster, 2001, p. 259.

25 Hazboun, Norma, "Israeli Resettlement Schemes for Palestinian Refugees in the West Bank and Gaza Strip", *Al-Shaml Monograph* Series 4, 1996.

26 Sharon, *Warrior*, pp. 258-260.

27 Hazboun, "Israeli Resettlement Schemes for Palestinian Refugees in the West Bank and Gaza Strip".

28 In 1977 when the Likud came to power the size of plots was reduced in to 125 square metres. The reduction was argued as a response to a shortage of suitable land, but must be understood as well against the background of the increased demand for land for the expansion of Jewish settlements in the Gaza Strip.

29 The policy was boosted again in 1976, during Rabin's government, when the then Minister of Defence Shimon Peres attempted to solicit international sponsorship for building homes for Gaza refugees.

30 The housing projects established by Israel included: The Canada project, 1972; 891 families in 488 houses; The Shuqairi project in Khan Younis, 1973; 135 families in 128 Houses; The Brazilian project in Khan Younis, 1973; 436 families in 422 Houses; 790 families in 809 houses; al-Amal project in Khan Younis, 1979; 802 families in 842 houses. Site were plots of lands and financial assistance was provided included: Nasr site in Gaza town, 1974; 36 houses were constructed on 36 plots of land, with 36 families; The Sheikh Radwan project, July 1976, where 1,000 plots of land were allocated, of which it accommodated 1,186 families; Beit Lahia project in Jabalia, October 1977; it had 472 houses constructed, with 832 families; Tal al-Sultan project in Rafah, April 1978; it had 943 houses with 1,041 families; Al-Amal project in Khan Younis, July 1979; 184 houses, with 343 families; Rafah Brazilian project, July 1979; 109 houses, with 161 families; Nazleh site in Gaza town, April 1981; 168 houses, 163 families. See Hazboun, "Israeli Resettlement Schemes for Palestinian Refugees in the West Bank and Gaza Strip".

31 According to Hazboun 95.6 per cent of the relocated refugees in the Sheikh Radwan resettlement scheme believe that their contribution to the national struggle is as strong as it was prior to relocation. See Hazboun, "Israeli Resettlement Schemes for Palestinian Refugees in the West Bank and Gaza Strip".

32 Fanon, Frantz, *The Wretched of the Earth*, London: Penguin books, 2003, p. 27.

33 One such, Al-Muqata in Ramallah, was originally constructed by the British as police headquarters, it was used as a base and prison by the Jordanian Army between 1948 and 1967 and in the same capacity by the IDF after 1967. In 1993 it became Arafat's compound-headquarters until its almost complete destruction by the Israeli military in spring 2002.

34 Sharon, *Warrior*, p. 400.

35 Daily Press Briefing by The Offices of the UN Spokesman for the Secretary-General and the Spokesperson for the General Assembly President. See Benn, Aluf, "Debris from Gaza homes razed in pullout may be sent to Sinai", *Ha'aretz*, 14 July 2005.

36 This text was first printed in *Did Someone Say Participate*, Markus Miessen and Shumon Basar eds., Cambridge MA.: MIT Press, 2006 and in *Log*, No. 6, Autumn 2005.

Lida Abdul: An Informal Architect
Sara Raza

1 Article adapted from the text "Travelling Light", first published by *n.paradoxa* in "Journeys", Vol. 17 (special Documenta 12 edition).

Landfills and Lifescapes: The Transformation of New York's Fresh Kills
Joel McKim

1 Field Operations, "Lifescape", *Praxis 4*, 2002, p. 24.

2 Waldheim, Charles, "Landscape Urbanism: A Genealogy", *Praxis*, No. 4, 2002, p. 15.

3 Waldheim, "Landscape Urbanism: A Genealogy", pp. 10-17.

4 Somol, RE and Sarah Whiting, "Notes Around the Doppler Effect and other Moods of Modernism", *Perspecta*, No. 33, 2002, pp. 72-77.

5 Allen, Stan, *Points and Lines: Diagrams and Projects for the City*, New York: Princeton Architectural Press, 1999.

6 Corner, James, "Terra Fluxus", *The Landscape Urbanism Reader*, Charles Waldheim ed., New York: Princeton Architectural Press, 2006, p. 30.

7 Pollock, Linda, "Sublime Matters: Fresh Kills", *Praxis*, No. 4, 2002, pp. 58-63.

8 Vandam, Jeff, "The Dump Was Closed, but the Rancor Never Ends", *The New York Times*, 5 February 2006.

9 Depalma, Anthony, "Landfill, Park…. Final Resting Place? Plans for Fresh Kills Trouble 9/11 Families Who Sense Loved Ones in the Dust", *The New York Times*, 14 June 2004.

10 Rancière, Jacques, "Who is the Subject of the Rights of Man?", *South Atlantic Quarterly*, No. 103, 2004, pp. 297-310.

11 Czerniak, Julia, "Introduction", *Case: Downsview Park Toronto*, Julia Czerniak ed., New York: Prestel, 2001, p. 15.

The Politics of Informal Production
Andrea Phillips

1 Agamben, Giorgio, *Means Without End: Notes on Politics*, Minneapolis: University of Minnesota Press, 2000.

2 Francis, Alÿs, *ArtForum*, Summer 2002.

3 Agamben, *Means Without End: Notes on Politics*,

4 Agamben, *Means Without End: Notes on Politics*.

5 Agamben, *Means Without End: Notes on Politics*.

Ruptures on the Architectural Grid: Brian Jungen's *Treaty Project*, Métis Road Allowance Houses and other models of inhabiting the 'in-between'.
Candice Hopkins

1 Cairns, Stephen "Introduction", *Drifting: Architecture and Migrancy*, London: Routledge, 2004.

2 After the Second World War, the summer camping area of the Dunne-Zaa people was sold by the Director

of the Veteran's Land act in 1945 who then sold it as farmland to returning veterans while the Dunne-Zaa were relocated permanently into three separate reserves further north. In what would become one of the most pivotal cases in the history of treaty land claims, the group argued that the reserve was wrongfully sold and that their best interests were not acted upon in the agreement to sell the land and its mineral rights. In 1995 the case, Apsassin vs the Queen, concluded that the Crown has certain fudiciary duties, which arise prior to the surrender of reserve land; in the other words, it has to act in the best interest of Aborginal people.

3 Lee, Pamela, *Object to be Destroyed: The Work of Gordon Matta-Clark*, Cambridge: MIT Press, 2001, p. 93.

4 Lee, *Object to be Destroyed: The Work of Gordon Matta-Clark*, p. 111.

5 Morgan, Jessica, "Brian Jungen's Other Projects", *Brian Jungen*, Rotterdam: WdW Publishers, 2006, p. 43.

6 Lee, *Object to be Destroyed: The Work of Gordon Matta-Clark*, p. 104.

7 There is little information on road allowance houses and much of the information that exists is through stories and oral records. See www.metismuseum.ca/browse/index.php/351

Temporary Territories
Marjetica Potrč

1 See Potrč, Marjetica, "Temporary Territories", *Emergencies*, MUSAC: Spain, p. 62–69, 2005, for an extended version of this text.

2 This research was carried out in 2003 as part of the *Caracas Case Project* and the Culture of the Informal City, sponsored by the Federal Cultural Foundation of Germany and the Caracas Think Tank.

Tent Embassies: Collapsing, Australia and Architecture
Gregory Cowan

1 See *New York Times* http://www.nytimes.com/2008/02/13/world/asia/13aborigine

2 Informal Architecture Programme: www.banffcentre.ca/programs/program.aspx?id=115

3 Bataille, Georges, *Documents*, No. 7, December 1929, cited in Hollier, D, *Against Architecture: The Writings of Georges Bataille*, Cambridge: MIT Press, 1989, p. 30.

4 Bey, Hakim, *TAZ: The Temporary Automous Zone*, New York: Autonomedia, 1985.

5 The Latin word *architectura* was only brought into the English language in the sixteenth century with John Shute's 1563 translation of Vitruvius' ten books: *The First and Chiefe Groundes of Architecture*.

6 "The war machine is exterior to the state apparatus.... The war machine seems to be irreducible to the state apparatus... it is outside its sovereignty and prior to its law." Deleuze, Gilles, *Nomadology*, Massumi trans., New York: Semiotext(e), 1986, pp. 1–2.

7 Ingraham, Catherine, "Architecture Lament and Power in the Journal of Visual Arts", *Architecture–Space–Painting*, London: Academy Group, 1992. Ingraham reread Vitruvius' aberrant book ten of *De Architectura Libri Decem* (Ten Books on Architecture).

8 Ingraham, Catherine, "Architecture Lament and Power in the Journal of Visual Arts".

9 Tench, Watkin, *A Narrative*, cited in Clark, Manning, *Sources of Australian History: World's Classics*, London: Oxford University Press, 1957, p. 8.

10 On 30 October 2002 Ngunnawal elders reportedly extinguished the sacred fire maintained by the Embassy as a national meeting place, prompting a controversy about corruption and the proper authority over the camp and symbolic meeting place at the fire, the

'Sacred Fire of Peace and Justice', said to contain the 'Dreamtime heroes': http://www.ohmsnotbombs.org

11 Parliament House was also losing public acceptablity as the central seat of government in Australia, according to architectural historian Jennifer Taylor in *Australian Architecture Since 1960*, Red Hill ACT: National Education Division, Royal Australian Institute of Architects, 1990, p. 100.

12 Parliament House was designed by Mitchell Giurgola and Thorpe.

13 ABC Radio The World Today report transcript for 19 February 2003: www.abc.net.au/worldtoday/s788025.

14 Vernon, Christopher, "Axial Occupation", *Architecture Australia*, September/October 2002.

15 Dow, Coral, "Aboriginal Tent Embassy: Icon or Eyesore?", *Chronology*, No. 3, 2001.

16 Bey, *TAZ: The Temporary Automous Zone*, p. 99.

17 In the sense D Hollier uses in *Against Architecture: The Writings of Georges Bataille*, pp. 31–36.

18 Hollier, D, *Against Architecture: The Writings of Georges Bataille*, pp. 31–32.

19 The etymology of 'tent' comes from the Latin *tentorium*, meaning 'stretched out'.

20 Aaron Betsky's critique posits the tent as primordial, the 'first' architecture; Betsky, Aaron, *Building Sex; Men, Women, Architecture and the Construction of Sexuality*, New York: Morrow, 1995, p. 18.

Portable Architecture:
Design Workshops at Domaine de Boisbuchet
Robert Kronenburg

1 Heidegger uses the example of a bridge establishing the location of a particular place (*locale*). See Heidegger, Martin, "Building, Dwelling, Thinking", *Martin Heidegger, Basic Writings*, David Krell ed., London: Routledge, 1993, pp. 355–356.

2 Le Corbusier, *Towards a New Architecture*, Frederick Etchells trans., London, Architectural Press: 1946, p. 89.

3 See Kronenburg, Robert, *Houses in Motion: The Genesis, History and Development of the Portable Building*, London: John Wiley, 2002, and Kronenburg, *Portable Architecture*, Oxford: Architectural Press, 2003.

4 The exhibition was curated by Mathias Schwart-Clauss who also co-edited the catalogue *Living in Motion: Design and Architecture for Flexible Dwelling*, Weil-am-Rhein: Germany, Vitra Design Museum, 2002.

Architecture of Motion
Sarah Bonnemaison and Christine Macy

1 Goethe, Johann Wolfgang von, *Von Deutscher Baukunst*, 1772.

2 Cited in Jormakka, Kari, *Flying Dutchmen: Motion in Architecture*, Basel: Birkhäuser, 2002, p. 80.

3 Tschumi, Bernard, *Architecture and Disjunction*, Cambridge, Massachusetts: MIT Press, 1996, p. 128.

4 Giedeon, Siegfried, *Mechanisation Takes Command: A Contribution to Anonymous History*, New York: Norton, 1948, p. 107.

5 Marcel Duchamp's *Nude Descending the Staircase*, 1912, and Umberto Boccioni's *Unique Form of a Continuous space*, 1913.

6 Edweard Muybridge's well-known stop-action photographs of animals and people in motion, 1870, Thomas Eakins' *The Double Jump*, 1880, Etienne-Jules Marey's chronophotographs, 1890, and Harold Edgerton's stroboscopic images, 1950. See also Wassily Kandinsky's *Movement of Paluca*, 1925, Herbert Matter's *Figure in movement*, 1941, László Moholy-Nagy's *Dance Movement*, 1946, and György Kepes' work at MIT. Dziga Vertov's *Kino-Eye*, Fritz Lang's use of shadow, and the

concept of *cineplastics* (See Vidler in Neumann, *Film Architecture*, p. 14).

7 Cohen, Jean-Louis, *Scenes of the World to Come: European Architecture and the American Challenge, 1893-1960*, Paris: Flammarion/Canadian Centre for Architecture, 1995, pp. 72-79.

8 Siegfried Giedeon's concept of *Durchdringung*, or transparency. See Heynen, Hilde, *Architecture and Modernity: A Critique*, Cambridge, MA: MIT Press, 2000, and Rowe, Colin, and Robert Slutzky, *Transparency: Literal and Phenomenal*, Boston: Birkhäuser, 1997.

9 Didi-Huberman, Georges, and Laurent Mannoni, *Mouvements de l'air: Étienne-Jules Marey, photographe des fluids*, Paris: Gallimard, 2004, p. 180.

10 See *Kitchen Diaries*, 2004, in which Norwegian researchers attempt to 'objectively' document the kitchen habits of bachelors in rural areas, only to find that most researchers befriended the subjects of study.

11 Barthes, Roland, "The Death of the Author", *Image/Music/Text*, Stephen Heath trans., New York: Hill and Wang, 1977, pp. 142-148.

12 Tschumi, *Architecture and Disjunction*, p. 3.

13 Paul Klee cited in Grohmann, Will, *The Drawings of Paul Klee*, New York: Curt Valentin, 1944. (Cited in *Mechanisation Takes Command*, p. 109).

14 Didi-Huberman, Georges, and Laurent Mannoni, *Mouvements de l'air*, p. 191.

15 Klee, Paul, *Pedagogical Sketchbook*, New York: Nierendorf Gallery, 1944. (Cited in *Mechanisation Takes Command*, p. 111).

16 Lars Spuybroek, NOX Architects, cited in Jormakka, Kari, *Flying Dutchmen*, Basel: Birkhäuser, 2002, p. 62.

17 Explored by Gerrit Rietveld and others. See Rowe, Colin and Robet Slutzky *Transparency*, Basel: Birkhäuser, 1997.

18 Schlemmer, Oskar, "Man in an Abstract Room" and "A Dancing Figure", *Bühne in Bauhaus*, László Moholy-Nagy ed., 1924. (Cited in Pelkonen, Eeva, "Transitions: Alvar Aalto's Approach to Organicism", *The Organic Approach to Architecture*, Deborah Gans and Zehra Kuz eds., Chichester: Wiley-Academy, 2003, pp. 41, 43.)

19 Forsythe, William, *Improvisation Technologies: a tool for the analytical dance eye*, Karlsruhe: Zentrum für Kunst und Medientechnologie, 1999, p. 18.

20 Duncan, Carol, and Alan Wallach, "The Museum of Modern Art as Late Capitalist Ritual: An Iconographical Analysis", *Marxist Quarterly*, 1979; Mark Wigley, *White Walls, Designer Dresses*, MIT Press, 2001.

21 Tschumi, *Architecture and Disjunction*, p. 139.

Between the Furniture and the Building (Between a Rock and a Hard Place)
Jimmie Durham

1 This text is adapted from a previous version originally published in *Jimmie Durham: Between the Furniture and the Building (Between a Rock and a Hard Place)*, Kunstverein München: Berliner Künstlerprogramm DAAD, Köln: König, 1998, with permission of the artist.

Caravans Are Cool
Sean Topham

1 Caravan Club of Great Britain: www.caravanclub.co.uk

2 Wallis, Allan D, *Wheel Estate*, New York: Oxford University Press, 1991, p. v.

3 Shafer, Jay, "The Complexity of Living Simply", *Designer/Builder Magazine*, Santa Fe: Kingsley Hammett, June 2001, pp. 17-25.

4 Rob Gray: www.robgray.com

Contributor Biographies

Lida Abdul

Abdul lives and works in Kabul, Afghanistan. Her work has been featured at the Venice Biennale 2005, São Paulo Biennial 2006, Gwanju Biennial 2006, Moscow Biennial 2007, Kunsthalle Vienna, ICA London, Tate Modern, Moma, ZKM among others.

Kim Adams

Adams has participated in the Sydney Biennale, InSite, America, Sculpture Projects 97, Germany, as well as projects at The Power Plant, Toronto, Jeu de Paume, Paris, Centraal Museum, Utrecht, Wino Aaltonen Museum, Turku, and Kunsthalle Friedericianum.

Paul Antick

Antick is Senior Lecturer in photography at Roehampton University, London, UK. He has recently exhibited in Europe and North America and has written for various publications on photography, fashion and advertising.

Lance Blomgren

Blomgren is a writer, curator, artist and teacher based in Vancouver, Canada. His publications and book projects include, *Manual For Beginners*, *Walkups*, *Oasis* and *Corner Pieces*. Blomgren's writings have recently appeared in *Art Asia Pacific*, *Ascent* and *Visual Codec*. He has exhibited internationally and is Director/Curator of Helen Pitt Gallery.

Eleanor Bond

Bond has exhibited internationally, participating in numerous biennials and group exhibitions and has had solo exhibitions at the Museum of Contemporary Art in São Paulo, Witte de With in Rotterdam, Clocktower in New York and the Museum of Contemporary Art in Montréal.

Sarah Bonnemaison and Christine Macy

Bonnemaison and Macy are professors of design, theory and history at the school of architecture of Dalhousie University. They are the authors of *Architecture and Nature: Creating the American Landscape*, 2003, and *Festival Architecture*, 2007.

The Center for Land Use Interpretation (CLUI)

CLUI is a research organisation interested in understanding the nature and extent of human interaction with the earth's surface. It was founded in 1994, and since that time it has produced over 30 exhibits on land use themes and regions, for public institutions worldwide. CLUI has published numerous books. CLUI Archive photographs illustrate journals, popular magazines, and books by other publishers, and have been used in non-CLUI exhibitions, and acquired by art collectors.

Gregory Cowan

Cowan has practiced as an architect, lecturer and researcher and promoted architecture and urbanism worldwide. He has researched, lectured, and participated in courses and workshops in Australia, The Netherlands, Croatia, Austria, Spain, Canada, Korea, the United Kingdom and Mongolia.

Jimmie Durham

Durham is a sculptor, essayist and poet. He has exhibited worldwide including the Whitney Biennial, Documenta IX, ICA London, Exit Art, the Museum of Contemporary Art, Antwerp and the Venice Biennale. Durham is the author of numerous essays and the anthology *A Certain Lack of Coherence*. In 1995 *Jimmie Durham*, a comprehensive survey of his art, was published.

Elle Flanders

Flanders is a filmmaker and photographer based in Toronto. Her most recent work includes: *What Isn't There*; *Bird on a Wire*; *A Five City Symphony*, *Zero Degrees of Separation* and *Once*. Her work has been screened and exhibited at the Museum of Modern Art New York, the Berlin International Film Festival, Hot Docs and festivals worldwide.

Dan Graham

Since the mid-1960s, Graham has produced an important body of art and theory that engages in a highly analytical discourse on the historical, social and ideological functions of contemporary cultural systems. Graham has published numerous critical and theoretical essays that investigate the cultural ideology of such contemporary social phenomena as punk music, suburbia and public architecture.

Donald Goodes

Goodes was a visual-art critic from 1984-1997 when he produced the manifesto *Complacent Criticism: I quit!*. He now works as a Web developer and artist. His mock television series *Each & Every One of You*, produced at The Banff Centre, developed a cult following and has been screened across Canada, America and Europe. He produced photo essays for the *Inside Television* exhibition catalogue, and for the publication *Obsession, Compulsion, Collection: On Objects, Display Culture and Interpretation*.

Arni Haraldsson

Haraldsson is an Associate Professor of Photography at Emily Carr Institute. He has written about art and photography for numerous publications. His work has been exhibited internationally. Haraldsson is represented by Catriona Jeffries Gallery in Vancouver.

David Hoffos

Hoffos has had many solo exhibitions, including Catastrophe, 1998, and Another City, 1999-2002. In 2003 he launched the first phase of Scenes from the House Dream, a five-year series of linked installations set to begin its national tour in October 2008. He recently represented Canada at the 48th Oberhausen Short Film Festival, Germany. His first work for the stage–*Hoffos/Clarke Conspiracy* (with Denise Clarke/One Yellow Rabbit)– debuted at Calgary's High Performance Rodeo in 2006. Hoffos is represented by Trépanier Baer, Calgary.

Candice Hopkins

Hopkins is Director and Curator of the Exhibitions Programme at the Western Front. She has been awarded the Ramapo Curatorial Prize for the exhibition Every Stone Tells a Story: The Performance Work of David Hammons and Jimmie Durham. Her writing is published by MIT Press, New York University, Catriona Jeffries Gallery, and Banff Centre Press and she is a contributor to *C Magazine*. She has given talks at Tate Modern, Dakar Biennale and the University of British Columbia.

Andrew Kearney

Kearney has exhibited internationally in such locations as the Irish Museum of Modern Art, Dublin, the Camden Arts Centre, London, and the Ottawa Art Gallery, Ontario Canada. He has participated in collaborative architecture and public art projects at Heathrow's Terminal 1 with the Public Art Development Trust.

Patrick Keiller

Keiller studied architecture at the Bartlett School and fine art at the Royal College of Art, both in London. His films include *London*, 1994, and *Robinson in Space*, 1997. He has contributed to the following publications: *The Unknown City*, 2000, *This Is Not Architecture*, 2002, *Re:CP*, 2003, and *London: from Punk to Blair*, 2003. Since 1974, he has taught and lectured in schools of architecture and fine art and universities across the UK.

Anthony Kiendl

Kiendl is Director of Plug In Institute of Contemporary Art in Winnipeg. He has taught art and architecture at the University of Regina and University of Manitoba. Kiendl was the Director of Visual Arts, Walter Phillips Gallery and the Banff International Curatorial Institute at The Banff Centre from 2002-2006. His numerous exhibitions include Little Worlds, 1998, Fluffy, 1999, Space Camp 2000: Uncertainty, Speculative Fictions and Art, 2000, and Godzilla vs Skateboarders: Skateboarding as a Critique of Social Spaces, 2001. Kiendl's writing has been published in *Parachute*, *FUSE*, *Flash Art* and *Canadian Art*.

Andrew King and Angela Silver
Silver is an interdisciplinary artist working both independently and collaboratively, based in Calgary. King is a graduate architect, author, critic, curator and educator.

Together, their collaborative practice has resulted in exhibitions at the Stride Gallery in Calgary, YYZ Gallery in Toronto, the Confederation Center Art Gallery in Charlottetown, Dalhousie University School of Architecture, arch3 gallery at the University of Manitoba, Owens Art Gallery and the Pratt Institute in Rome.

Knowles Eddy Knowles
Knowles Eddy Knowles formed in 2004. Since meeting in Halifax, Nova Scotia, all three members have dispersed to different locales (Jon Knowles to Montréal, Canada, Michael Eddy to Frankfurt, Germany, Robert Knowles to London, England). They work remotely but also come together to engage research, commissions, residencies and exhibitions in Rotterdam, Frankfurt, London, Vancouver, New York City, Montréal and Banff.

Robert Kronenburg
Kronenburg is an architect and holds the Chair of Architecture at the University of Liverpool, School of Architecture, in the UK. His books include *Houses in Motion: The Genesis, History and Development of the Portable Building*, *Portable Architecture*, *Spirit of the Machine* and he is editor of *Transportable Environments*.

Aoife Mac Namara
Mac Namara is Director of the AHRC Spaces Buildings Make project, programme leader for the MA Film and Visual Culture and a member of the SSHRC Informal Architectures research group. Recent curatorial work includes projects at the Lighthouse, Scotland's Centre for Architecture and the City, 2006; the Walter Phillips Gallery, Canada, 2004; the Ottawa Art Gallery, Canada, 2004; the Letterkenny Arts Centre, Ireland, 2003; the Limerick City Art Gallery, Ireland, 2002, and MoDA, London, UK, 2001.

Corywn Lund
Corwyn Lund's formative public art projects have culminated in the exhibitions *Swingsite, MusicBox RevolvingDoor and Parlour of Twilight* and *Microphone Bouquet Series*. His work has been shown internationally and is held in the Library and Archives of the National Gallery of Canada and the Canada Council Art Bank.

Marie-Paule Macdonald
Macdonald is a registered architect, member of the Order of Architects of Québec and the RAIC. Her book, *rockspaces*, was published by Art Metropole in Toronto in 2000. Other publications include *Wild in the Streets*, 1994.

Luanne Martineau
Martineau can be found in the public collections of the Vancouver Art Gallery, the Art Gallery of Greater Victoria, the Musee d'art Contemporain de Montréal, and The National Gallery of Canada. She has recently published *FREAKOUT (Temporal Bodies)*.

Gordon Matta-Clark
Matta-Clark was born in New York in 1943 and died in 1978. His work has been presented in Documenta V, Kassel, Germany; and at exhibitions in São Paolo, Berlin, Zurich, and in the Ninth Biennale de Paris. Major projects by Matta-Clark were staged in Aachen, Paris and Antwerp.

Rita McKeough
McKeough works in installation, audio and performance and has been exhibiting installations and site works throughout Canada since 1977.

Joel McKim
Joel McKim is a lecturer in the Department of Communication Studies at Concordia University, Montreal and a PhD candidate at the Centre for Cultural Studies, Goldsmiths College. He writes for several architecture and art publications.

Bernie Miller
Miller has exhibited worldwide and been commissioned to do major public artworks in Canada. He has co-edited a collection of essays featured in *Crime and Ornament: The Arts and Popular Culture in the Shadow of Adolf Loos*.

Alex Morrison
Morrison has exhibited internationally at Catriona Jeffries Gallery, Büro Friedrich, Künstlerhaus Bethanien, Henry Art Gallery, Contemporary Art Gallery and Frankfurt Kunstverein.

Ryan Nordlund
Nordlund has exhibited at Art Gallery of Calgary, Alberta Biennial of Contemporary Art and the Nickel Arts Museum in Calgary. In 2004, he participated in the Informal Architecture Thematic Residency at The Banff Centre.

Edgar Arceneaus, Matthew Sloly, Olga Koumoundouros and Vincent Galen Johnson
Arceneaux has had solo exhibitions at the Kunstverein Ulm, Germany; Galerie Kamm, Berlin; Frehrkring Wiesehoefer, Cologne; Susanne Vielmetter Los Angeles Projects; The Studio Museum of Harlem, New York and the Project, New York. Sloly has exhibited at Neuer Aachener Kunstverein, The Beall Center for Art and Technology (University of California, Irvine), the Museum of Contemporary Art (Chicago), The Saidye Bronfman Centre for The Arts (Montréal) and Art Gallery of Nova Scotia (Halifax). Johnson has exhibited at PS 1 Museum, the SK Stiftung, Cologne, the Santa Monica Museum of Art, the Museum of Contemporary Art, Chicago, Center on Contemporary Art, Seattle and the Studio Museum, Harlem. Koumoundouros' solo exhibitions include Thieves Vinegar and Designated Hitters.

William Pope.L
Pope.L is a visual and performance-theatre artist whose street performances have been featured in several publications, including *Art in America*. He was included in the 2002 Whitney Biennial and has toured nationally with the retrospective eRacism, and its companion monograph, *William Pope.L: The Friendliest Black Artist in America*.

Marjetica Potrč
Potrč's work has been featured in exhibitions worldwide, including the São Paulo Biennial in Brazil, 1996 and 2006; Skulptur Projekte in Münster, Germany, 1997; The Structure of Survival at the Venice Biennial, 2003 and FarSites at the San Diego Museum of Art, San Diego, CA, 2005.

Sara Raza
Raza is a writer and curator currently based in London. She has curated public programmes at Tate Modern and is editor for *ArtAsiaPacific*. In 2005 she co-curated the Central Asian Biennale, In the Shadow of Heroes, and has been a curatorial and regional adviser to Goldsmiths College MFA in Creative Curating.

Kyohei Sakaguchi
Sakaguchi's written works include *Tokyo House*, *Zero Yen Houses* and *ROAD IN*. Sakaguchi's work has been shown at Vancouver Art Gallery and in exhibitions elsewhere in Canada, Europe, Africa and Asia.

Mark Soo
Soo is a Vancouver based artist. His work, which often undertakes a humourous post-institutional critique, has been exhibited in New York, Manchester, Melbourne, Toronto and Vancouver.

Sean Topham
Topham is the author of several books including *Blow-up: Inflatable Art, Architecture and Design*, 2002, *Where's My Space Age?*, 2003, and *Move House*, 2004, and co-author of *Xtreme Houses*, 2002.

Ehryn Torrell
Torrell is a visual artist who has exhibited at Centre des arts actuels Skol, 2008, Gallery Connexion, 2007, and Anna Leonowens Gallery, 2005. In Autumn 2004, she participated in the Informal Architectures residency at The Banff Centre.

Eyal Weizman
Weizman is director of the Centre for Research Architecture at Goldsmiths College, University of London and, previously, Professor of Architecture at the Academy of Fine Arts in Vienna. His books include *Hollow Land*, *A Civilian Occupation*, the series *Territories* 1, 2 and 3, *Yellow Rhythms* and many articles in journals, magazines and edited books.

Acknowledgements

This book was made possible by a Social Sciences and Humanities Research Council grant for Creation in Fine Arts. Research was further supported by a Leverhulme Visiting Research Fellowship at the School of Arts, Middlesex University, London and grants from the Canada Council for the Arts.

I am indebted to the support of numerous institutions that made the various aspects of the Informal Architectures project possible. They include Plug In ICA, The Banff Centre, including the Banff International Curatorial Institute, Visual Arts, Walter Phillips Gallery, Creative Electronic Environment, and the Paul D Fleck Library and Archives, Middlesex University, Department of Visual Culture, Black Dog Publishing, Tate Modern and Tate Britain, University of Manitoba Department of Architecture, the Canadian Centre for Architecture, Dunlop Art Gallery, Regina Public Library and the National Gallery of Canada.

I would like to thank various groups and individuals that made all this work possible including: The SSHRC Informal Architectures research team: Aoife Mac Namara, Candice Hopkins, Melanie Townsend, Mark Wasiuta, David Hoffos, Andrew King, Rita McKeough, Luanne Martineau; the Spaces Buildings Make AHRC research team in Visual Culture at Middlesex University (www.visual-culture.com), (lead by Aoife Mac Namara); the artists in the Informal Architectures residency at The Banff Centre in 2004: Lance Blomgren, Trevor Boddy, Sandra Buckley, Sigrid Dahle, Rebecca Duclos, Dennis Evans, Leah Garnett, Lucy Gunning, David Hoffos, Gul Ilgaz, Andrew Kearney, Andrew King, Johnathan Knowles, Robert Knowles, Adrienne Lai, Corwyn Lund, Kourosh Mahvash, Shauna McCabe, Alexandra McIntosh, Randall McKay, Rita McKeough, Bernie Miller, Douglas Moffat, Gailan Ngan, Ryan Nordlund, Vessna Perunovich, Alex Pilis, Jeanne Randolph, Stuart Reid, David Ross, Mark Soo and Ehryn Torrell; and the and the University of Manitoba Department of Architecture graduate theory seminar in 2007.

Thank you to the speakers and participants in symposia related to this project in Banff and London, too numerous to list here. Further, I would like to thank other individuals who have contributed in numerous and countless ways: Sylvie Gilbert, Pauline Martin, Charlene Quantz-Wold, Nicole Burisch, Mimmo Maiolo, Kevin Tweed, Ian August, Katie Spicer, Alissa Firth-Eagland, Katia Meir, Scott Felter, Naomi Potter, Jen Hutton, Paul Smith, Milena Placentile, Sara Diamond, Luke Azevedo, Joanne Morrow, Susan Kennard, Kitty Scott, Tara Nicholson, Kelly Holmes, Claudia Hasan, Matthew Walker, Wendy Tokaryk, Ed Bamiling, Sarah Fuller, Sara Raza, Karin Streu, Daniel Ellingsen, Steven Matijcio, Henry Kuzia, Collin Zipp, Kevin Waugh, Suzanne Gillies, Shoshanna Paul, Duncan McCorquodale, Matthew Pull, Aimee Selby, Nat Chard, Neil Minuk, Noam Gonick, Meeka Walsh, Richard W Hill, Adrian Rifkin, Andrew Kearney, Paul Antick, Marcos Sanchez, Ashok Mathur, Michael Boyce, Heidi Reitmaier, Peter Poole, Laura Millard, Brian Jungen, Tom Cuckle, Yves Trepanier and Kevin Baer, Catriona Jeffries, Gwendolyn Owens, Lida Abdul, Elizabeth McLuhan, Joyce Clark, Dan Graham, Pablo Helguera, Don Goodes, Gregory Cowan, Layda Gongora, Robyn Moody, Lydia Gray, David Ross and Kevin Finlayson, Jane Crawford and the Estate of Gordon Matta-Clark, Electronic Arts Intermix, and all the contributors to this volume.

Parts of this book originated in different form in the publications *Godzilla vs. Skateboarders: Skateboarding as a Critique of Social Spaces*; *The Edge of Everything: Reflections on Curatorial Practice* and *Ethics of Luxury* by Jeanne Randolph.

Thank you to the publishers, archives and galleries who granted permission to reprint works in this volume. The Canada Council for the Arts, Alberta Foundation for the Arts, Saskatchewan Arts Board, Manitoba Arts Council, Winnipeg Arts Council, Creative Capital, Canada House, Department of Foreign Affairs, and Arts Council of England, all supported the organisations and individuals that made this work possible. I would like to thank all lenders of images and artworks to the exhibition and this publication.

This project could not have happened without the artists in the Informal Architectures exhibition at Walter Phillips Gallery and Plug In ICA, including those not already listed above: Eleanor Bond, William Pope.L, and Kiyohei Sakaguchi and Jimmie Durham.

Blanche Craig and Vanessa Kroeker should be especially acknowledged for their dedicated work in producing this publication. Finally I would like to thank my best friend Joanne Bristol for critical feedback and companionship, and my family for their support.

Anthony Kiendl

Edited by Blanche Craig at Black Dog Publishing.
Designed by Matthew Pull at Black Dog Publishing.

© 2008 Black Dog Publishing Limited, London, UK,
the artists and authors. All rights reserved.

Black Dog Publishing Limited
10A Acton Street
London WC1X 9NG
United Kingdom

Tel: +44 (0) 20 7713 5097
Fax: +44 (0) 20 7713 8682
info@blackdogonline.com
www.blackdogonline.com

ISBN: 978 1 906155 33 9
British Library Cataloguing-in-Publication Data.
A CIP record for this book is available from
the British Library.

Printed in Turkey

Black Dog Publishing Limited, London, UK, is an
environmentally responsible company. *Informal
Architectures* is printed on Sappi Magno Satin,
a chlorine-free, FSC certified paper.

The Informal Architectures exhibition was organised
by the Walter Phillips Gallery at The Banff Centre. It
was held at the Walter Phillips Gallery, Banff, Alberta
22 June–23 September 2007 then circulated to Plug In
Institute for Contemporary Art, Winnipeg, Manitoba,
3 May–28 June 2008. www.informalarchitecture.net

Walter Phillips Gallery,
The Banff Centre
Box 1020
Banff, Alberta,
Canada T1L 1H5
www.banffcentre.ca/wpg

The Walter Phillips Gallery gratefully acknowledges
the support of the Social Sciences and Humanities
Research Council of Canada, Canada Council for
the Arts, Alberta Foundation for the Arts, and the
Department of Canadian Heritage National Arts
Training Contribution Programme.

Plug In Institute of Contemporary Art
286 McDermot Avenue
Winnipeg, Manitoba,
Canada R3B 0T2
Tel (204) 942-1043
www.plugin.org
Plug In Editions is the imprint of Plug In ICA.

Plug In ICA is a centre for research in contemporary
art including film, architecture, television, new media
and sound. Plug In acknowledges the support of the
Canada Council for the Arts, Manitoba Arts Council,
Winnipeg Arts Council, the Department of Canadian
Heritage, the Winnipeg Foundation, the WH and SE
Loewen Foundation, Investors Group, our donors,
patrons and volunteers.